A PROGRAMMED GERMAN GRAMMAR

A Programmed
German Grammar

with exercises

Alan K. Tyrer

VANTAGE PRESS
New York / Washington / Atlanta
Los Angeles / Chicago

FIRST EDITION

Published by Vantage Press, Inc.
516 West 34th Street, New York, New York 10001

Manufactured in the United States of America
ISBN: 533-04927-X

CONTENTS

PART 2

PREFACE

Whatever enthusiasts for any particular method of teaching languages may say, there is no way of learning a foreign language without effort—"through the pores," as advocates of direct-method teaching used to say.

Experience shows that where students of foreign languages (particularly of fairly highly inflected languages like German) most often come to grief is with the grammar—the way in which words may change their aspect or shape in association with other words in the same sentence.

Personally I have always found the study of grammar fascinating, but, as a teacher of foreign languages for many years, I have been forced to admit that most people who wish to learn a foreign language do not share my fascination.

This course, which I think I may claim is the first, and indeed so far the only one designed to teach the concepts of grammar by programmed methods, is intended to remove as far as possible the grief and tears from the learning of a foreign language by bringing into it the interest that many people seem to find in crossword puzzles. In particular, it is meant to keep interest alive by giving the information that must be learnt in only small steps at a time and providing a little test immediately, with the answers also immediately available. The student thus plays a little game with himself; if he has answered correctly, he is encouraged to go on, while the student who has made a mistake knows exactly where and, so, to what point he must return to correct it.

This book is intended primarily for mature students working at home alone, but has also been used successfully in schools in Britain.

I do not claim that it is a course that, by itself, will enable a learner to speak fluent German. So as not to distract attention from the essential grammar, the vocabulary has been deliberately limited to about three hundred words, which means that the variety of the examples that I can give has also had to be limited. There is therefore a lot of essential vocabulary that the learner will have to supply for himself. In addition, practice in speaking and listening to the language, either with the help of someone whose mother tongue is German or by means of one of the many oral courses now on the market, will be highly desirable, if not indispensable.

However, I do claim that, without a knowledge of the basic grammar such as this course seeks to give, and in which many other courses offered in recent years seem terribly defective, it will hardly be possible for the student to speak or write correct German.

I should also like to think that, at least as regards the indexing, this course is superior to most other language courses. All the German words used are indexed in both the German/English and the English/German vocabularies, together with the number of the item in which the word is first introduced, and the grammatical features dealt with have been indexed as comprehensively as possible in the Grammatical Index, many of them under two or three different headings, so that the occasions on which the learner has to guess what is in the mind of the indexer are, I hope, reduced to a minimum. There should therefore be no need for the student ever to lose his way.

My thanks are due to Mr. Desmond Fleming and Miss Alexandrina Smith, who worked through the course without any previous knowledge of German and helped me to identify inaccuracies and passages which needed further clarification. I should be grateful for suggestions for further improvement in any case where inspiration may have been lacking.

Finally I should like to pay a tribute to my wife, Linda, who, while still at school, helped me to check the first draft and who has remained the greatest help and source of my inspiration ever since.

—A. K. TYRER
Luxembourg City
September 1, 1980

A PROGRAMMED GERMAN GRAMMAR

Part 1

GERMAN PRONUNCIATION AND SPELLING

Do not attempt to memorize the contents of this Introductory Section to begin with: simply read it through, making sure that you understand it, but without trying to learn all that it contains. Then refer back to it later whenever you find it necessary.

Phonetic symbols are given in some places, in case you are already familiar with them, to help you with the pronunciation. If you are not familiar with phonetics you can still understand the explanations given. Wherever phonetic symbols are used they are placed in square brackets – thus: [ka:m].

The letters of the German alphabet are the same as ours, but there is an accent which may be placed on three of the vowels, and there is a special symbol for double 's' in some words. Each of these matters is dealt with later.

VOWELS		EXAMPLES	
	GERMAN		ENGLISH
As in English, vowels may be short or long.			
Long **a** is pronounced as in the English* word *rather*.	**kam** [ka:m]	is like	*calm* [ka:m]
Short **a** is like a shortened version of the long **a**, or rather like the first vowel in English *Monday*. It may be compared also with the flat **a** heard in the North of England.	**Kamm** [kam]	is like	*come* [kam]
Short **a** is never pronounced like the vowel in standard English *hat*. This vowel sound, half way between **a** and **e**, does not exist in German.	**hat** [hat]	is NOT like *hat*	[hæt]
Long **e** is pronounced like the first vowel sound of the English diphthong in *say* [sei] or *name* [neim].	**den** [den]	is NOT like *Dane*	[dein]

* Except where otherwise mentioned, references to English pronunciation are intended as references to standard English and not to any regional pronunciation.

2

('Diphthong' means two vowels pronounced in rapid succession but so as to
make one syllable.) Be careful not to go
on to the second vowel sound of this
diphthong [i].

Short **e** is pronounced like short *e* in English.	**Bett** [bɛt]	is like	*bet* [bɛt]
Unstressed **e**, which occurs as the ending of many German words, sometimes fol-lowed by a consonant, is like the first vowel in English *again* or like the first and last vowels in *America* [əmɛrɪkə].	**kommen** [kɔmən]	is like	*common* [kɔmən]
The vowel **e** is always sounded, so the silent *e* (*e* mute) found in French and English (e.g. *plume*) is absent in German.	**Tone** [tonə]	is NOT like *tone* [toːun]	
Long **i** is pronounced as in the English word *machine* [məʃiːn], never as in English 'mine' [main].	**mir** [miːr]	is rather like *mere* [miːɹ]	
Short **i** is pronounced rather like the same letter in English.	**bin** [bɪn]	is like	*bin* [bɪn]
Long **o** is pronounced like the first vowel sound in the diphthong in English *home* [houm] or *rose* [rouz]. Be careful not to go on to the second vowel sound of this diphthong [u].	**bot** [boːt]	is NOT like *boat* [boːut]	
Short **o** is pronounced like the same letter in English.	**Kost** [kɔst]	is like	*cost* [kɔst]
Long **u** is pronounced like the same letter in the English words *Susan* [Suːzən] or *flue* [fluː]. It is never pre-ceded by the semi-vowel heard in English 'you' or 'use' [juː, juːz].	**du** [duː]	is like NOT like	*do* [duː] due [djuː]
Short **u** is pronounced as in the English word *put* [put], never as in English *mud* [mad].	**Futter** [futer] **Mutter** [mutər]	is like is NOT like *mutter*	*footer* [futəɹ] [matəɹ]

3

	GERMAN		ENGLISH

Vowel combinations.

There are six sets of combined vowels in German, not all of them true diphthongs – **ai, au, äu, ei, eu** and **ie.** It will be convenient to take them out of alphabetical order and to postpone **äu** until we have dealt with the Umlaut.

The diphthong **au** is pronounced like the vowel sound in English *how* [hau].	**Haus** [haus]	is like	*house* [haus]
The diphthong **eu** is pronounced like the vowel sound in English *boy* [bɔi]	**Heu** [hɔi]	is like	*hoy* [hɔi]
The diphthongs **ai** and **ei**★ are both pronounced like the *i* in English *fine* [fain].	**mein** [main]	is like	*mine* [main]
	Hai [hai]	is like	*high* [hai]
The digraph **ie**★ is pronounced like the German long **i** or as the *i* in English *machine* [məʃiːn]. ('Digraph' means two letters representing a single sound.)	**die** [diː]	is like	*Dee* [diː]

The Umlaut.

There is only one accent in German. It consists of two dots which may be placed over certain vowels and is called an **Umlaut** (pronounced 'úm-lout' [umlaut]) This means 'change of sound'.†
Three vowels and one diphthong may take an Umlaut – **ä, ö, ü** and **äu.**

The vowel **ä** is pronounced like the *e* in the English word *fell*.	**fällen** [fɛlən]	is like	*felon* [fɛlən]

★ If you have difficulty in distinguishing between the combinations **ei** and **ie** it may help to remember that the pronunciation is the same as the English name for the second letter of the combination in each case. Thus **ei** is pronounced like the letter 'I' and **ie** is pronounced like the letter 'E'.

† This change of sound was originally caused by the presence of an **i** or **j** in the following syllable in an earlier form of the word, and may be compared with the sound change in such English pairs of words as *hat – hate, rod – rode, cut – cute.*

4

	GERMAN		ENGLISH
The vowel **ö** [ø, œ] is rather like French 'eu' in 'neuf' [nœf] and roughly equivalent to the vowel sound in English *bird* [bᴧɹd] or *her* [hᴧɹ].	**Föhn** [fø:n]	is something like	*fern* [fᴧɹn]
The vowel **ü** has no equivalent in English but is similar to French 'u' in 'mur' [my:r]. The sound is produced by pronouncing the English letter *e* with rounded lips. The sound of English *u* is altogether absent.	**für** [fy:r]	is like pronounced with rounded lips	*fear* [fy:r]
The diphthong **äu** is pronounced in the same way as German diphthong **eu,** namely like English *oy*.	**-bäu** [bɔi]	is like	*boy* [bɔi]

Consonants.

The German consonants are pronounced rather like the English consonants, with the following exceptions:

C, in modern German, is found only in the compounds **ch, ck** and **sch.**

The letters **ch** when following **a, o, u** and **au** (the vowels pronounced at the back of the throat) are pronounced as in Scottish *loch* [lɔx]. Be careful not to clip this final sound short like *k*; it can be carried on as long as your breath lasts.	**Loch** [lɔx]	is like Scottish	*loch* [lcx]
The letters **ch,** when following letters other than the back vowels, are pronounced like the *h* in English *human* [hju:mən].	**ich** [ıç]	is like the capital letters in	reallY Huge [riəlı HJu:dz]
The letters **chs,** if they occur in the stem of a word, are pronounced like the English letter *x*.	**Ochs** [ɔks]	is like	*ox* [ɔks]
The letter **g** is hard as in English *go*, never as in English *gem*.	**gieß** [gis]	is like	*geese* [gis]

5

	GERMAN		ENGLISH
The letter **h** is pronounced as in English except that when following a vowel it has the effect of lengthening the vowel and is not then itself pronounced.	**hemm** [hɛm] **ihn** [iːn]	is like is like	*hem* [hɛm] *e'en* [iːn]
The letter **j** is pronounced like English *y* in *yes* [jɛs]	**ja** [ja]	is like	*yah* [ja]
The letters **qu** (always found together as in English) are pronounced *kv*.	**quetsch** [kvɛtʃ]	is like the capital letters in	*blaCK VETCH* [blæK VƐTʃ]
The letter **r** is made in the throat, not, as in English, with the tongue. It can be pronounced when the tongue is held down with one finger (English *r* cannot).			
It is always pronounced and does not affect the sound of a previous vowel.	**her** [heːr]	is NOT like	*her* [hʌɹ]
The letter **s** at the beginning of a word is pronounced like English *z*.	**sink** [zɪnk]	is like	*zinc* [zɪnk]
The letters **sch** are pronounced like English *sh*.	**schien** [ʃiːn]	is like	*sheen* [ʃiːn]
The letters **sp** and **st** at the beginning of a word are pronounced as if spelt *schp* and *scht*.	**spitz** [ʃpɪts]	is like the capital letters in	*aSH PITS* [æʃ PɪTS]
	[ʃtɪl]	still is like the capital letters in	*casH TILL* [kæʃ TIL]
The letter **v** is pronounced like English *f*.	**viel** [fiːl]	is like	*feel* [fiːl]
The letter **w** is pronounced like English *v*.	**weil** [vail]	is like	*vile* [vail]
The letter **z** is pronounced like English *ts*. Be careful always to make a good clear *t* sound.	**Zeit** [tsait]	is like the capital letters in	*aT SIGHT* [əT SAIT]

	EXAMPLE		
	GERMAN		ENGLISH
Final **b** is pronounced like *p*.	**Lieb'**	is like	*leap*
	[li:p]		[li:p]
Final **d** is pronounced like *t*.	**lud**	is like	*loot*
	[lut]		[lut]
Final **g** is usually pronounced like *k*	**mag**	is like	*mark*
	[ma:k]		[ma:k]
But if the word ends in **ig** the **g** is usually	**innig**	is like the	
pronounced like German **ch.**	[ɪnɪç]	the capital	
		letters in	*MINNIE*
			Hughes
			[mɪNɪ
			HJu:z]

THE SYMBOL 'ß'

A special symbol, 'ß', is used instead of double **s**. The symbol stands for **sz** and is called **ess-tset** (the German names for the letters **sz**). However, **ss** must be used between two vowels of which the first is short. The word **groß** must be so spelled because there is only one vowel. The word **Grüße** must be so spelled because, although there are two vowels, the first is long. The word **Flüsse** is so spelled because the first of the two vowels is short.

STRESS

The stress occurs as a rule on the first syllable of a German word – **Mörder, König.**

But words borrowed from French have the stress on the last syllable – **Generál** (which comes from French).

In addition, inseparable verbs, about which you will learn later, and a small number of other words, take the stress on the second syllable – **erhálten** (an inseparable verb).

GENERAL NOTE ON ENUNCIATION

Each German word must be clearly enunciated and crisply separated by a slight pause in the voice from the following word. Sounds are never carried on from one word to the next. This is the exact opposite of French; in German 'liaisons' (the carrying on of the last sound of one word into the first sound of the next) MUST NOT be made. Where a single word is made up of more than one component this pause in the voice (sometimes called a 'glottal stop') is heard between the separate components – thus **er/innern, Haus/arbeit.**

7

HOW TO SET TO WORK

(If you do not know how to pronounce German words, you should first study the section on Pronunciation and Spelling.)

Have ready writing materials and a card 5 to 6 inches wide.

Set the upper edge of your card to the figure 2 on the page opposite.

Read item 1. It ends with a threefold choice: *man/woman/house*.
Choose the word you think is correct and write it in your notebook.
Next, bring your card down to figure 3. The left-hand column shows the correct answer to item 1.

If you were correct, read item 2, in which the last word is missing. Think of the word and then proceed as before.

If your choice ever proves to be wrong, you must find out what is wrong with it before you go on. If you do not you may get into difficulties.

Do not miss out any items, or you may lose the thread.

Do not look back at previous items before writing your answers. Some of the benefit of the course will be lost if you do. If you find it difficult to avoid looking back, cut a slot 1½ in. deep and ½ in. across in the edge of a card, about the middle, and use the card upright to cover the left-hand column only. The slot will reveal one answer at a time.

This is a way of learning, not a test; there are no trick questions or questions you cannot be expected to answer.

Gender

1

In English, nouns which denote male creatures are sometimes said to be of the MASCULINE GENDER. Which of the following words is of the masculine gender? *Man/woman/house.*

Man

2

Similarly, *boy* is of the masculine —.

gender

3

Man, boy, widower are all of the — gender.

masculine

4

Nouns which denote female creatures are said to be of the FEMININE GENDER. Which of the following words is of the feminine gender? *Man/woman/house.*

woman

5

Similarly, *girl* is of the — gender.

feminine

6

Nouns which denote creatures or things which are neither of the masculine nor the feminine gender are said to be of the NEUTER GENDER. ('Neuter' is another word for 'neither'). Which of the following is of the neuter gender? *Man/woman/house.*

house

7

Similarly, *table* is of the — gender.

neuter

8

Notice that although gender may be connected with sex, it is not quite the same thing. Although a ship has no sex we may sometimes call it *she*, thus treating it as being of the — gender.

feminine	**9** Similarly we may occasionally refer to a child, whatever its sex, as *it*, thus treating it as being of the — gender.
neuter	**10** Gender is something which belongs to which parts of speech?
nouns	**11** From now on instead of always saying that a noun is of the neuter or feminine or masculine gender we shall often say simply that it is neuter, or feminine, or masculine. Thus *schoolmaster* is —.
masculine	**12** In English a noun may belong to one of *one/two/three/four* genders.
three	**13** In German, too, as in English, nouns may have one of — genders.
three	**14** These three genders are the same as in English, namely —, — and —.
masculine, feminine and neuter	**15** As we shall now be speaking a good deal about articles, we had better be sure that you understand the word. The DEFINITE ARTICLE is the word for *the* and the INDEFINITE ARTICLE is the word for *a* or *an*. The word *the is/is not* the definite article.
is	**16** 'The definite article' means *a/the*.
the	**17** *A* or *an* is the — article.
indefinite	**18** You say *a man, a woman, a house; the man, the woman, the house*. In English, the gender of the noun makes *a/no* difference to the form of the article.

no	19 In German the definite article varies according to the gender of the noun. **Der Mann** *the man* is masculine, so the definite article for a masculine noun is —.
der	20 Notice that all nouns in German begin with a — letter.
capital	21 **Junge** (*boy*) is also masculine, so the German for *the boy* is — —.
der Junge	22 **Die Frau** (*the woman*) is feminine, so the definite article for a feminine noun is —.
die	23 **Dame** (*lady*) is also feminine, so the German for *the lady* is — —.
die Dame	24 The German for *the man is* — —.
der Mann	25 The German for *the woman* is — —.
die Frau	26 **Das Haus** (*the house*) is neuter, so the definite article for a neuter noun is —.
das	27 **Buch** (*book*) is also neuter, so the German for *the book* is — —.
das Buch	28 The German for *the house* is — —.
das Haus	29 The definite articles for masculine, feminine and neuter words are —, — and — respectively.

	30
der, die, das	You remember that gender is not exactly the same as sex. Although it has no sex we sometimes treat the English word — as being feminine.
	31
ship	In German this happens very often indeed and nouns used for things which are neither male nor female may be of the — or the — or the — gender.
	32
masculine, feminine neuter	Thus, **der Tisch** (*the table*) is masculine, although tables cannot be of the — sex.
	33
male	Similarly, **die Wand** (*the wall*) is — although walls are not female.
	34
feminine	The most that can be said is that if a noun stands for a person or one of the higher animals its sex may be a guide to the — of the noun.
	35
gender	Thus a male cat is — **Kater.**
	36
der	. . . and a female cat is — **Katze.**
	37
die	Even this does not always follow however: for example, **das Mädchen** (the girl) is —.
	38
neuter	This is because **das Mädchen** belongs to a special class of noun called DIMINUTIVES. A diminutive is a smaller version of something. Thus *booklet* is the diminutive of —.
	39
book	The diminutive of *eye* is —.
	40
eyelet	In English *doggie, keylet, duckling* are all —.

12

diminutives	**41** In German, diminutives can be made from almost any noun and usually end in **-chen** or **-lein**. *The girl* is **das Mäd—**.
-chen	**42** The diminutive of **der Tisch** (*the table*), is **das Tischlein.** The gender of diminutives is —.
neuter	**43** The German for *the girl* is — —.
Das Mädchen	**44** **Das Mädchen** is neuter because the word is a —.
diminutive	**45** In general the only way of knowing the gender of a noun is to learn it. Always learn the definite article with a noun, e.g., **das Brot** (*the bread*). Go to next item.
	46 — **Frau ist** (*is*) **gut** (*good*).
Die	**47** — **Haus ist groß** (*big*).
Das	**48** — **Wand ist grün** (*green*).
Die	**49** — **Mädchen ist schön** (*beautiful*).
Das	**50** — **Mann ist stark** (*strong*).
Der	**51** — **Tisch ist braun** (*brown*).
Der	**52** — **Tischlein ist nicht** (*not*) **groß**.
Das	**53** — **Katze ist klein** (*small*).

Die	54 — **Kater ist schwarz** (*black*).
Der	55 — **Buch ist offen** (*open*).
Das	56 — **Junge ist schmutzig** (*dirty*).
Der	57 — **Männlein** (*little man*) **ist nicht froh** (glad).
Das	

Determinatives

58
You do not really need to know at this stage what the heading to this section means but, in case you are curious, a determinative is a word which *defines* or *determines* something – e.g., *the* book (more definite than just 'book'), *this* woman, *my* table, etc. Go to the next item.

59
You have already met the *definite article*. In English the definite article is —.

the

60
In German the definite article varies according to the — of the noun.

gender

61
The definite article is — for a masculine noun, — for a feminine noun and — for a neuter noun.

der, die, das

62
The words *the*, **der**, **die** and **das** are all known as the — —.

14

definite article	**63** In addition to the definite article there is also an important class of determinative called DEMONSTRATIVE ADJECTIVES. 'Demonstrative' means 'pointing out' so demonstrative adjectives are adjectives which — something —.
point out	**64** In English, adjectives like *this, that, such, each* are used for pointing out. They are therefore — —.
demonstrative adjectives	**65** In German, demonstrative adjectives have the same endings as the definite article. **Dieser Mann** means *this man*. Which two letters show that **Mann** is masculine?
-er	**66** **Diese Frau** means *this woman*. Which letter shows that **Frau** is feminine? —
-e	**67** **Dieses Haus** means *this house*. Which two letters show that **Haus** is neuter? (Notice that the ending of **das** has undergone a slight change.)
-es	**68** Since **dieser Mann** means *this man* the German for *this table* is — —. (**Tisch,** masc.)
dieser Tisch	**69** Since **diese Frau** means *this woman* the German for *this cat* is — —. (**Katze,** fem.)
diese Katze	**70** Since **dieses Haus** means *this house* the German for *this girl* is — —. (**Mädchen,** neut.)
dieses Mädchen	**71** **Dieser, diese, dieses** is a de — ive adjective.
demonstrative	**72** The demonstrative adjectives have the same endings as the words — or — or —.

der, die, das	**73** Another demonstrative (pointing out) adjective is the German for *that* – **jener** (masc.), **jene** (fem.), **jenes** (neut.). The German for *that tom-cat* is — —. (**Kater, masc.**)
jener Kater	**74** The German for *that wall* is — —. (**Wand,** fem.)
jene Wand	**75** The German for *that book* is — —. (**Buch,** neut.)
jenes Buch	**76** *Each* (**jeder, jede, jedes**) is another de — ve adjective.
demonstrative	**77** *Each* (**jeder, jede, jedes**) has the same endings as —, —, —.
der, die, das (or **jener** or **dieser**)	**78** *Each boy* is — —. (**Junge,** masc.)
jeder Junge	**79** *Each cat* (fem.) is — —.
jede Katze	**80** *Each girl* is — —.
jedes Mädchen	**81** **Solcher, solche, solches** means *such* and is like the other demonstrative adjectives. It has the same endings as —, —, —.
der, die, das	**82** *Such* = **solcher, solche, solches**. *Such cheese* (**Käse,** masc.) is — —.
solcher Käse	**83** *The coal* is **die Kohle**. *Such coal* is — —.
solche Kohle	**84** *The grass* is **das Gras**. *Such grass is* — —.

16

	85
solches Gras	**Mancher** means *many a*. (Note that there is only one word for the two in English). It too has the endings of **der, die das.** *Many a man* is — —.
	86
mancher Mann	*Many a lady is* — —. (**Dame,** fem.)
	87
manche Dame	*Many a book* is — —.
	88
manches Buch	**Welcher** means *which* and is no different from the other words you have just met. *Which girl?* is — —.
	89
welches Mädchen?	*Which table?* is — — .
	90
welcher Tisch?	*Which wall?* is — —.
	91
welche Wand?	Remember that we are dealing with words which behave like **der, die, das.** To show that you have not forgotten them – *the mouse* is — —. (**Maus.** fem.)
	92
die Maus	**Hund** (masc.) = *dog. The dog* is — —.
	93
der Hund	**Fräulein** = *young lady*. It is a diminutive of **Frau** and you notice that apart from **-lein** there has been the addition of an —.
	94
Umlaut or (··)	(The vowel of a noun always takes an Umlaut if it can when forming a diminutive). *The young lady* is — —.
	95
das Fräulein	In the next 10 items write out all the German words given, adding the correct endings in place of the dashes – e.g. **Welch- Mann? – Welcher Mann?** Go to next item.

17

	96 Dies- Gras ist grün.
	97
Dieses Gras ist grün	Jed- Maus ist flink (*lively*).
	98
Jede . . . etc.	Manch- Buch ist interessant (*interesting*).
	99
Manches . . . etc.	Jen- Junge ist intelligent.
	100
Jener . . . etc.	Welch- Kohle ist teuer? (*expensive*).
	101
Welche . . . etc.	Solch- Käse schmeckt gut (*tastes good*).
	102
Solcher . . . etc.	Dies- Frau ist froh (*glad*).
	103
Diese . . . etc.	Jen- Fräulein ist sehr (*very*) schön.
	104
Jenes . . . etc.	Nicht jed- Hund ist schwarz (*black*).
	105
Nicht jeder . . . etc.	Dies- Wein ist alt (*old*). (**Wein,** masc. = *wine*).
	106
Dieser . . . etc.	Solch- Kohle brennt (*burns*) nicht.
Solche . . . etc.	

Demonstrative Pronouns

107

The definite article **der, die, das** can be used without a noun as a demonstrative pronoun – *the one, this one, that one*, etc. **Ist die Katze groß? Nein, die ist klein** (*that is small*). **Ist die Wand schwarz? Nein, — ist grün.**

die	108
	Ist der Mann stark? Nein, — ist nicht stark.
der	109
	Ist — das Haus?
das	

Determinatives – Ein, Kein, and Possessive Adjectives

110

Up to now we have been dealing with determinatives (defining words) which behave like **der, die, das.** Now we come to a group which behave differently, the chief of which is the INDEFINITE ARTICLE, namely (in English) — or —.

a an

111

In German the indefinite article for a masculine word is **ein.** The German for *a man* is — —.

ein Mann

112

The words *a*, *an*, **ein** are called the — —.

indefinite article

113

For a neuter word the indefinite article is also **ein.** The German for *a house* is — —.

ein Haus

114

The German for *a girl* (remember the word is neuter, not feminine!) is — —.

ein Mädchen

115

The German for *a boy* is — —.

ein Junge

116

The indefinite article for a masculine noun *is/is not* the same as for a neuter word.

is

117

For both masculine and neuter nouns the indefinite article (*a*, *an*) is —.

19

ein	118 Compare the masculine forms of the definite and indefinite articles – **der Mann, ein Mann. Der** shows that **Mann** is masculine, but **ein** does not show whether **Mann** is — or —.
masculine or neuter	119 **Ein** does not show whether it is masculine or neuter but **der** shows clearly that it is masculine because it ends in the two letters —.
-er	120 Compare similarly **ein Haus, das Haus. Ein** could be either neuter or —.
masculine	121 But in **das Haus, das** could not be anything but —.
neuter	122 In **der Mann, der** has a special masculine ending, but in **ein Mann, ein** *has/has not* a special masculine ending.
has not	123 In **das Haus, das** has a special neuter ending, but in **ein Haus, ein** *has/has not* a special neuter ending.
has not	124 The feminine form of the indefinite article is **eine.** (Remember that the **-e** must be clearly pronounced.) *A woman* is — —.
eine Frau	125 The masculine, feminine and neuter forms of the indefinite article are — (masc.), — (fem.), — (neut.)
ein, eine, ein	126 *A dog is* — —.
ein Hund	127 *A cat* (fem.) *is* — —.
eine Katze	128 *A book is* — —.

20

ein Buch	**129** There is a negative form of the indefinite article **kein** which must be used instead of **nicht ein**. It behaves just like **ein**. The meaning is *no, not a, not any*. *No dog is* — —.
kein Hund	**130** *No mouse* (remember it is fem.) is — —.
keine Maus	**131** *Not any girl* is — —.
kein Mädchen	**132** The *possessive adjectives* (*my, your, their*, etc.) also behave just like **ein**. *My* is **mein**. *My cheese* (**Käse,** masc.) is — —.
mein Käse	**133** *My house* is — —.
mein Haus	**134** *My cat* (fem.) is — —.
meine Katze	**135** *Their* is **ihr**. *Their dog* is — —.
ihr Hund	**136** *Their girl* is — —.
ihr Mädchen	**137** *Their coal* (**Kohle,** fem.) is — —.
ihre Kohle	**138** Other possessive adjectives will be given after you have learnt the personal pronouns. Go to next item.
	139 In the next 10 items, rewrite the phrase given, substituting the correct form of the word given in brackets for **der, die** or **das**. E.g. **Die Frau (Ein)** – **Eine Frau**. Go to next item.
	140 **Der Käse (Mein).**

Mein Käse	141 **Die Maus (Jener).**
Jene Maus	142 **Das Mädchen (Mancher).**
Manches Mädchen	143 **Die Kohle (Ihr).**
Ihre Kohle	144 **Der Hund (Ein).**
Ein Hund	145 **Das Gras (Dieser).**
Dieses Gras	146 **Das Gras (Kein).**
Kein Gras	147 **Der Wein (Solcher).**
Solcher Wein	148 **Die Dame (Kein).**
Keine Dame	149 **Das Fräulein (Jeder).**
Jedes Fräulein	## *Personal Pronouns and the Verb 'To Be'*
	150 The German for *I am* is **ich bin.** The German for *I* (first person singular) is —.
ich	151 Notice that although in English *I* has a capital letter the German pronoun has a — letter.
small	152 The German for *I am* is — —.
ich bin	153 *You are* is **du bist.** The German for *you* (2nd person singular) is —.

22

du	**154** *You are* (2nd person sing.) is — —.
du bist	**155** However, the 2nd person is more complicated than in English because there are three different words for *you*. **Du** is 2nd person *singular* so it can only be used when speaking to *one/two/more* person(s).
one	**156** **Du** is not only singular, but *familiar*, so that it must only be used when speaking to one person whom we *know very well/hardly know at all*.
know very well	**157** **Du** is also used when speaking to a child. The German for *you are* when speaking to a child or a person whom we know very well is — —.
du bist	**158** *I am* is — —.
ich bin	**159** *He is* is **er ist** (3rd person singular masculine). The German for *he* is —.
er	**160** *She* is **sie** (3rd person singular feminine). *She is* is — —.
sie ist	**161** *He is* is — —.
er ist	**162** *It* is **es** (3rd person singular neuter). *It is* is — —.
es ist	**163** Write the German for *I am, you are* (familiar singular), *he, she, it is* — —, — —, —, —, — —.
ich bin, du bist, **er, sie, es ist**	**164** Those are the singular personal pronouns. Now for the plural. *We are* is **wir sind**. *We* (1st person plural) is —.

23

wir	165 *We are* is — —.
wir sind	166 You remember that **du** means *you* for *one* person whom we *know well/hardly know at all.*
know well	167 The plural of **du** is **ihr,** so that it means *you* for *one/more than one* person whom we know well.
more than one	168 *You are* (fam. plural) is **ihr seid.** It would be *right/wrong* to use this for one person whom we know well.
wrong	169 The German for *you are* when addressing more than one person whom we know well is — —.
ihr seid	170 **Du** and **ihr** both mean *you* and both are *familiar/polite.*
familiar	171 The difference between **du** and **ihr** is that (though both are familiar) **du** is for *one/more than one* person.
one	172 . . and **ihr** is for *one/more than one* person.
more than one	173 *You are* (fam. pl.) is — —.
ihr seid	174 *We are* is — —.
wir sind	175 *They are* is **sie sind** (3rd person plural). You will notice that the verb for the 1st and 3rd persons plural (*we* and *they*) is *the same/different.* (This is true of all verbs).
the same	176 *They are* is — —.

sie sind	177 You will also notice that the word for *they* is the same as for *he/she/it*.
she	178 This does not lead to any confusion as the verb is different. *She is* is — — and *they are* is — —.
sie ist, **sie sind**	179 You have met two ways of saying *you* to a person whom you know well, namely — (sing.) and — (plural).
du, ihr	180 But you do not know how to say *you* to someone you do not know well. It is the same as *they*, but to distinguish them the word for *you* is written with a capital letter. *You* (polite) is —.
Sie	181 This capital letter is the *only* difference between *they* and *you* (polite). *They are* is — —.
sie sind	182 *You are* (polite) is — —.
Sie sind	183 Whether you are speaking to one person or more than one the polite way of saying *you* is always —.
Sie	184 However, since **Sie** really means *they* the verb that goes with it must always be in the 3rd pers. sing./plural.
plural	185 Write the German for *we are, you are* (fam. pl.), and *they are*.
wir sind, ihr seid, **sie sind**	186 The German for *you are* (fam. sing.) is **du bist/ihr seid/ Sie sind.**

du bist	187 The German for *you are* (polite) is **du bist/ihr seid/Sie sind.**
Sie sind	188 The German for *you are* (fam. pl.) is **du bist/ihr seid/Sie sind.**
ihr seid	189 When using a 3rd person pronoun (**er, sie, es**) instead of a noun you must be careful to use the correct pronoun according to the gender of the noun. In English the pronoun to use for *a table*, for example, would be *he/she/it*.
it	190 But in German the word for *table* is masculine, so we must call a table *he*. The pronoun to use instead of **der Tisch** is —.
er	191 The pronoun to use for **die Wand** (*wall*) is —.
sie	192 The pronoun to use for **das Haus** (*house*) is —.
es	193 Note. It is usual to use the pronoun **sie** rather than **es** for **das Fräulein** and **das Mädchen**. Go to next section.

Infinitive and Present Tense of Regular Verbs

	194 In English a verb has several forms – e.g. *am, is, been, to be, being* are all forms of *the same/a different* verb.
the same	195 The form of the verb which is preceded by the word *to* is called the INFINITIVE – e.g. the infinitive of *looking* is *to* —.

look	**196** The infinitive of *having* is — —.
to have	**197** The infinitive of *been* is — —.
to be	**198** *To be, to have, to look* are all in the —.
infinitive	**199** In German the infinitive of all verbs ends in **-n.** Thus **kommen** means — *come*.
to	**200** In dictionaries, verbs are always given in the infinitive. If you meet a part of a verb **komme** or **kommt** you will look it up under —.
kommen	**201** German dictionaries show verbs in the — form.
infinitive	**202** Notice that although English infinitives consist of two words, German infinitives consist of *one/two/three* word(s).
one	**203** *To come* is —.
kommen	**204** The infinitive of all German verbs ends in the letter —.
-n	**205** You already know the German for *I am* (**ich bin**) etc. The infinitive of this verb is **sein. Sein** means — —.
to be	**206** The form of a verb used to describe actions which are taking place (or do take place) at the present time is called the PRESENT TENSE. The verb **ich bin** (*I am*) is in the — —.

27

present tense	**207** In English the present tense may have several forms: *I come, I am coming, I do come* are all forms of the — —.
present tense	**208** The verb *to come* is not in the present tense but in the —.
infinitive	**209** The verb *I come* is in the — —.
present tense	**210** The first person singular (the **ich** form) of most German verbs ends in **-e** and is usually formed by removing the **-n** of the infinitive, e.g., **kommen, ich** —.
komme	**211** If when the **-n** of the infinitive has been removed the last letter is not **-e,** one must be added, e.g. **tun** (*to do*); *I do* is **ich** —.
tue	**212** You know that English has several forms of present tense but German has only one form of present tense. *I come, I am coming, I do come* are all represented by — —.
ich komme	**213** **Stehen** is *to stand, I stand* is — —.
ich stehe	**214** *I am coming* is — —.
ich komme	**215** *I do come* is — —.
ich komme	**216** (**Stehen** is *to stand*.) *I am standing* is — —.
ich stehe	**217** Here now is the present tense of the verb **kommen.** Study it for a few moments, then go on.

1st sing.	**ich komme**	1st plural	**wir kommen**
2nd sing.	**du kommst**	2nd plural	**ihr kommt**
3rd sing.	**er kommt**	3rd plural	**sie kommen**

218

The first person singular of most German verbs (the **ich** form) ends in the letter —.

-e

219

The 2nd person sing. (**du** form) of German verbs ends in -st (This is just the same as Old English *thou dost, thou goest,* etc. but as you remember in German it is still the familiar singular form of address.) You remember that the German for *you are* (fam. sing.) is — —.

du bist

220

The -st is not usually preceded by an **e** unless the word would be hard to pronounce without the **e**. So *you come* (fam. sing.) is not **du kommest** but — —.

du kommst

221

Öffnen is *to open.* You could not very well pronounce the German for *you open* (fam. sing.) without the **e**, so the correct form is — —.

du öffnest

222

You are standing (fam. sing.) using **stehen** is — —.

du stehst

223

You are doing (fam. sing.) using **tun** is — —.

du tust

224

The 3rd person sing. (**er, sie, es** form) of German verbs usually ends in **-t. Gehen** is *to go. He goes* is — —.

er geht

225

She comes is — —.

sie kommt

226

It stands is — —.

es steht

227

As with the **du** form there is no **e** before the **t** unless the word otherwise cannot be pronounced. Thus with **tun** there is no need for an **e**. *He is doing* is — —.

29

er tut	228 But with **arbeiten** (*to work*) there would be a difficulty in pronunciation, so *she is working* is — —.
sie arbeitet	229 Notice that for the 3rd person singular if the stem (e.g., *arbeit*) already ends in a **t** you must *add* —et/*leave it as it is*).
add -et	230 The 1st person sing. (**ich** form) of the present tense ends in the letter —.
-e	231 *I go, I am going, I do go* (using **gehen**) are — —.
ich gehe	232 The 2nd person sing. (fam.) of the present tense ends in the two letters —.
-st	233 *You go* (fam. sing.) is — —.
du gehst	234 The 3rd person sing. of the present tense ends in the letter —.
t	235 **Machen** is *to make. It makes* is — —.
es macht	236 **Schwimmen** is *to swim. I, you* (fam. sing.) *swim, he swims* are — —, — —, — —.
ich schwimme, **du schwimmst,** **er schwimmt**	237 The 1st person plural of the present tense almost always has the verb in the same form as the infinitive. *We are coming* is — —.
wir kommen	238 *We go* is — —.
wir gehen	239 *We do* (using **tun**) is — —.

wir tun	240 *We are opening* is — —.
wir öffnen	241 The **wir** form of the verb ends in the letter —.
n	242 You remember that the 2nd person plural (fam. pl.) is the **ihr** form. The verb almost always ends in **t**. *You are coming* (fam. pl.) is — —.
ihr kommt	243 *You are opening* (fam. pl.) is — —.
ihr öffnet	244 *You do* (fam. pl.) (using **tun**) is — —.
ihr tut	245 As usual, an **e** is only added before the **t** if necessary for the pronunciation. *You work* (fam. pl.) is — —.
ihr arbeitet	246 You learnt with **sein** that the verb is always the same in 1st and 3rd persons plural. *They are coming* is — —.
sie kommen	247 *They go* is — —.
sie gehen	248 *They do* (using **tun**) is — —.
sie tun	249 *They are opening* is — —.
sie öffnen	250 The 3rd person plural verb always ends in the letter —.
n	251 You learnt that the polite *you* for one person or more is the same as *they* except that it has a — letter.
capital	252 *You work* (polite) is — —.

Sie arbeiten	**253** Write the singular of the present tense of **machen,** with the pronouns in each case.
ich mache **du machst** **er (sie, es) macht**	**254** Write the plural of the present tense of **machen.** (Include both ways of saying *you* and note that the polite form is usually placed after the 3rd person pl.)
wir machen **ihr macht** **sie (Sie) machen**	**255** If the infinitive of the verb ends in **-eln** or **-ern,** the **e** preceding the **l** or **r** (but not of course the final e of the personal ending) is dropped in the 1st person sing. **Zittern** = to tremble. *I tremble* is — —.
ich zittre	**256** **Klingeln** is *to ring. I ring* is — —.
ich klingle	**257** This dropping of the **e** only occurs in the 1st person sing., so *you tremble* (fam. sing.) is **du zitter**—.
zitterst	**258** . . . and *he trembles* is — —.
er zittert	**259** The 1st and 3rd persons plural of such verbs end in **n,** not **-en.** *We ring* is **wir klingel**—.
klingeln	**260** . . . and *they ring* is — —.
sie klingeln	**261** Here to sum up is the whole present tense of **klingeln:**

ich klingle   **wir klingeln**
du klingelst   **ihr klingelt**
er klingelt   **sie klingeln**

Go to next item when you know this.

	262
	In this and the next 9 items write the correct form of the verbs in brackets. (**Stehen**) **du, oder** (**kommen**) **du?** [**Oder** = *or*]
	263
stehst, kommst	**Dieser Junge** (**kommen**) **und ich** (**gehen**).
	264
kommt, gehe	**Was** (**tun**) **Sie?** (**Was** = *what*).
	265
tun	**Ihr** (**kommen**) **und** (**schwimmen**).
	266
kommt, schwimmt	**Wir** (**machen**) **einen Spaziergang** (*a walk*) **und** (**arbeiten**) **nicht.** (Notice that in German one speaks of *making* a walk, not of going for one.)
	267
machen, arbeiten	**Jenes Mädchen** (**tun**) **nichts** (= *nothing*).
	268
tut	**Er** (**arbeiten**), **aber das Fräulein** (**machen**) **nichts** (**aber** = *but*).
	269
arbeitet, macht	**Hans und Lotte** (**kommen**) **nach Hause** (*home*).
	270
kommen	**Was** (**machen**) **ihr dort?** (*there*).
	271
macht	(**Gehen**) **Sie jetzt** (*now*) **nach Hause?**

Present Tense of 'Haben'

Gehen

272

Haben is *to have*. The first person singular is regular. *I have* is — —.

33

ich habe	273 The 2nd and 3rd persons are irregular as the **b** of the stem is omitted. *You have* (fam. sing.) is **du hast;** *he has* is — —.
er hat	274 *You have* (fam. sing.) is — —.
du hast	275 The plural persons are not in any way irregular, so that the **b** of the infinitive returns. *We have* is — —.
wir haben	276 *You have* (fam. pl.) is **ihr** —.
habt	277 *They have* is — —.
sie haben	## Some Irregular Present Tenses 278 Some verbs show certain variations in the present tense. You will realize that **sein** and **haben** are amongst these. Some verbs (called STRONG verbs, but don't bother about the meaning of this just yet) may show a change of vowel in some persons. Go to next item.
	279 Nearly all such verbs have a regular 1st person. sing. **Tragen** = *to wear* (or *carry*). *I am wearing* is — —.
ich trage	280 Some such verbs however show a vowel change in the 2nd and 3rd persons sing. If the vowel in the stem of the infinitive is **a** (e.g. **tragen**) the change is usually to **ä**. Thus *you wear* (or *carry*) (fam. sing.) is — —.
du trägst	281 The vowel in the 3rd pers. sing. is always the same as in the 2nd pers. sing. so *he carries* (*wears*) is — —.

er trägt	282 All the other persons in such verbs revert to the same vowel as the 1st person sing. The plural of the present tense of **tragen** is therefore **wir** —, **ihr** —, **sie** (**Sie**) —.
wir tragen, ihr tragt, sie (Sie) tragen	283 The only persons affected by such a vowel change are the *1st and 2nd/2nd and 3rd* persons *singular/plural*.
2nd and 3rd persons singular	284 In verbs which show a vowel change in the present tense the vowel **a** usually changes to —.
ä	285 **Fangen** (*to catch*) is another such verb. *I catch* is — —.
ich fange	286 *You catch* (fam. sing.) is — —.
du fängst	287 *She is catching* is — —.
sie fängt	288 *You catch* (fam. plural) is — —.
ihr fangt	289 **Fallen** (*to fall*) shows a similar change. *You fall* (fam. sing.) is — —.
du fällst	290 *It falls* is — —.
es fällt	291 *We fall* is — —.
wir fallen	292 If the vowel of the infinitive is **e** the 2nd and 3rd persons sing. of such verbs is likely to change to **i**. **Helfen** = *to help. I help* is — —.
ich helfe	293 *He helps* is — —.

35

er hilft	**294**
	Another important verb where the **e** changes to **i** is **geben** (*to give*). *I give* is — —.
ich gebe	**295**
	You give (fam. sing.) is — —.
du gibst	**296**
	She gives is — —.
sie gibt	**297**
	Nehmen (*to take*) is a verb of this kind but here there is more than just a vowel change. The first person is regular. *I take* is — —.
ich nehme	**298**
	He takes = **er nimmt.** Remember that 2nd and 3rd persons sing. show the same change, so that *you take* (fam. sing.) is — —.
du nimmst	**299**
	He takes is — —.
er nimmt	**300**
	But *we take* is — —.
wir nehmen	**301**
	Another important verb rather like this is **werden** (*to become*). *I become* is — —.
ich werde	**302**
	He becomes = **er wird** (notice the **d** instead of **t**). *She becomes* is — —.
sie wird	**303**
	You become (fam. sing.) = **du wirst.** As usual the other persons are regular, so *they become* is — —.
sie werden	**304**
	You become (fam. sing.) is — —.

du wirst

305

There is a fairly long list of verbs which have a vowel change in these two persons of the singular. The only thing to do is to learn them as you meet them. So that you do not have too many all at once we will give you three or four at a time later on. Go to next section.

Plural of Nouns

306

In English it is usually easy to form the plural of a noun. The plural of *cat* is —.

cats

307

So all we need usually do to make a noun plural is to add the letter —.

s

308

However there are some nouns where this is not possible. The plural of *tooth* is not *tooths* but —.

teeth

309

The plural of *child* is not *childs* but —.

children

310

The plural of *ox* is not *oxes* but —.

oxen

311

The plural of *man* is not *mans* but —.

men

312

The plural of *mouse* is not *mouses* but —.

mice

313

Most German nouns form their plurals rather like one or other of the English nouns you have just dealt with. We will start with feminine nouns as they mostly follow one simple pattern. Go to next item.

	314
	Most feminine German nouns form their plural by adding **en** (or **n** if there is already an **e** there). The plural of **die Frau** is — —.
	315
die Frauen	The plural of **die Katze** is — —.
	316
die Katzen	The plural of **die Dame** is — —.
	317
die Damen	Sometimes it is possible to turn a noun standing for a male creature into the feminine by adding **in**. So with **der Schüler** (*schoolboy*); *the schoolgirl* is — —.
	318
die Schülerin	To form the plural of such feminine nouns we must add **nen**. The plural of **die Schülerin** is — —.
	319
die Schülerinnen	**Der Lehrer** (*schoolmaster*) is similar. *The schoolmistress* is — —.
	320
die Lehrerin	*The schoolmistresses* is — —.
	321
die Lehrerinnen	Most feminine nouns form their plural by adding the letters — (or if the noun ends in **e**, the letter —).
	322
en (n)	If the feminine noun ends in **in**, then to form the plural we must add the letters —.
	323
nen	Amongst the exceptions to the rule that feminine plurals end in **n** we must learn **die Mutter** (*mother*), which forms its plural by adding an Umlaut. (You can compare it with *mouse–mice* or *tooth–teeth*). The plural of **die Mutter** is — —.

die Mütter	**324** **Die Tochter** (*daughter*) forms its plural like **die Mutter**. The plural of **die Tochter** is — —.
die Töchter	**325** If a feminine noun ends in **el** or **er** we must add **n**, not **en** to form the plural. **Die Tafel** = *the board*. The plural is — —.
die Tafeln	**326** **Die Nummer** = *the number*. The plural is — —.
die Nummern	**327** A few feminine monosyllables form their plurals by adding an Umlaut and **e**. **Die Maus** (*the mouse*) is such a noun. *The mice* is — —.
die Mäuse	**328** Another such noun is **die Wand** (*the wall*). *The walls* is — —.
die Wände	**329** **Die Hand** (*the hand*) forms its plural in the same way. *The hands* is — —.
die Hände	**330** The German for *the mice* is — —.
die Mäuse	**331** The German for *the walls* is — —.
die Wände	**332** The German for *the hands* is — —.
die Hände	## Four More Verbs with Irregular Present **333** You remember that with the verbs which show a vowel change in the 2nd and 3rd persons sing. an **e** in the infinitive often changes to **i** (e.g. **helfen, geben, nehmen, werden**). So with **sprechen** (*to speak*); *you speak* (fam. sing.) is — —.

du sprichst	334 *He speaks* is — —.
er spricht	335 You remember that this vowel change only affects those two persons, so *we speak* is — —.
wir sprechen	336 Similarly with **treffen** (*to meet*). *You meet* (fam. sing.) is — —.
du triffst	337 *She meets* is — —.
sie trifft	338 But *you meet* (fam. plural) is **ihr** —.
trefft	339 Sometimes the **e** of the infinitive changes to **ie.** This is the case with **sehen** (*to see*). *You see* (fam. sing.) is — —.
du siehst	340 *He sees* is — —.
er sieht	341 **Lesen** (*to read*) behaves like **sehen** except that the 2nd pers. sing. has a contracted form **du liest.** The 3rd pers. sing. is the same as the 2nd person, so *he reads* is — —.
er liest	342 *You read* (fam. sing.) is — —.
du liest	## Plural of Nouns, continued
	343 We have dealt with the plural of most feminine nouns. For the plural of masculine and neuter nouns there are several rules, but there are exceptions to all of them.

	344
	If a <u>masculine</u> or <u>neuter</u> noun ends in **el** the plural is likely to be unchanged. **Der Onkel** = *the uncle*. The plural is **die —**.
Onkel	**345**
	You notice that we changed **der** to **die** for the plural. This is the plural of the definite article for all genders. The plural of **der Löffel** (*spoon*) is — —.
die Löffel	**346**
	The plural of **das Viertel** (*quarter*) is — —.
die Viertel	**347**
	Similarly, masc. or neut. nouns ending in **en** usually remain the same in the plural. **Der Wagen** = *car* or *cart*; *the cars* is — —.
die Wagen	**348**
	Der Morgen = *morning*. *The mornings* is — —.
die Morgen	**349**
	Masc. and neut. nouns ending in **er** also usually remain unchanged in the plural. **Der Schüler**, plural — —.
die Schüler	**350**
	Der Bäcker = *baker*. *The bakers* is — —.
die Bäcker	**351**
	Das Messer = *knife*. *The knives* is — —.
die Messer	**352**
	Similarly, all diminutives remain unchanged in the plural. You remember that diminutives end in **-chen** or **-lein** and that their gender is —.
neuter	**353**
	The plural of **das Mädchen** is — —.
die Mädchen	**354**
	The plural of **das Tischlein** is — —.

die Tischlein	355 Let us sum up what we have learnt about plurals up to now: feminine nouns mostly form their plurals by adding — or —.
n or **en**	356 The plural of the definite article for all genders of noun is —.
die	357 *Masculine* and *neuter* nouns ending in **el, en, er, chen** or **lein** usually *change/do not change* in the plural.
do not change	358 If you add the above endings together you get **Elener Chenlein** which is rather like a girl's name. This may help you to remember which masc. and neut. nouns *change/do not change* in the plural.
do not change	359 Note. Some *masc.* nouns ending in **el, en,** or **er** add an Umlaut in the plural. **Der Vogel** (*bird*) is one such noun. *The birds* is — —.
die Vögel	360 Similarly the plural of **der Vater** (*father*) is — —.
die Väter	361 . . . and the plural of **der Boden** (*floor, ground*) is — —.
die Böden	362 There is a special rule for the plural of neuter nouns of one syllable (or NEUTER MONOSYLLABLES, as it is easier to call them). **Das Buch** is a neuter m—.
monosyllable	363 **Das Mädchen** *is/is not* a neuter monosyllable.
is not	364 **Das Mädchen** is not a monosyllable because it has *one/more than one* syllable.

more than one	**365** Most neuter monosyllables form their plural by adding an Umlaut to the vowel if it can take one and adding **er** at the end. *The books* is — —.
die Bücher	**366** The plural of **das Kind** (*child*) is — —. (It is interesting to remember that in parts of England children are still called *childer*.)
die Kinder	**367** The plural of **das Haus** is — —. (Remember which vowel takes the Umlaut.)
die Häuser	**368** The plural of **das Gras** is — —.
die Gräser	**369** A few *masculine* nouns form their plural in the same way as most neuter monosyllables, that is to say, by adding an — and the letters —.
Umlaut er	**370** So the plural of **der Mann** is — —.
die Männer	**371** . . . and the plural of **der Wald** (*forest*) is — —.

---

die Wälder	## The Meaning of 'Case'
	372 In English, as you know, pronouns have several forms. We say for example 'Wait for *me* until — am ready'.
I	**373** We could not say 'Me am ready'. On the other hand we cannot say 'Can you see I ?' but 'Can you see — ?'

43

me	**374** The pronoun *I* can only be used as the *subject* of a verb. The subject means the person or thing which is doing the action in any sentence. In *You are speaking* the subject is —.
you	**375** Similarly in the sentence *You see me* the pronoun *you* is the —.
subject	**376** In the sentence *The man gives a bone to the dog*, the noun *the man* is the —.
subject	**377** Notice that when we are dealing with grammar the word SUBJECT has nothing to do with the everyday meaning of the matter under discussion but refers only to the person or thing which is doing the — in any sentence.
action	**378** In the sentence *The man gives a bone to the dog*, the subject *is/is not 'the dog'*.
is not	**579** In the sentence *The man gives a bone to the dog, 'the dog'* is not the subject because it is the man who is performing the —.
action (or the giving)	**380** *The dog eats a bone.* Here the dog is doing the action (the eating) so *the dog* is the —.
subject	**381** When a word is the subject of a sentence we say it is in the NOMINATIVE CASE. In the sentence *I look at my book* the pronoun *I* is in the — case.
nominative	**382** *You see me.* The pronoun *me is/is not* in the nominative case.

is not	**383** *You see me.* The pronoun *you is/is not* in the nominative case.
is	**384** Most of the personal pronouns have a special form for the nominative case and this form can only be used for the — of a sentence.
subject	**385** If we use the wrong case for a pronoun instead of the nominative case, the result is likely to be odd, as some of the following examples show: *You see me; Me see you.* The nominative of *me* is —.
I	**386** But *I see you; You see me.* The nominative of *you* is —.
you	**387** *I see him; Him sees me.* The nominative of *him* is —.
he	**388** *I see her; Her sees me.* The nominative of *her* is —.
she	**389** *I see it; It sees me.* The nominative of *it* is —.
it	**390** *You see us; Us see you.* The nominative of *us* is —.
we	**391** *You see them; Them see you.* The nominative of *them* is —.
they	**392** You will see therefore that of the personal pronouns, only y— and i— can be used unchanged in anything but the nominative case.
you, it	**393** The subject of a sentence is the person or thing which is performing the —.
action	**394** The subject of a sentence must be in the — case.

45

nominative	**395** The *object* of a sentence is the person or thing which is *receiving* the action (or to which the action is being done). *You see me.* Here the object is —.
me	**396** Note. In this section we are concerned only with the *direct object* and not with the indirect object, which means *to someone* or *to something.* In the sentence *I see you* the direct object is —.
you	**397** In the sentence *He sees us* the word *he is/is not* the direct object.
is not	**398** The sentence *They see we* is incorrect because *we* is not the direct object form of the pronoun but the — form.
subject (or nominative)	**399** The object of a sentence is the person or thing which is — the action.
receiving	**400** The direct object of a sentence is said to be in the ACCUSATIVE CASE. In the sentence *Can you see me?* the word *me* is in the — case.
accusative	**401** In the sentence *Can you see me?* the word — is in the accusative case.
me	**402** The NOMINATIVE is the word used to describe the *subject/ object* of a sentence.
subject	**403** *He sees us.* The word — is in the accusative case.
us	**404** *He sees us.* The word — is in the nominative case.

46

he	**405**
	Them see us is incorrect because *them* is intended as the subject of the sentence but is not in the — case.
nominative	**406**
	She sees I is incorrect because *I* is intended as the direct object of the sentence but is not in the — case.
accusative	

Plural of Nouns, continued

	407
	Nearly all *masculine* nouns ending in **e** add an **n** to form the plural. So the plural of **der Junge** is — —.
die Jungen	**408**
	. . . and the plural of **der Name** (*name*) is — —.
die Namen	**409**
	Let us now sum up again the rules you have learnt for plurals up to now. Most feminine nouns add the letters — or the letter — to form their plural.
en n	**410**
	Masculine and neuter nouns ending in **el, en, er, chen** and **lein** *change/do not change* in the plural.
do not change	**411**
	Write the name of the girl who may help you to remember these endings: **E— C—**.
Elener Chenlein	**412**
	But some *masculine* nouns with the endings **el, en** or **er** add an —.
Umlaut	**413**
	Most neuter (and a few masculine) monosyllables form their plural by adding an — and the letters —.
Umlaut **er**	**414**
	Masculine nouns ending in **e** form their plural by adding the letter —.

47

n

415

Of the nouns which are not covered by the above rules most form their plural by adding **e**. This applies to nearly all masculine and neuter words of more than one syllable. So the plural of **der Bleistift** (*pencil*) is — —.

die Bleistifte

416

. . . and the plural of **der Abend** (*evening*) is — —.

417

die Abende

Similarly the plural of **das Geschäft** (*business*) is — —.

die Geschäfte

Accusative of Personal Pronouns

418

You saw how in English it is important to put a pronoun in the correct case – that is, to use the proper form of pronoun according to whether it is nominative or accusative. Go to next item.

419

You already know enough to be able to say that in the sentence **Ich bin ein Schüler** the pronoun **ich** is in the — case.

420

nominative

The accusative of **ich** is **mich** (*me*). The German for *He sees me* is **Er sieht** —.

421

mich

He sees me is — — —.

422

er sieht mich

In the sentence **Er sieht mich** the pronoun **mich** is the — of the verb.

423

object

Because in the sentence **Er sieht mich** the pronoun **mich** is the direct object of the verb it must be in the — case.

48

	424
accusative	The accusative of **du** is **dich.** The German for *He see you* (fam. sing.) is **Er sieht** —.
	425
dich	*He sees you* (fam. sing.) is — — —.
	426
er sieht dich	In the sentence **Er sieht dich** the pronoun **dich** is in the — case.
	427
accusative	The accusative of **er** (*he*) is **ihn** (*him*). The German for *I see him* is **ich sehe** —.
	428
ihn	*I see him* is — — —.
	429
ich sehe ihn	The accusative of **ich, du** and **er** are —, — and —.
	430
mich, dich, ihn	Just as in English there were two pronouns *you* and *it* which had no separate form for the accusative case, so in German **sie** (*she*) and **es** (*it*) do not change in the accusative. *He sees her* is — — —.
	431
er sieht sie	. . . and *He sees it* is — — —.
	432
er sieht es	The accusative or **wir** (*we*) is **uns.** *He meets us* is **er trifft** —.
	433
uns	*He meets us* is — — —.
	434
er trifft uns	The accusative of **ihr** (*you*, fam. pl.) is **euch.** *He meets you* is — — —.
	435
er trifft euch	**Sie** (*they*) is another pronoun which does not change for the accusative, so *He meets them* is — — —.

49

er trifft sie	**436** . . . and since, as you remember, the polite way of saying *you* is always the same as the 3rd person plural, except for the capital letter, *He meets you* (polite) is — — —.
er trifft Sie	**437** The accusative of **wir, ihr, sie** and **Sie** is —, —, — and —.
uns, euch, sie, Sie	**438** Here is a table to sum up the Nom. and Acc. of the pronouns:

Sing.   1   2 3m. 3f. 3n. Pl. 1   2   3

	1	2	3m.	3f.	3n.	Pl. 1	2	3
Nom.	**ich**	**du**	**er**	**sie**	**es**	**wir**	**ihr**	**sie (Sie)**
Acc.	**mich**	**dich**	**ihn**			**uns**	**euch**	

If you feel doubtful about this, copy the table down and keep it by you till you know it. Go to next section.

Four More Verbs with Irregular Present

	439 With verbs which change their vowel in the 2nd and 3rd pers. sing. of the present tense an **a** in the infinitive stem usually changes to —.
ä	**440** So with **schlafen** (*to sleep*), *he sleeps* is — —.
er schläft	**441** *You sleep* (fam. sing.) is — —.
du schläfst	**442** . . . whilst of course *I sleep* is — —.
ich schlafe	**443** **Laufen** (*to run*) works the same way, so *he runs* is — —.

50

	444
er läuft	Remember that with the diphthong **au** the Umlaut always goes on the first vowel. *You run* (fam. sing.) is — —.
	445
du läufst	Similarly with **lassen** (*to let* or *leave*), *he lets* is — —.
	446
er läßt	As with some other verbs which have an **s** or **z** at the end of the infinitive stem (e.g. **les-en**) the 2nd person sing. simply adds **t** instead of **est**, so that the verb in *you let* (fam. sing.) is the same as in the 3rd pers. sing., namely **du** —.
	447
du läßt	*He lets* is — —.
	448
er läßt	*You let* (fam. sing.) is — —.

du läßt	## Plural of Nouns, continued
	449
	Most masculine nouns of one syllable add an **e** like those of more than one syllable, but also add an Umlaut. The plural of **der Ball** (*ball*) is — —.
	450
die Bälle	The plural of **der Sohn** (*son*) is — —.
	451
die Söhne	The plural of **der Stuhl** (*chair*) is — —.
	452
die Stühle	Let us now have a final recapitulation of the major rules for forming plurals. Most feminine nouns add the letters — or the letter —.
	453
en n	Masculine and neuter nouns remain unchanged in the plural if they end in the letters —, —, —, — or —.

el, en, er, chen or **lein**	**454** But some masculine nouns ending in **el, en** or **er** add an —.
Umlaut	**455** Most neuter (and a few masculine) monosyllables form their plural by adding an — and the letters —.
Umlaut **er**	**456** Masculine nouns ending in **e** form the plural by adding the letter —.
n	**457** Masculine and neuter nouns of more than one syllable form the plural by adding the letter —.
e	**458** Masculine monosyllables add an — and the letter —.
Umlaut **e**	**459** As you can see, the position with regard to plurals is not always straightforward, so the best plan is always to learn the plural as well as the gender of any noun you meet from now on. Go to next section.

Accusative of Nouns

	460 Do not forget what you have learnt about the nominative and accusative cases. The subject of a sentence, e.g. *I meet you* must be in the — case.
nominative	**461** The object of a sentence, e.g. *I meet YOU* must be in the — case.
accusative	**462** You know the accusative of the personal pronouns, e.g. *I meet him* is **ich treffe** —.

52

ihn	463 In German not only pronouns but masculine nouns as well have a special accusative case, e.g., **Ich sehe den Mann.** Here **den Mann** is in the — case.
accusative	464 As you noticed, the accusative is shown by a change in the definite — rather than by a change in the noun itself.
article	465 (There are some cases in which the noun also changes, but you will not learn about these till later.) Thus in **Ich sehe den Mann** the word which is actually in a different form from the nominative is —.
den	466 The form of the definite article for a masculine singular noun in the accusative is therefore —.
den	467 *I see the table* (remember **Tisch** is masc.) is — — — —.
ich sehe den Tisch	468 *I meet the son* (**Sohn**) is **ich treffe** — —.
den Sohn	469 *The father meets the uncle* is **der Vater trifft** — **Onkel**.
den	470 Remember that it is only the direct — which goes into the accusative case.
object	471 *The father meets the uncle* is (write the full sentence): **Der/den Vater trifft der/den Onkel.**
Der Vater trifft den Onkel	472 Only masculine nouns show a special accusative case, so *The father meets the daughter* (**Tochter**). is **Der Vater trifft** — —.

die Tochter	**473** . . . and *The father sees the house* is **Der Vater sieht —** —.
das Haus	**474** What is more, it is only masculine *singular* nouns which show a special accusative case, so *the father meets the uncles* is **der Vater trifft — —.**
die Onkel	**475** Think back to the section called 'Determinatives', which we explained meant words like *the, this, my, a (an),* etc. The masc. accusative sing. of all these determinatives ends in **en.** *I see a man* is **ich sehe ein— Mann.**
einen	**476** You remember that there are two types of determinative – first those like the definite article, **der, jener, dieser, welcher,** etc., all of which in the masc. nominative singular end in —.
er	**477** To form the masc. accusative singular this nominative **er** ending must be *changed* to —.
en	**478** *I see this man* is **ich sehe dies— Mann.**
diesen	**479** *I see that man* is **ich sehe jen— Mann.**
jenen	**480** *I see this man* is — — — —.
ich sehe diesen Mann	**481** *I see that man* is — — — —.
ich sehe jenen Mann	**482** The other type of determinative is like the indefinite article —.

ein (eine, ein)	483 Apart from **ein** itself, this group includes **kein** (*no, not any*) and the possessive adjectives such as **mein** (*my*), **ihr** (*their*), etc.; the words in this group show *a/no* special masculine nominative ending.
no	484 With determinatives like **ein** therefore, to obtain the masc. accusative sing. form we must *add* the letters —
en	485 So *I see a man* is **ich sehe ein— Mann**
en	486 *I see a man* is — — — —.
ich sehe einen Mann	487 *I see no man* (using **kein**) is — — — —.
ich sehe keinen Mann	488 *I meet their uncle* is **ich treffe ihr— —.**
ihren Onkel	489 . . . but *I meet a lady* is **ich treffe — Dame.**
eine	490 *I see a girl* (remember the gender of **Mädchen**) is — — — —.
ich sehe ein Mädchen	491 Here is a table to sum up the Nom. and Acc of the definite article:

Sing. Masc. Fem. Neut. Pl. (all genders).

	Masc.	Fem.	Neut.	Pl.
Nom.	dER	dIE	dAS	dIE
Acc.	dEN			

Go to next item when you are quite sure you know this.

492
Here is a table to sum up the Nom. and Acc. of the indefinite article:

55

Sing.	Masc.	Fem.	Neut.	

Nom. **ein** ⎰ **einE** ⎰ **ein**   As in English, there is
Acc. **einEN** ⎱   ⎱   no plural.

Make sure that you know this (including the way in which the endings differ from those of the definite article – i.e. no endings in the Nom. Masc. and Nom. and Acc. Neut.) Then go to next section.

Plural of Determinatives

493

The nominative plural of all determinatives ends in **e**, e.g. **diE Frauen, diesE Mädchen, keinE (meinE, ihrE) Onkel.** *My teachers* is — —.

---
meine Lehrer

494

Of course with the words like **ein (kein, mein, ihr,** etc.) we must *add* this letter — to the word. (Naturally **ein** itself, which means *one*, has no plural).

---
e

495

Their uncles is **ihr**— —.

---
ihre Onkel

496

With **der**-type determinatives (e.g. **dieser, diese, dieses; jener, jene, jenes**) which have a special ending in the masc. and neut. nominative sing. this ending must be removed before we add the letter — for the plural.

---
e

497

The plural of **dieser Schüler** is — —.

---
diese Schüler

498

You can see how important this plural **e** is, as with the many nouns which do not change in the plural it may be the only sign that the word *is* plural. Thus the plural of **mein Wagen** is — —.

56

meine Wagen	499 . . . and the plural of **kein Mädchen** is — —.
	500
keine Mädchen	The plural of **dieses Fräulein** is — —.
	501
diese Fräulein	The plural of **jene Schülerin** is — —.
	502
jene Schülerinnen	You would notice that feminine determinatives are the same for singular and plural, but this never leads to confusion as no feminine nouns remain unchanged in the plural. Go to next item.
	503
	The plural of **meine Mutter** is — —.
	504
meine Mütter	Here is a table to sum up the Nom. and Acc. of **der**-type determinatives (last letter always the same as that of **der, die, das** etc.):

Sing. Masc.   Fem.   Neut.   Pl. (all genders).

Nom.	**diesER** ⎰	**diesE** ⎰	**diesES** ⎰	**diesE**
Acc.	**diesEN** ⎱			

Go to next section.

Four More Irregular Feminine Plurals

505

You remember that nearly all feminine nouns form their plural by adding **n** or **en**. The plural of **die Tür** (*door*) is — —.

506

die Türen   The plural of **die Insel** (*island*) is — —.

507

die Inseln   But there are a few feminine monosyllables, as you know, which form the plural by adding an Umlaut and **e**. Thus the plural of **die Maus** is — —.

die Mäuse	**508** Another such feminine noun is **die Frucht** (*fruit*), so the plural is — —.
die Früchte	**509** Similarly with **die Kuh** (*cow*). *The cows* is — —.
die Kühe	**510** So too with **die Nacht** (*night*). The plural is — —.
die Nächte	**511** *The fruits* is — —.
die Früchte	**512** *The cows* is — —.
die Kühe	**513** *The nights* is — —.

---

die Nächte

Four More Verbs with Irregular Present

	514 Here are four more verbs in which an **e** in the infinitive stem changes to **i** in the 2nd and 3rd pers. sing. **Brechen** = *to break*. *He breaks* is — —.
er bricht	**515** ... and accordingly *you break* (fam. sing.) is — —.
du brichst	**516** **Sterben** = *to die*. (English *starve* comes from this although the two verbs no longer mean exactly the same.) *You die* (fam. sing.) is — —.
du stirbst	**517** *He dies* is — —.
er stirbt	**518** **Werfen** = *to throw*. *He throws* is — —.
er wirft	**519** ... and *you throw* (fam. sing.) is — —.

du wirfst	**520** **Gelten** (*to be worth*) is usually only used impersonally (i.e. with *it* as subject). It is also slightly irregular as no extra **t** is added for the 3rd pers. sing. *It is worth* is therefore — —.
es gilt	**521** *It is worth* is — —.
es gilt	**522** *He breaks* is — —.
er bricht	**523** *He dies* is — —.
er stirbt	**524** *He throws* is — —.
er wirft	**525** *It is worth* is — —.

es gilt	## The Dative Case: Pronouns
	526 We have already met two cases in dealing with nouns and pronouns: first, the nominative case, which is the form for a noun or pronoun when it is the — of a verb.
subject	**527** ... and secondly, the accusative case, which is the form for a noun or pronoun when it is the direct — of a verb.
object	**528** Now we come to the INDIRECT OBJECT, which represents the person or thing to which (or for the benefit of which) an action is done. So in the sentence *I give the dog a bone* the indirect object is — —.

the dog	**529** If there is an indirect object in a sentence you can almost always put *to* or *for* in front of it without making the meaning absurd – so with *I give the dog a bone* we could very well say *I give — the dog a bone*.
to	**530** Since we could say *I give TO the dog a bone*, we know that *the dog* is the — object of the sentence.
indirect	**531** Let us try putting *to* in front of another word in the sentence as a test e.g. *I give the dog to a bone*. This is nonsense, so that *a bone* clearly *is/is not* the indirect object.
is not	**532** Try another example – *Tell me a story*: *Tell me to a story*. *Story is/is not* the indirect object.
is not	**533** Try again with the same example. *Tell (to) me a story*. This makes sense, so *(to) me is/is not* the indirect object.
is	**534** We said that you can sometimes put *for* (instead of *to*) in front of the indirect object. Take the sentence *Buy me a book*. Try *Buy me for a book*. Rubbish! So *book is/is not* the indirect object.
is not	**535** Try again with the same example. *Buy (for) me a book*. This works, so the indirect object *is/is not (for) me*.
is	**536** If you have identified the indirect object correctly, then (as in the sentence *Give the dog a bone*) you can insert the word — in front of it;
to	**537** . . . or else (as in the sentence *Buy me a book*) you can insert the word — in front of the indirect object.

for	**538** Of course sometimes the preposition *to* or *for* is already there. Thus you could not omit the preposition in the sentence *Give a bone — the dog.*
to	**539** . . . or in the sentence *Buy a book — me.*
for	**540** (You can omit this item if you wish.) It is interesting to note that in English we usually omit the words *to* and *for* from the indirect object if it precedes the direct object: *Tell (to) the class a story.* But if the direct object comes first the preposition cannot be omitted — *Tell a story TO the class.* Go to next item.
	541 In English, then, the indirect object must have, either expressed or understood, the preposition — or the preposition —.
to for	**542** In German however the indirect object is not shown by adding a preposition but by changing the form of the word. Just as we had the nominative case for the —,
subject	**543** . . . . and as we had the accusative case for the —,
direct object	**544** . . . so we have the DATIVE CASE for the — object.
indirect	**545** The case used for the indirect object is called the — case.
dative	**546** The word *dative* comes from Latin and means *giving* because it is the case to use when you speak about giving something — someone.

to	**547**
	The dative of the pronoun **ich** is **mir**, which means — *me* or — *me*.
	548
to me, *for* me	*He gives (to) me a book* is **Er gibt** — **ein Buch.**
	549
mir	Notice how important it is to get the case right. If you said **Er gibt mich** (Acc.) instead of **Er gibt mir** (Dat.) it would mean *He gives me (away to somebody)*! *To me* is —.
	550
mir	The dative of **du** is **dir**. **Dir** means — *you* or — *you* (fam. sing.).
	551
to you, *for* you	*He shows (to) you a book* is **Er zeigt** — **ein Buch.**
	552
dir	The dative of **er** is **ihm**, which means — *him* or — *him*.
	553
to him, *for* him	*We show (to) him a house* is **Wir zeigen** — **ein Haus.**
	554
ihm	The datives of **ich** and **du** are — and —.
	555
mir dir	The dative of **er** is —.
	556
ihm	The dative of **sie** (*she*) is **ihr**, which means — *her* or — *her*.
	557
to her *for* her	*He shows (to) her the child* is **Er zeigt** — **das Kind.**
	558
ihr	The dative of **es** is the same as the dative of **er**, namely —.
	559
ihm	**Ihm** therefore means not only *to* (or *for*) *him*, but — (or) — —.

to (or *for*) *it*	**560** *To* (or *for*) *her* is —.
ihr	**561** (You can omit this item if you wish). Have you noticed how some of the German dative pronouns are like some of the English accusative pronouns ? (**Ihm** is like *him*, **ihr** is like *her*.) Old English used to have separate accusative forms for the pronouns – *hine* for *him*, *hie* for *her*, etc. These old accusative forms for all the pronouns except *it* were lost several hundred years ago and the dative forms (*him*, *hire* (= *her*), etc.) were taken over to do duty as accusatives instead. Probably this was how we first began to omit *to* from our indirect object pronouns – because they really are dative. Go to next item.
	562 The datives of all the singular personal pronouns (**ich, du, er, sie, es**) are —, —, —, —, —.
mir, dir, ihm, **ihr, ihm**	**563** The dative of **wir** is **uns,** which therefore means — *us* or — *us*.
to us, *for* us	**564** *They show* (*to*) *us their dog* is **sie zeigen — ihren Hund.**
uns	**565** The dative of **ihr** (= *you*, fam. pl.) is **euch. Euch** means — *you* or — *you*.
to you, *for* you	**566** *He shows* (*to*) *you* (fam. pl.) *his dog* is **er zeigt — seinen Hund.**
euch	**567** The dative of **sie** (= *they*) is **ihnen**, which means — *them* or — *them*.
to them, *for* them	**568** *I show them my car* is **ich zeige — meinen Wagen.**

ihnen	**569** As you know by now, the polite way of saying *you* is the same as the 3rd pers. pl. *To you* (polite) is —. (Be careful how you write it!)
Ihnen	**570** *I show you* (polite) *my book* is **ich zeige** — **mein Buch**.
Ihnen	**571** The datives of all the plural personal pronouns (**wir, ihr, sie, Sie**) are —, —, —, —.
uns, euch, ihnen **Ihnen**	**572** Here is a table to sum up the Nom., Acc. and Dative of the pronouns:

Sing. 1　2　3m. 3f. 3n. Pl. 1　2　　　3

Nom.	ich	du	er	⌠ sie ⌠ es	wir ihr	⌠ sie	(Sie)
Acc.	mich	dich	ihn	⌊ ⌊	uns euch	⌊
Dat.	mir	dir	ihm	ihr ihm	uns euch ihnen	(Ihnen)

If you feel doubtful about this, copy the table down and keep it by you till you know it. Go to next section.

The Imperative

	573 The IMPERATIVE is the name given to the form of the verb when it is used to give a command. In the sentence *Go away!* the verb is in the —.
imperative	**574** As you know, you cannot just use the present tense to give a command. You cannot say 'Are quiet!' or 'Is quiet!' but — *quiet!*
Be	**575** Similarly in German there are special ways of giving a command, and these vary according to which of the forms of address (polite, fam. sing. or pl.) you are using. Go to next item.

576

The polite form is quite straightforward. It consists of the present tense *followed* by the pronoun – e.g. *Give!* is **Geben Sie!** *Show!* (using **zeigen**) is — —!

zeigen Sie!

577

With regard to punctuation, notice that the imperative in German is normally followed by an — mark, even though it may be omitted in English.

exclamation

578

Come! (polite) is — —.

kommen Sie!

579

Go! (polite) is — —.

gehen Sie!

580

The 2nd pers. sing. imperative (fam. sing.) usually consists of adding **e** to the stem of the verb. There is no pronoun. Thus **mach-en** (the hyphen is put in simply to show you how it is done and is not part of the spelling) gives —.

mache!

581

The fam. sing. imperative of **geh-en** is —.

gehe!

582

The fam. sing. imperative of **tu-n** is —.

tue!

583

Often in speaking this final **e** is omitted, so that instead of **Mache! Gehe!** or **Tue!** we may get —, — or —.

mach'! geh'! tu'!

584

If the verb is one in which an **e** in the infinitive stem changes to **i** or **ie** in the 2nd and 3rd pers. sing. of the present tense (e.g., **nehmen – nimmst, sehen – siehst**) the fam. sing. imperative shows the vowel change and no final **e** is added, e.g. **Nimm!** *See!* (fam. sing.) is —.

sieh!

585

Give! (fam. sing.) is —.

gib!	586 *Break!* (fam. sing.) is —.
brich!	587 The 2nd pers. pl. imperative (fam. pl.) is straightforward. It consists of the 2nd pers. pl. of the present tense of the verb without the pronoun, e.g., **gebt!, kommt!** *See!* (fam. pl.) is —.
seht!	588 *Go!* (fam. pl.) is —.
geht!	589 *Give!* (fam. pl.) is —.
gebt!	590 **Sein** (*to be*) has irregular imperatives. The polite form is **seien Sie!** *Be quiet!* (quiet = **still**) is — — —.
seien Sie still!	591 *Be careful!* (**vorsichtig**) (polite) is — — —.
seien Sie vorsichtig!	592 The 2nd pers. sing. imperative of **sein** is **sei!** *Be quiet!* is — —.
sei still!	593 *Be careful!* (fam. sing.) is — **vorsichtig!**
sei	594 The 2nd pers. pl. imperative of **sein** is the same as the present tense without the pronoun, namely —.
seid!	595 *Be quiet!* (fam. pl.) is — —.
seid still!	

'Essen' and 'Fressen'

596
Essen (*to eat*) is another verb where the **e** of the infinitive stem changes to **i** in the 2nd and 3rd pers. sing. *He eats* is — —.

er ißt	597 As in the case of other slightly irregular verbs having **s** at the end of the infinitive stem, the 2nd pers. sing. simply adds **t** instead of **est**, so *you eat* (fam. sing.) is — —.
du ißt	598 You must not use **essen** to describe an animal eating. For animals the verb is **fressen,** which behaves just like **essen.** *The mouse eats* is — — —.
die Maus frißt	599 Of course you will not usually meet **fressen** in the 2nd pers. sing. You may like to know that **fressen** is simply the modern way of spelling **ver-essen,** which means *to gobble up.* Go to next item.

The Dative Case: Nouns

	600 You remember that in dealing with pronouns you learnt that the indirect object (*to* or *for* someone) had to go into the — case.
dative	601 You will not be surprised to hear that nouns, too, have a dative case. The dative of **der Mann** is **deM Mann,** which means — or — *the man.*
to or *for* the man	602 The dative of neuter nouns is formed in exactly the same way as that of masc. nouns. The dative of **das Haus** is — —.
dem Haus	603 *Give (to) the man a book* is **Geben Sie** — **Mann ein Buch.**
dem	604 *He shows the girl a picture* is **Er zeigt** — — **ein Bild.**

dem Mädchen	605 Sometimes with masc. and neuter monosyllables an **e** may be added to the noun, so that instead of **dem Mann** we could say **dem Mann—**.
dem Manne	606 . . . and instead of **dem Haus** we could say — —.
dem Hause	607 However there is not usually any need to do this. And with **dem Geschäft**, for example, it would be wrong to add an **e** because **Geschäft** is not a —.
monosyllable	608 The other determinatives as well as the definite article (that is, **dieser, jener, ein, mein,** etc.) also end in **em** for the dative of masc. and neut. sing. nouns. *To this man* is **dies— Mann(e)**.
diesem	609 *To a man* is **ein— Mann(e)**.
einem	610 *To no man* is — —.
keinem Mann(e)	611 Feminine nouns form their dative case differently. The dative of **die Maus** is **dER Maus,** which means — or — — —.
to or *for the mouse*	612 *Give (to) the woman a book* is **geben Sie** — — **ein Buch.**
der Frau	613 With feminines, the noun itself never changes in the singular, unlike masc. or neut. sing. nouns where, if they are monosyllables, it is possible (though not usually necessary) to add an —.
e	614 *Show the lady a picture* is **zeigen Sie** — — **ein Bild.**

68

der Dame	**615** As in the case of the definite article, all the other determinatives (**dieser, jener, ein, ihr,** etc.) end in **er** in the feminine dative singular. *To a woman* is — —.
einer Frau	**616** *To this lady* is — —.
dieser Dame	**617** *To my daughter* is — —.
meiner Tochter	**618** All plural nouns form their dative in the same way. (Remember there are *some/no* distinctions of gender in the plural).
no	**619** The dative of **die Frauen** is **den Frauen,** so we shall expect all determinatives in the dative plural to end in the letters —.
en	**620** *To the girls* is — —.
den Mädchen	**621** *To these schoolgirls* is — —.
diesen Schüler-innen	**622** *To my cats* is — —.
meinen Katzen	**623** However, there may be a further change to make for the dative plural, since all dative plural nouns *must* end in **n,** and one must be added if it is not there already. *To the mice* is — —.
den Mäusen	**624** *To their bakers* is — —.
ihren Bäckern	**625** *To no birds* is — —.

69

	626
keinen Vögeln	Here is a table to sum up the Nom., Acc. and Dat. of the definite article:

Sing. Masc. Fem. Neut. Pl. (all genders).

Nom.	**dER** ⎰	**dIE** ⎰	**dAS**	⎰ **dIE**
Acc.	**dEN** ⎱	⎱		⎱
Dat.	**dEM**	**dER**	**dEM**	**dEN**

If you feel doubtful about any of this, copy the table down and keep it by you till you know it. Go to next section.

More Verbs with Vowel Change in Present

627

You already know **lesen** and **sehen,** where the **e** changes to **ie** in 2nd and 3rd pers. sing. of the present tense.
Befehlen (*to command* or *order*) behaves similarly. *You command* (fam. sing.) is — —.

	628
du befiehlst	*He commands* is — —.
	629
er befiehlt	**Stehlen** (*to steal*) changes in the same way. *He steals* is — —.
	630
er stiehlt	**Geschehen** (*to happen*) does the same. (Of course it is an impersonal verb.) *It happens* is — —.
	631
es geschieht	*You steal* (fam. sing.) is — —.
	632
du stiehlst	*It happens* is — —.
	633
es geschieht	**Befehlen** has another peculiarity: it requires to be followed by a dative (not accusative) case. So *He commands the men* is **er** — — —.

70

befiehlt den Männern	634 *We command you* (polite) is — — —.
wir befehlen Ihnen	## Prepositions Requiring Dative
	635 Up to now we have only dealt with the dative where it corresponds to the English — object.
indirect	636 However another important use for the dative is after many prepositions. One preposition which must be followed by the dative is **aus** (*out of*). *Out of the house* is — — —.
aus dem Haus(e)	637 **Die Klasse** = *the class. Out of the class* is — — —.
aus der Klasse	638 *Out of the car* is — — —.
aus dem Wagen	639 Another preposition requiring the dative is **bei** (*at the house of* – like French 'chez'). *He lives at his uncle's house* is **er wohnt** — — —.
bei seinem Onkel	640 *They live with their aunt* is **sie wohnen** — — **Tante.**
bei ihrer Tante	641 **Gegenüber** (*opposite*) requires the dative. (This looks like a long word but it is really two – **gegen** = *against* and **über** = *over,* so it really means *over against,* which is the same as *opposite*). It usually comes after the noun or pronoun to which it belongs. *Opposite the house* is **dem Haus(e)** —.
gegenüber	642 *Opposite the wall* is — — —.

der Wand gegen- **über**	**643** *Opposite the chair* is — — —.
	644
dem Stuhl gegen- **über**	**Mit** (*with*) requires the dative. *With me* is — —.
	645
mit mir	*With his daughters* is — — —.
	646
mit seinen **Töchtern**	*With you* (polite) is — —.
	647
mit Ihnen	You have now met four prepositions requiring the dative. Try to memorize them (in the next item you will be asked to write them out). **Aus, bei, gegenüber, mit.** Go to next item.
	648
	Write the four prepositions requiring the dative which you have met up to now —, —, —, —.
aus, bei, **gegenüber, mit**	

Word Order: Inversion

649

You may have noticed how, when we begin a sentence in English with certain expressions we must alter the order of verb and subject. So, *I had hardly seen you when you left*, but *Hardly — — seen you when you left.*

650

had I	Similarly *I will not only come but stay a week*, but *Not only — — come but stay a week.*
	651
will I	In German, word order is especially important. In a main sentence the verb must always be the *second* idea (except in a question, when of course it must come —.)

72

first	**652**
	In a main sentence in German (other than a question) the verb must be the *first/second/third* idea.
second	**653**
	Der Vater (1) **spricht** (2) **nach der Schule** (3) **mit dem Sohn** (4). *The father speaks with the son after school.* We have divided the sentence up by numbering the various ideas and the verb is no. —.
(2)	**654**
	Let us change the order and make **Nach der Schule** the first idea, **Nach der Schule** (1) **spricht** (2) **der Vater** (3) **mit dem Sohn** (4). The verb is still idea no. —.
(2)	**655**
	Here is the sentence again for reference: **Nach der Schule spricht der Vater mit dem Sohn.** As we started with an idea which was not the subject, and the verb has to come second, it has been necessary to put the subject — the verb.
after	**656**
	Let us begin with yet another idea: **Mit dem Sohn** (1) **spricht** (2) **der Vater** (3) **nach der Schule** (4). The verb is still idea no. —
(2)	**657**
	You have no choice about this rule, which is sometimes called the INVERSION RULE, because if you begin with something which is not the subject the verb and its — are inverted. (Here is the sentence for reference: **Nach der Schule spricht der Vater mit dem Sohn.**)
subject	**658**
	Note. The conjunctions **und** (*and*), **aber** (*but*), **oder** (or) do not cause inversion so it is *right/wrong* to say . . . **und der Vater spricht**

GG—F

right	**659** . . . and it is *right/wrong* to say . . . **aber der Vater spricht.**
right	## Test on Inversion
	660 In this and the next five items, rewrite the sentences beginning with the words in capitals and make any other changes in word order which you think are required. **Der Sohn kommt AUS DER SCHULE.**
Aus der Schule kommt der Sohn	**661** **Er geht MIT SEINEM HUNDE aus dem Walde.**
Mit seinem Hunde geht er aus dem Walde	**662** . . . **die Katze geht nicht mit ihnen./ABER.**
aber die Katze geht nicht mit ihnen	**663** **Sie haben keine Nachricht** (*news*) **VON MIR** (*of me*).
Von mir haben sie keine Nachricht	**664** . . . **er spricht mit der Klasse./UND.**
und er spricht mit der Klasse	**665** **Er liest ein Buch MIT EINEM BLEISTIFT IN DER HAND.**
Mit einem Bleistift in der Hand liest er ein Buch	## Prepositions Requiring Dative, continued **666** You have met four prepositions, **aus, bei, gegenüber, mit,** which need to be followed by the — case.

dative	**667** **Nach** is another preposition requiring the dative. It has two meanings – *after* and *to* (*towards*). *The sons come after their father* is **Die Söhne kommen — — —**.
nach ihrem Vater	**668** *After him* is — —.
nach ihm	**669** *To England* is — *England*.
nach	**670** *The father is walking to the town* (**Stadt** fem.) is **Der Vater geht — — —**.
nach der Stadt	**671** **Nach** means — and —.
after to (towards)	**672** **Nach Hause** is an important expression involving this preposition. It means *home(wards)*. *He is going home* is **er — — —**.
geht nach Hause	**673** Notice that in the expression **nach Hause**, the final **e**, which is a sign of the — case, is always required.
dative	**674** *I am coming home* is **ich — — —**.
komme nach Hause	**675** **Seit** (since) also requires the dative. *Since the morning* (**Morgen** masc.) is — — —.
seit dem Morgen	**676** *Since the evening* (**Abend** masc.) is — — —.
seit dem Abend	**677** **Von** (*of, from*) also requires the dative. *From the house* is — — —.
von dem Haus(e)	**678** *From the wood* (**Wald** masc.) is — — —.

	679
von dem Wald(e)	*News of the woman* is **Nachricht** — — —.
	680
von der Frau	**Von** means — or —.
	681
of from	**Zu** (*to*) also requires the dative. It is usually used in the sense of going up to something. Do not use it for the indirect object. *He goes up to the teacher* is **er geht** — — —.
	682
zu dem Lehrer	*They go to the table* is **sie gehen** — — —.
	683
zu dem Tisch(e)	An important expression involving **zu** is **zu Hause** which means *at home*. Notice that as with **nach Hause** the dative **e** is essential. *I am at home* is — — — —.
	684
ich bin zu Hause	You have now had a fairly complete list of the prepositions which always require the dative. Later you will meet others which sometimes require the dative. The best thing to do is to memorize those you have now met. In alphabetical order they are **aus, bei, gegenüber, mit, nach, seit, von, zu.** Go to next frame.
	685
	The eight prepositions you have just been dealing with require the dative *sometimes/always*.
	686
always	We shall omit two at a time until you have learnt them all. **AUS, BEI, gegenüber, mit, nach, seit, von, zu.** Go to next item.
	687
	—, —, **GEGENÜBER, MIT,** nach, seit, von, zu. Write the missing prepositions.
	688
aus, bei	—, —, —, —, **NACH, SEIT,** von, zu.

76

aus, bei, **gegenüber, mit**	**689** —, —, —, —, —, —, **VON, ZU.**
	690 Write out the eight prepositions which always require to be followed by the dative case.
aus, bei, **gegenüber, mit,** **nach, seit**	

aus, bei,
gegenüber, mit,
nach, seit, von, zu

More Verbs with Vowel Change in Present

691

You remember that where a verb changes its stem vowel in the 2nd and 3rd pers. sing. **a** usually becomes **ä**. So with **fahren** (*to travel*), *He travels* is — —.

er fährt

692

You travel (fam. sing.) is — —.

du fährst

693

(You can omit this item if you wish). **Fahren** is the verb which gives us our English words *thoroughfare*, *welfare* and *farewell*. Go to next item.

694

Schlagen (*to strike*) shows the same changes. *You strike* (fam. sing.) is — —.

du schlägst

695

He strikes is — —.

er schlägt

696

Wachsen = *to grow*. (This is the same word as the verb *to wax* which we find in the Bible – '. . . and the child grew and waxed strong in spirit . . .' – Luke ii, 40). **Wachsen** is like the other verbs mentioned above. *He grows* is — —.

er wächst	**697** You remember that these slightly irregular verbs with stems ending in **s** usually add only **t** (instead of **est**) in the 2nd pers. sing. *You grow* (fam. sing.) is — —.
du wächst	**698** **Halten** (*to hold*) is slightly irregular in another way – it adds an Umlaut but no extra **t** (or **et**) in the 3rd pers. sing. *He holds* is — —.
er hält	**699** The 2nd pers. sing. adds an Umlaut but is otherwise not remarkable. *You hold* (fam. sing.) is — —.
du hältst	**700** You have now met most of the really common verbs which show a vowel change of this kind in the present tense. Go to next section.

Three More Irregular Feminine Plurals

	701 You remember that most feminine nouns form their plural by adding the letters — or the letter —.
en n	**702** . . . but that some monosyllables add an — and the letter —.
Umlaut **e**	**703** Amongst the latter are the following – **die Gans** (*the goose*). *The geese* is — —.
die Gänse	**704** . . . **die Nuß** (*nut*) has for its plural — —.
die Nüsse	**705** . . . and the plural of **die Stadt** (*town*) is — —.
die Städte	**706** *The geese* is — —.

die Gänse	707 *The nuts is — —.*
die Nüsse	708 *The towns is — —.*
die Städte	

Prepositions Requiring the Accusative

709
Just as some prepositions require the dative case, there are a few (very important ones) which require the accusative. **Durch** (*through*) is one of these. *Through the house is — — —.*

durch das Haus	710 *Through the wood (**Wald** masc.) is — — —.*
durch den Wald	711 *Through the town is — — —.*
durch die Stadt	712 **Für** (*for*) is another preposition requiring the accusative. *For me is — —.*
für mich	713 *For the sons is — — —.*
für die Söhne	714 *For the girl is — — —.*
für das Mädchen	715 **Gegen** (*against*) also requires the accusative. *Against my father is — — —.*
gegen meinen Vater	716 *The chair is against the wall is — — — — — —.*
der Stuhl ist gegen die Wand	717 *Against him is — —.*

79

gegen ihn	718 **Ohne** (*without*) is another preposition requiring the accusative. *Without me* is — —.
ohne mich	719 *Without my dog* is — — —.
ohne meinen Hund	720 *Without their teachers* is — — —.
ohne ihre Lehrer	721 (Omit this item if you like). You may be interested to know that it is from this preposition (**ohne**) that both we and the Germans get our negative prefix *un-*, as in *unpleasant, untie* or German **unvorsichtig**. (Go to next item.)
	722 **Um** (around) is the last of the common prepositions requiring the accusative. *Round the table* is — — —.
um den Tisch	723 *Round the town* is — — —.
um die Stadt	724 *Round them* is — —.
um sie	725 **Um** also has an important use with time, when it means *at*. *At two o'clock* is **um zwei Uhr**. *At three o'clock* is — **drei** —. (Note that **Uhr** does not mean *hour* but *o'clock*.)
um drei Uhr	726 When **um** is used in connexion with time it does not mean *round* but —.
at	727 We have been dealing with the prepositions which always require the — case.

80

accusative	**728** You should learn the list so as not to confuse them with other prepositions. **Durch, für, gegen, ohne, um.** Go to next item. **729** —, —, **gegen, ohne, um.**
durch, für	**730** —, —, —, **ohne, um.**
durch, für, gegen	**731** Write the list of the 5 prepositions which always require the accusative case.

durch, für, gegen
ohne, um

Plural of Nouns, continued

732
A few nouns, mostly of obviously foreign origin, form their plural by adding **s**. Thus the plural of **das Auto** (*motor-car*) is **die Auto—**.

Autos

733
. . . and the plural of **das Büro** (*office*) is — —.

die Büros

734
Such nouns do not add **n** in the dative plural. *With the cars* is **mit den —**.

Autos

735
Out of the offices is **aus** — —.

den Büros

The Rest of the Possessive Adjectives

736
You have already met the possessive adjectives **mein** (*my*) and **ihr** (*their*). You will remember that these words belong to the **ein**-group of determinatives, which have *a/no* special nominative ending in the masc. and neut. sing.

81

	737
no	*My book* is — —.
	738
mein Buch	. . . and *their son* is — —.
	739
ihr Sohn	. . . whereas *this book* is **dies—** **Buch** (because **dieser, diese, dieses** belongs to the **DER**-group of determinatives).
	740
diesES Buch	. . . and *each son* is **jed— Sohn**.
	741
jedER Sohn	To go back to the possessive adjectives – you will also remember that they, like the rest of the **ein-**group, do show a *feminine* ending in the nominative singular. So *my mother* is — —.
	742
meine Mutter	The possessive adjective for **du** is **dein**. *Your dog* (fam. sing.) is — —.
	743
dein Hund	*Your class* (fam. sing.) is — —.
	744
deine Klasse	*Your house* (fam. sing.) is — —.
	745
dein Haus	The possessive adjective from **er** and **es** is **sein**. There is therefore no difference in German between *his* and —.
	746
its	(Omit this item if you wish.) In English, too, there was until comparatively recently no difference between *his* and *its* – which is a comparatively modern invention. The Authorized Version of the Bible uses *his* only: '. . . a tree that bringeth forth his fruit in his season.' (Psalms I).
	747
	His father is — —.

	748
sein Vater	*His number* (**die Nummer**) *is* — —.
	749
seine Nummer	*Its number is* — —.
	750
seine Nummer	*His picture* (**das Bild**) *is* — —.
	751
sein Bild	The possessive adjective from **sie** (*she*) is **ihr**. (Yes, this is the same as *their* but this does not seem to lead to any confusion.) *Her uncle is* — —.
	752
ihr Onkel	*Her aunt is* — —.
	753
ihre Tante	*Her knife* (**das Messer**) *is* — —.
	754
ihr Messer	Special note for those who have learnt French: In French 'son, sa, ses' mean both *his* and *her*. If you learnt French before German you will probably need a special effort to remember that German is different and that there are separate words for *his* (—) and *her* (—).
	755
sein, ihr	The possessive adjective from **wir** is **unser**. *Our boy is* — —.
	756
unser Junge	Note that with **unser** the **er** is an essential part of the word and not just a grammatical ending. *Our town is* — —.
	757
unsere Stadt	*Our house is* — —.
	758
unser Haus	The possessive adjective from **ihr** (*you*, fam. pl.) is **euer**. *Your name* (**der Name**) *is* — —.

	759
euer Name	Here too the **er** of **euer** is part of the word, but when any grammatical ending is added the **e** before the **r** is dropped, e.g., **eure Häuser.** *Your cow* is — —.
	760
eure Kuh	*Your business* (**das Geschäft**) is — —.
	761
euer Geschäft	You already know the German for *their*; it is —.
	762
ihr	You therefore also know the word for *your* (polite), namely —.
	763
Ihr	*Your baker* (polite) is — —.
	764
Ihr Bäcker	*Your daughter* (polite) is — —.
	765
Ihre Tochter	*Your knife* (polite) is — —.
	766
Ihr Messer	So far in this section all these adjectives have been given in the nominative case, but you already know how to deal with them in other cases as well. *He shows it to my father* is **er zeigt es mein— Vater** (dative).
	767
meinEM Vater	*We speak with his mother* (remember **mit** requires dative) is **wir sprechen mit sein— Mutter.**
	768
mit seinER Mutter	*I take my car* is **ich nehme mein— Wagen** (Acc.).
	769
meinEN Wagen	Similarly you remember that the nominative plural (and the accusative too, since in the plural there is no change) of all determinatives ends in **e.** Thus **die Mäuse.** *My mice* is — —.

meine Mäuse	770 *Our woods* (**Wälder**) is — —.
unsere Wälder	771 *Your towns* (fam. pl.) is — —.
eure Städte	772 You also know that in the dative plural both the determinative and the noun must end in the letter—.
n	773 *Out of these woods* is **aus dies**— **Wälder**—.
aus diesEN WälderN	774 *He gives it to your daughters* (polite) is **er gibt es** — —.
Ihren Töchtern	## The Genitive Case
	775 German, like English, has a GENITIVE (or POSSESSIVE) CASE. In the singular in English we denote the genitive case by adding *'s* to the noun, e.g. *the boy — book*.
's	776 In the phrase *the boy's book*, the noun *boy's* is in the — (or possessive) case.
genitive	777 The genitive of *daughter* is —.
daughter's	778 The genitive case of German nouns is in some respects very like the English genitive. So with most masc. and neut. nouns the genitive is formed by adding **s** to the noun. The genitive sing. of **Onkel** is —.
Onkels	779 Notice that in German there is no apostrophe before the **s**. The genitive of **Vogel** is —.

85

Vogels	780 With **Haus** and similar nouns we could not pronounce an additional **s**, so to make it pronounceable we add **es**. The genitive of **Gras** is —.
Grases	781 The genitive of **Haus** is —.
Hauses	782 However, the determinative (**der, jener, ein, kein,** etc.) must also end in **es**, e.g. **dES Bäckers**. So the genitive sing. of **der Onkel** is — —.
des Onkels	783 Did you remember to change both the article and the noun? The gen. sing. of **ein Haus** is — —.
eines Hauses	784 The gen. sing. of **euer Bäcker** is — —.
eures Bäckers	785 In German the genitive usually comes after the noun to which it relates. So *the father's book* is **das Buch** — —.
des Vaters	786 It is possible however to have it the other way round and to say, rather like we do in English, — — —.
des Vaters Buch	787 In any event, however, for masc. and neut. nouns you must remember to change both the determinative and the —.
noun	788 Masc. and neut. monosyllables may add **es** instead of just **s** for the genitive singular even when the sound does not require it. So you will see, e.g., both **des Kind** — and **des Kind**—.
Kinds Kindes	789 The genitive sing. of *feminine* nouns is rather different. Here the determinative must end in **er** and the noun does not change, e.g. **der Frau,** *the woman's*. The genitive of **eine Maus** is **ein**— **Maus**.

	790
einER Maus	For the gen. sing. of feminine nouns the determinative ends in **er** and the noun *does/does not* change.
	791
does not	For the gen. sing. of feminine nouns the noun does not change and the determinative ends in —.
	792
er	The gen. sing. of **die Gans** is — —.
	793
der Gans	The gen. sing. of **unsere Klasse** is — —.
	794
unserer Klasse	The gen. sing. of **Ihre Mutter** is — —.
	795
Ihrer Mutter	The German for *this cat's mouse* is **die Maus** — —.
	796
dieser Katze	*Each schoolgirl's chair* is **der Stuhl** — —.
	797
jeder Schülerin	Plural nouns form their genitive in the same way as feminine singular nouns, i.e., the determinative ends in the letters —.
	798
er	Of course the noun is in the plural form but there is no genitive ending to add to it. *Of the mice* is **d— Mäuse.**
	799
dER Mäuse	*Of the fathers* (**Väter**) is — —.
	800
der Väter	In this and the next five items, rewrite the words of which portions have been omitted: **Der Name dies— Frau.**
	801
dieser	**Der Onkel d— Schüler—.**
	802
des Schülers	**Der Lehrer ein— Schülerin.**

einer	803
	Die Bleistifte mein— Töchter.
meiner	804
	Das Geschäft jen— Bäcker—.
jenes Bäckers	805
	Das Geschäft jen— Bäcker. (Think carefully before deciding whether this is singular or plural!)
jener	806
	You have now learnt all four cases which exist in German. To systematize your knowledge, the next two items give tables of nouns of all three genders with **der**-type and **ein**-type determinatives.

807

	MASC.	**FEM.**
Nom.	**dER, ein Mann**	**diE, einE Frau**
Acc.	**dEN, einEN Mann**	,, ,, ,,
Gen.	**dES, einES Mann(E)S**	**dER, einER** ,,
Dat.	**dEM, einEM Mann(E)**	,, ,, ,,

	NEUT.
Nom.	**daS, ein Haus**
Acc.	,, ,, ,,
Gen.	**dES, einES HausES**
Dat.	**dEM, einEM Haus(E)**

Go to next item when you are satisfied that you know all this.

808

	PLURAL (all genders)
Nom.	**diE, keinE Häuser**
Acc.	,, ,, ,,
Gen.	**dER, keinER Häuser**
Dat.	**dEN, keinEN HäuserN**

Go to next section when you are satisfied that you know all this.

Weak Nouns

809

There is a special class of *masculine* nouns known grammatically as WEAK NOUNS, which behave rather differently from other nouns, as they add an **n** (or **en**) in every case except the nominative sing. **Der Junge** is such a noun. *I see the boy* is **ich sehe den Junge**—.

den Jungen

810

Der Mensch (*human being*) is another weak noun. *The cat sees a human being* is **die Katze sieht** — —.

einen Menschen

811

In the genitive sing. the **n** takes the place of the usual **s.** *The boy's uncle* is **der Onkel** — —.

des Jungen

812

Nearly all masculine nouns ending in **e** are weak, e.g. **der Franzose** (*Frenchman*). *He speaks to (with) the Frenchman* is **er spricht mit** — —.

dem Franzosen

813

Of course such nouns form their plural with the letter — also.

n

814

The boys is — —.

die Jungen

815

Masculine nouns which add **n** or **en** in every case except the nom. sing. are called — nouns.

weak

816

All weak nouns belong to the — gender.

masculine

817

Der Knabe, which is another word for *boy*, is another weak noun. (Incidentally, we get the English *knave* from this, although it does not now *mean* the same as **Knabe.**) *She meets the boy* is **sie trifft** — —.

den Knaben	818 **Der Held** (*the hero*) is weak. *The hero's father* is — — — —.
der Vater des Helden (or **des Helden Vater**)	819 **Der Löwe** (*lion*) is another weak noun. *He gives the meat to the lion* is **Er gibt** — — **das Fleisch.**
dem Löwen	820 Many foreign words ending in **ent** are also weak – **der Student, der Korrespondent, der Präsident.** *The correspondent's pencil* is **der Bleistift** — —.
des Korrespond-enten	821 A word which needs special attention is **der Herr** (*gentleman, lord* or *Mr*). Although it is weak, it adds **n** only in the sing. but **en** in the pl. *To Mr Schmidt* (dat.) is — —.
Herrn Schmidt	822 But *the gentlemen* is — —.
die Herren	823 Note that in writing the name and address on a letter we put the name in the dative, so that in a letter to Mr Braun the name will read — —.
Herrn Braun	# Prepositions with either Accusative or Dative
	824 We have met the prepositions **aus, bei, gegenüber, mit, nach, seit, von, zu,** which always require the noun or pronoun with which they are used to be in the — case.
dative	825 . . . and the prepositions **durch, für, gegen, ohne, um,** which always require the pronoun to be in the — case.

accusative	**826** In addition there are some prepositions which require either the accusative or the dative according to the circumstances in which they are used. In the sentence **Er kommt in das Haus** the words **das Haus** are in the — case.
accusative	**827** In the sentence **Er ist in dem Hause** the words **dem Hause** are in the — case.
dative	**828** In the case of **Er kommt in das Haus** there is movement *towards* the house, so that when there is movement towards a place the preposition **in** requires the — case.
accusative	**829** In the case of **Er ist in dem Hause** there is rest *at* the house. If there is rest at a place, **in** requires the — case.
dative	**830** We can easily see the distinction with the preposition **in** because if there is movement towards a place we do not in English usually say *in* but *in—*.
into	**831** The accusative case is used if there is movement — a place.
towards	**832** *He goes into the wood* – **Er geht in — Wald.**
den	**833** The dative case is used if there is rest — a place.
at	**834** *He is in the wood* is **Er ist in — Wald.**
dem	**835** If there is movement towards a place the preposition **in** requires the — case.

91

accusative	**836** If there is rest at a place the preposition **in** requires the —— case.
dative	**837** We use the prepositions *on* and *on to* in rather the same way as *in* and *into*. *He is* —— *the grass,* but *He runs* —— —— *the grass.*
on, on to	**838** Notice that it is only in American that *onto* can be written as one word. In English *onto* is *right/wrong.*
wrong	**839** The German preposition which means *on* or *on to* is **auf.** When it means *on* (i.e. rest at a place) **auf** requires the —— case.
dative	**840** When it means *on to* (i.e. movement towards a place) **auf** requires the —— case.
accusative	**841** Note. **Auf** only means *on* when we are referring to a horizontal surface. In such a sentence as *The picture hangs on the wall* it would be *right/wrong* to use **auf.**
wrong	**842** *He is on the grass* is **er ist** —— —— ——.
auf dem Gras(e)	**843** But *He runs on to the grass* is **er läuft** —— —— ——.
auf das Gras	**844** Remember that **auf** means *on* or *on to,* especially when referring to a —— surface.
horizontal	**845** There is another word, **an,** which means *on* or *on to* for a surface which is not horizontal. *The picture is on the wall* is **das Bild ist** —— —— **Wand** (fem.).

92

	846
an der	*He hangs the picture on the wall.* Here there is obviously movement towards the wall, even though we do not express it in English: a picture cannot be hung on a wall without being brought towards it. So in German the sentence is **er hängt das Bild — — —.**

846

He hangs the picture on the wall. Here there is obviously movement towards the wall, even though we do not express it in English: a picture cannot be hung on a wall without being brought towards it. So in German the sentence is **er hängt das Bild — — —.**

an der

847

an die Wand

An can also mean *at* or *to*. *He is sitting at the table* is **er sitzt an — Tisch.**

848

dem

He comes to the table is **er kommt an — Tisch.**

849

den

Hinter (*behind*) is another preposition with which we make no distinction between movement and rest, but the Germans insist on the appropriate case. *He is behind the house* is **er ist — — —.**

850

hinter dem Haus(e)

. . . but *He runs behind the house* is **er läuft — — —.**

851

hinter das Haus

So far we have met four of these prepositions which require the — case if there is rest. . . .

852

dative

. . . but the — case if there is motion towards the noun.

853

accusative

In alphabetical order, these prepositions so far are: **an, auf, hinter, in.** Remember them; we will come back to this question later.

Separable Verbs

854

In German it is very common to use a preposition or adverb as a prefix in front of a verb, e.g. **ausgehen** (*to go out*). In a main sentence the prefix becomes detached from

93

the verb when not in the infinitive and is put at the end of the sentence. *I go out is* — — —.

855

ich gehe aus

It does not matter how long the sentence is, the prefix still goes at the end; so *I am not going out today with my daughter* is **ich gehe heute mit meiner Tochter nicht** —.

856

aus

Ankommen (*to arrive*) behaves like **ausgehen,** that is, it is separable. *I arrive is* **ich** — —.

857

komme an

I arrive with my son (**mit meinem Sohne**) is — — — — — —.

858

ich komme mit meinem Sohne an

Aufstehen (*to get up*) is separable. *I get up at 9 o'clock* (**um neun Uhr**) is — — — — — —.

859

ich stehe um 9 Uhr auf

Zumachen (*to shut*) is separable. *We shut the door* (**die Tür**) is — — — — —.

860

wir machen die Tür zu

Einschlafen (*to fall asleep*) is separable. *He falls asleep at night* (**in der Nacht**) is — — — — — —. (Remember what you know about the present tense of **schlafen.**)

861

er schläft in der Nacht ein

Most of the prefixes to separable verbs (like the four you have met above) are separable whatever the verb to which they are attached, but there are a few which are not always separable. There is a verb **unterhalten** (*to hold under*) which is separable. *She holds him under* is — — — —.

862

sie hält ihn unter

But there is another verb spelt in just the same way – **unterhalten** (*to entertain*), which is inseparable, so *she entertains him* is — — —.

94

sie unterhält ihn	**863** You will have to learn which verbs are separable and which are inseparable. One difference in speaking is that in a separable verb the prefix has the stress. Thus **ankommen** (separable) is pronounced **ánkommen.** Mark the stress in **aufstehen** (*to get up*) (separable).
aúfstehen	**864** Mark the stress in **zumachen** (*to shut*) (separable).
zúmachen	**865** If a verb is inseparable the verb part, not the prefix, has the stress; thus **únterhalten** (*to hold under*) but **unterhálten** (*to entertain*) (inseparable). **Übersetzen** (*to translate*) is inseparable. Mark the stress.
übersétzen	**866** We will deal with separable and inseparable verbs again later.

Prepositions
with Accusative or Dative, continued

	867 We have already met **an, auf, hinter, in** – four prepositions which take the — case if there is motion towards a a place . . .
accusative	**868** . . . but which require the — case if there is rest in relation to the place.
dative	**869** **Neben** (*near to*) is another such preposition. *He stands near the door* is **er steht neben — Tür** (fem.).
der	**870** *He comes near to the door* is **er kommt neben — Tür.**

die	**871** **Über** (*over*) behaves similarly. *The picture is over the door* is **das Bild ist über — —**.
der Tür	**872** But *He hangs the picture over the door* (which must involve motion as the picture was presumably not there before) is **er hängt das Bild — — —**.
über die Tür	**873** **Unter** (*under*) acts in just the same way. *The dog is under the table* is **der Hund ist — — —**.
unter dem Tisch	**874** But *The dog runs under the table* is **der Hund läuft — — —**.
unter den Tisch	**875** **Unter** also means *amongst*. *The dog runs amongst the cows* is **der Hund läuft — — —**.
unter die Kühe	**876** **Vor** (*in front of*) similarly takes dative or accusative. *She is in front of me* is **sie — — —**.
ist vor mir	**877** But *She runs in front of me* is **sie — — —**.
läuft vor mich	**878** **Vor** (used in front of the noun) also means *ago* and in this sense always takes the dative. *Two days ago* is **— — —**.
vor zwei Tagen	**879** The last of these prepositions taking either dative or accusative is **zwischen** (between). *They stand between the houses* is **sie stehen — — —**.
zwischen den Häusern	**880** But *They walk between the houses* (i.e. they are not there to begin with) is **sie gehen — — —**.

zwischen die Häuser	**881** You should now try to memorize these 9 prepositions. In alphabetical order they are: **AN, AUF, hinter, in, neben, über, unter, vor, zwischen.** We shall omit them two at a time.
	882 —, —, HINTER, IN, neben, über, unter, vor, zwischen.
an, auf	**883** —, —, —, —, NEBEN, ÜBER, unter, vor, zwischen.
an, auf, hinter, in	**884** —, —, —, —, —, —, UNTER, VOR, zwischen.
an, auf, hinter, in, neben, über	**885** —, —, —, —, —, —, —, —, zwischen.
an, auf, hinter, in, neben, über, unter, vor	**886** Write out the 9 prepositions which require either the dative or the accusative.

an, auf, hinter, in, neben, über, unter, vor, zwischen

Contractions of Prepositions with Article

887
Many prepositions may (but need not) form a compound with the definite article if the sound will allow it. Thus we might meet (instead of **auf das Haus**) **aufs Haus.** What might we have instead of **in das Haus?** — —.

ins Haus

888
Instead of **bei dem Onkel** we might meet **beim Onkel,** and for **zu dem Vater** we might see — —.

zum Vater

889
Similarly instead of **zu der Tür** we might have **zur Tür** and instead of **durch das Haus** — —.

97

durchs Haus	**890** As the form of the preposition changes slightly in two cases you should make a special note of these. Instead of **an dem** we sometimes have **am** and for **in dem** we may meet **im. Im Hause** stands for — — —.
in dem Hause	**891** With all these contractions (which are quite optional) remember that the definite article is present, even though abbreviated. Thus **am Tisch** means *at* — *table.* . . .
the	**892** . . . and **im Hause** means *in* — *house.*

the

Word Order: Accusative and Dative

893
When there are two pronouns, one dative and one accusative (indirect object and direct object), the accusative pronoun must come first. *He gives it to me* is **er gibt** — —.

es mir	**894** *She shows them to us* is **sie zeigt** — —.
sie uns	**895** *Give it to her* is **geben Sie** — —.
es ihr	**896** But with two *nouns,* one dative and one accusative, the order is reversed – the dative noun must come first: *He gives the ball* (**Ball,** masc.) *to the boy* is **Er gibt** — — — —.
dem Jungen (or **Knaben**) **den Ball**	**897** *He shows the picture to the girl* is **er zeigt** — — — —.
dem Mädchen das Bild	**898** *She reads a book aloud to her sons* is **sie liest** — — — — **vor.** (*To read aloud* is **vorlesen,** sep.)

	899
ihren Söhnen ein Buch	With one noun and one pronoun the pronoun comes first, whatever the case. So *He shows it to the men* is **er zeigt — — —.**
	900
es den Männern	*Read it aloud to the class* is **lesen Sie — — — vor.**
	901
es der Klasse	*He shows her to his father* is **er zeigt — — —.**
	902
sie seinem Vater	To avoid confusion you had better memorize three 'pattern' sentences. Order of two pronouns – accusative before dative. *He gives it to me,* **er gibt — —.**
	903
es mir	Order of two pronouns (repeated): accusative before dative. *He gives it to me* **— — — —.**
	904
er gibt es mir	Write the pattern sentence for order of two pronouns (accusative before dative).
	905
er gibt es mir	Order of two nouns – dative before accusative. *He shows the picture to the girl* is **er zeigt — — — —.**
	906
dem Mädchen das Bild	Order of two nouns (repeated) – dative before accusative. *He shows the picture to the girl* is **— — — — — —.**
	907
er zeigt dem Mädchen das Bild	Write the pattern sentence for order of two nouns – dative before accusative.
	908
er zeigt dem Mädchen das Bild	Order of one noun and one pronoun – pronoun first. *He shows it to the men* is **er zeigt — — —.**
	909
es den Männern	Order of one noun and one pronoun (repeated) – pronoun first. *He shows it to the men* **— — — — —.**

99

er zeigt es den Männern	**910** Write the pattern sentence for order of one noun and one pronoun (pronoun first).
er zeigt es den Männern	**911** *Note:* In the above section about word order, when we mention the dative case we mean a simple dative noun or pronoun (used as indirect object), not a preposition + dative.

Interrogative Pronouns

912
The commonest interrogative pronouns in English are
who? and *what?*; *who?* has three cases. *Who is that?*
Here we are using it in the — case.

nominative	**913** *Whom can you see?* Here, *Whom?* is in the — case.
accusative	**914** *Whose is that book?* Here, *Whose?* is in the — case.
genitive	**915** *Note* (which you can omit if you wish). *Who?* has no dative case today, but if you remember what you were told about *him* and *her* you will not be surprised to learn that *whom?* is in fact an old dative case (notice how often **m** is the dative singular ending in German and Old English) and that the accusative of *who?* used to be *whone?* or more correctly, *hwone?*. Go to next item.
	916 The German for *who?* is **wer?**. *Who is there?* (**da**) is — — —.
wer ist da?	**917** In the sentence **Wer ist da?**, **wer?** is of course in the — case. (For its shape you can compare it with **er** or **der**, which are in the same case.)

100

nominative	**918** The accusative of **wer?** is **wen?** (Compare with **ihn** and **den**). *Whom do you see?* (polite) is — — —.
wen sehen Sie?	**919** The dative of **wer?** is **wem?** (compare with **ihm** and **dem**). *To whom do you give it?* is — **geben Sie es?**
wem	**920** *With whom are you going?* is — — — —.
mit wem gehen Sie?	**921** The genitive of **wer?** is **wessen?** (*whose?*). It is used just like *whose?* in English. *Whose book is there?* is — — — —.
wessen Buch ist da?	**922** The German for *what?* is **was?** *What is there?* is — — —.
was ist da?	**923** The accusative of **was?** is the same as the nominative (because the pronoun is neuter in form – compare with **es** and **das**). *What do you see?* (polite) is — — —.
was sehen Sie?	**924** The genitive of **was?** is **wessen?** but you will not find it used very often.
	925 **Was?** has no dative form because, for a reason that you will see in the next section, none is really needed.

Prepositions with Pronouns for Inanimate Objects

926
You now know quite a lot about prepositions. Let us recall one or two examples of their use with personal pronouns. *With me* is — —.

101

	927
mit mir	*For me* (using the preposition **für**) is — —.
	928
für mich	*After him* is — —.
	929
nach ihm	*Behind them* (not implying movement) is — —.
	930
hinter ihnen	You noticed earlier on that the dative of **es** is the same as the dative of **er**, namely —.
	931
ihm	If therefore we were to say **nach ihm** to mean *after it* we should tend to get it confused with the same words meaning *after* —.
	932
him	Perhaps to avoid this confusion, German has a special way of combining prepositions with pronouns standing for inanimate objects. Thus *behind it* is not **hinter ihm** but **DAhinter** – that is, the word — is put in front of the preposition.
	933
da	**Da** means *there,* so saying **danach** in German is the same as saying —*after* in English.
	934
thereafter	*Thereafter* is of course a good English word (though it is going out of use now except in legal documents). Similarly we can say —*to* . . .
	935
thereto	. . . —*in* and so on.
	936
therein	In German (as in English) the stress falls on the second part of the word, e.g. **danách.** What is the German for *with it* (*therewith*) ? (Mark the stress).

102

	937
damít	The German for *in front of it* (using **vor**) is —. (Mark the stress again.)
	938
davór	Note that although we introduced this section by mentioning **es**, this rule applies to all inanimate objects, whatever their gender or number. *With the knives* is **mit den Messern;** *with them* is —.
	939
damit	*From the board* is **von der Tafel;** *from it* is —.
	940
davon	*To the town* is **zu der Stadt;** *to it* is —.
	941
dazu	If the preposition begins with a vowel **dar-** is added instead of **da-**. *In it* (or *them*) ('*therein*') is —.
	942
darin	*Out of it* (or *them*) is —.
	943
daraus	*Round it* (or *them*) is —.
	944
darum	Remember that this rule only applies to inanimate objects, so that although *to it* is **dazu**, *to her* is — —.
	945
zu ihr	. . . and though *with it* is **damit**, *with him* is — —.
	946
mit ihm	The same sort of compound is formed in the case of the interrogative pronoun **was?**. In English, instead of *with what?* in the Bible we read *wherewith?* and instead of *in what?* we read *—in?*
	947
*where*in	In German a compound of this kind is made with the word **wo-**, which means the same as the English word used in similar compounds, namely —.

where	**948** *With what ? (wherewith ?)* is —.
womit?	**949** The stress, as before, is on the second part of the word, so the pronunciation of **womit** is — (mark stress).
womít?	**950** *To what ? (whereto ?)* (using **zu**) is —.
wozu?	**951** As with **da-**, if the preposition begins with a vowel the letter **r** is inserted. *In what ?* is —.
worin?	**952** *Out of* (**aus**) *what ?* is —.
woraus?	## Word Order: Main and Dependent Sentences
	953 Up to now we have spoken about main sentences, though without defining what we mean. Now we must go further into this. Sentences which have one subject and one verb belonging to it are called SIMPLE SENTENCES. *I see you* is a — sentence.
simple	**954** A COMPLEX SENTENCE is one which has a simple sentence with another sentence depending on it. *I see you when you come* is a — sentence.
complex	**955** A sentence which *depends* upon another is called a DEPENDENT SENTENCE. In the complex sentence *I see you when you come*, the *when you come* is a — sentence.
dependent	**956** The principal sentence on which another sentence depends is called a MAIN SENTENCE. In the complex sentence *I see you when you come*, the *I see you* is a — sentence.

104

	957
main	In the complex sentence *I am glad when you go* the main sentence is — — —.
	958
I am glad	In the complex sentence *I am glad when you go* the dependent sentence is — — —.
	959
when you go	You can see from the above examples that a main sentence is complete in itself (i.e. it will make some sort of sense even though it may not tell you all you want to know). In the complex sentence *I am glad when you go*, the *I am glad is/is not* complete in itself.
	960
is complete	On the other hand, a dependent sentence (including the word or words joining it to the main sentence) does not make sense by itself. In the complex sentence *I am glad when you go*, the *when you go is/is not* complete in itself.
	961
is not complete	. . . *when you go* is therefore a *main/dependent* sentence.
	962
dependent	In the complex sentence *I speak German if I can*, the *I speak German* in itself *makes/does not make* sense.
	963
makes sense	*I speak German* is therefore a *main/dependent* sentence.
	964
main	In the same complex sentence: *I speak German if I can*, the *if I can* in itself *makes/does not make* sense.
	965
does not make sense	Of course, the main sentence does not always have to come first. In the complex sentence *When she comes I go* the main sentence is — —.

GG—H

I go	**966** You should now be able to say which is the dependent sentence in most complex sentences. This is very important because in German in a dependent sentence *the verb comes last.* In the complex sentence **Sie sehen, daß ich einen Bleistift habe** (*You see that I have a pencil*), the last word of the dependent sentence is —.
habe	**967** In the same complex sentence **Sie sehen, daß ich einen Bleistift habe,** the verb **habe** is at the end because it is in a *main/dependent* sentence.
dependent	**968** In a dependent sentence in German the word which comes last is the —.
verb	**969** In a dependent sentence in German the verb must be the — word.
last	**970** You will remember from English grammar that a CONJUNCTION is a word joining two sentences or parts of sentences together. In the complex sentence **Sie sehen, daß ich einen Bleistift habe,** the conjunction is — (Notice that it is spelt differently from the neut. definite article.)
daß	**971** Join the following sentences together, using the conjunction **daß** and altering the word order if you think it necessary: (1) **Er sieht.** (2) **Ich bin müde** (*tired*). *He sees that I am tired* is — —, — — — —.
Er sieht, daß ich müde bin	**972** **Wenn** is a conjunction meaning *when* or *if.* Join these two sentences together using **wenn**: (1) **Ich schlafe.** (2) **Es ist Nacht.** *I sleep when it is night* is — — ,— — — —.

106

Ich schlafe, wenn es Nacht ist	973 Compare the punctuation in English and German: *I sleep when it is night.* **Ich schlafe, wenn es Nacht ist.** In German the main sentence must be separated from the dependent sentence by a —.
comma	974 In a German dependent sentence the verb comes at the —.
end	975 What punctuation mark must separate the main sentence from the dependent sentence in German? A —.
comma	976 If the dependent sentence comes first in German the verb and subject in the main sentence must be inverted. **Ich schlafe, wenn es Nacht ist.** Turn this complex sentence round so as to begin with the dependent sentence: **Wenn es Nacht ist, — —.**
schlafe ich	977 Join the following two sentences together, using **wenn**: (1) **Ich gehe.** (2) **Sie kommt heute.** *I am going if she comes today* (**heute**) is **Ich —, — — — —.**
(ich) gehe, wenn sie heute kommt	978 Join the same two sentences together with **wenn** as before, but starting with the dependent sentence: (1) **Ich gehe.** (2) **Sie kommt heute.** *If she comes today I am going* is **— — — —, — —.**
Wenn sie heute kommt, gehe ich	979 **Ob** (pronounced 'op') means *whether.* **Fragen** = *to ask.* *I ask whether you* (polite) *come* is **— —, — — —.**
Ich frage, ob Sie kommen	980 *I ask whether you are coming today* (**heute**) is **— —, — — — —.**

107

Ich frage, ob Sie heute kommen	981 *I ask him* is **ich frage ihn. Fragen** therefore requires the — case.
accusative	982 (If you have studied French before German you might feel a temptation to use a dative with **fragen.** If so, resist it!) **He asks me** is — — —.
er fragt mich	983 *We ask you* (polite) is — — —.
wir fragen Sie	984 *They ask whether we are coming today* is **sie fragen,** — — — —.
ob wir heute kommen	985 *Before* (conjunction) is **bevor.** *I swim* (**schwimme**) *before I go home* is — —, — — — — —.
Ich schwimme, bevor ich nach Hause gehe	986 *Before I go home I swim* is — — — — —, — —.
Bevor ich nach Hause gehe, schwimme ich	987 Another word for *before* (conjunction) is **ehe** (compare English *ere*). Using this word, *before I go home* is — — — — —.
ehe ich nach Hause gehe	988 **Da** (conjunction) means *since* or *as* (in the sense of *because*). *I sleep as I am tired* (**müde**) is — —, — — — —.
Ich schlafe, da ich müde bin	989 *Since I am tired I sleep* is — — — —, — —.

108

Da ich müde bin, schlafe ich	**990**
	After (conjunction) is **nachdem** (for the form of this word compare French 'après que' or Biblical English 'after that they had tarried', etc.) *The cat sleeps after she catches* (**fängt**) *a mouse*) is — — —, — — — — —.
	991
Die Katze schläft, nachdem sie eine Maus fängt	*After she catches a mouse the cat sleeps* is — — — — —, — — —.
	992
Nachdem sie eine Maus fängt, schläft die Katze	*While* is **während**. *She works* (**arbeitet**) *while I sleep* is — —, — — —.
	993
Sie arbeitet, während ich schlafe	*While I sleep she works* is — — —, — —.
	994
Während ich schlafe, arbeitet sie	Another important conjunction of this kind is **weil** (*because*). *I don't work because I am tired* is — — —, — — —.
	995
Ich arbeite nicht, weil ich müde bin	*Because I am tired I don't work* is — — — —, — — —.
	996
Weil ich müde bin, arbeite ich nicht	Of course, not every conjunction introduces a dependent sentence. Some conjunctions like **und** simply join two simple sentences together without affecting word order. *I don't work and I am not tired* is — — —, **und** — — — —.
	997
Ich arbeite nicht, und ich bin nicht müde	**Aber** (*but*) is like **und** – i.e. it joins two main sentences together. *I sleep but I am tired* is **Ich schlafe,** — — — —

109

aber ich bin müde	**998**
	Oder (*or*) also joins two main sentences without affecting word order. *The cat plays or she catches mice* is **Die Katze spielt, oder — — —.**
	999
sie fängt Mäuse	**Denn** (*for*) is another important conjunction which does not affect word order. *I sleep, for I am tired* is **Ich schlafe, — — — —.**
	1000
denn ich bin müde	*I don't walk, for I have a car* is **Ich gehe nicht, — — — — —**
	1001
denn ich habe einen Wagen	**Sondern** is another conjunction which does not affect word order. It is used after a negative to mean *but, on the contrary*. *I don't work but sleep* is **Ich arbeite nicht, — —.**
	1002
sondern schlafe	*I don't travel by car but I go by foot* is **Ich fahre nicht mit dem Wagen, — — — zu Fuß.**
	1003
sondern ich gehe	*I don't work, but I sleep at night* is **Ich arbeite nicht, — — — in der Nacht.**
	1004
sondern ich schlafe	Of the conjunctions which you have now met, **bevor, ehe, da, daß, ob, während, weil** and **wenn** introduce *dependent* sentences and therefore require the verb to go at the — of the sentence.
	1005
end	But **und, aber, oder, denn** and **sondern** simply join main sentences together and therefore *do/do not* affect word order.
	1006
do not	You had better learn the conjunctions which do not alter word order; they are **und, aber, oder, denn, sondern.**

1007

The conjunctions which do not alter word order are —, —, **oder, denn, sondern.**

und, aber

1008

The conjunctions which do not affect word order are —, —, —, —, **sondern.**

und, aber, oder, denn

1009

Write the five conjunctions which do not affect word order.

und, aber, oder, denn, sondern

Modal Verbs

1010

Modal verbs are so called because they help to form what are called grammatical MOODS.

1011

English has modal verbs such as *can, will, shall, must, may.* They are all defective in some way – that is, they have not the same number of different parts as other verbs. For example, one cannot say 'to can', 'to shall', 'to must', etc., so that these verbs have no —.

infinitive

1012

Further, English modal verbs do not add an 's' in the 3rd pers. sing. We do not say 'he cans' or 'he mays' but '*he* —' and '*he* —'.

can, may

1013

When English modal verbs are used with another verb the second verb must be in the infinitive, but without the word 'to' which we usually expect with the infinitive. We say neither 'I can am' nor 'I can to be' but '*I can* —'.

111

be	**1014** German modal verbs also show certain peculiarities, though not always the same ones as ours. One German modal verb is **können** (*can* or *to be able*). From this you will see that German modal verbs do have an —.
infinitive	**1015** *I can* is **ich kann.** Notice that as compared with the infinitive, **können,** there has been a change of — in the stem.
vowel	**1016** German modal verbs, like English, are used with an infinitive. *I can go* is — — **gehen.**
ich kann	**1017** The 2nd pers. sing. *you can* (fam. sing.) is **du kannst.** *You can go* is — — —.
du kannst gehen	**1018** In the 3rd pers. sing. the verb is the same as the 1st pers. sing. (as it is in English). *He can* is — —.
er kann	**1019** *She can be* is — — —.
sie kann sein	**1020** *We can* is **wir können**; so the vowel has gone back to the vowel of the —.
infinitive	**1021** *You can* (fam. pl.) is **ihr könnt.** *You can read* is — — —.
ihr könnt lesen	**1022** You remember that the verb in 1st and 3rd pers. plural is always the same, so *they can* is — —.
sie können	**1023** *We can speak* is — — —.
wir können sprechen	**1024** The 1st, 2nd and 3rd pers. sing. of **können** are **ich** —, **du** —, **er** —.

112

kann, kannst, kann	1025 In the plural the vowel goes back to that of the —.
infinitive	1026 The 1st, 2nd and 3rd pers. plural of **können** are **wir** —, **ihr** —, **sie** —.
können, könnt, können	1027 This is the pattern for most modal verbs. **Können – ich kann**; the vowel of the sing. of the present tense *is/is not* the same as in the infinitive.
is not	1028 **Können – wir können.** In the plural the vowel *is/is not* the same as in the infinitive.
is	1029 **Ich kann – er kann.** 1st and 3rd sing. are *the same/ different*.
the same	1030 **Du kannst gehen.** When a modal verb is used with another verb the latter verb is in the —.
infinitive	1031 **Müssen** (*must*) is another modal verb. 1st pers. sing. (*I must*) is **ich muß** (no Umlaut). 3rd pers. sing. (*he must*) is — —.
er muß	1032 As with some other verbs, as the stem ends in **s** the 2nd pers. sing. (fam. sing.) does not add **est** but only **t**. *You must ask* (fam. sing.) is — — —.
du mußt fragen	1033 The infinitive, remember, is **müssen.** *We must* is — —.
wir müssen	1034 *You must* (fam. pl.) is — —.
ihr müßt	1035 *They must* is — —.

113

sie müssen	**1036** *We must come* is — — —.
wir müssen kommen	**1037** **Wollen** is another modal verb. It means *to want* or *to be willing. I want* is **ich will.** *He wants* is — —.
er will	**1038** *You want* (fam. sing.) is — —.
du willst	**1039** *She wants to go out* (**ausgehen**) is — — —.
sie will ausgehen	**1040** *We want* is — —.
wir wollen	**1041** *You want* (fam. pl.) is — —.
ihr wollt	**1042** *They want* is — —.
sie wollen	**1043** *Note:* **Wollen** means *will* only in the sense of *to be willing,* not in the sense of a future tense. Could you therefore use it in such a sentence as *Will it rain tomorrow? Yes/No.*
no	**1044** Can you use **wollen** in the sense *Will you please tell me the time? Yes/No.*
yes	**1045** *Will you read? (= Are you willing to read?)* (polite) is — — —.
wollen Sie lesen?	**1046** **Wir wollen** is sometimes used to mean *let's* (a sort of 1st pers. pl. imperative). *Let's go!* is — — —.
wir wollen gehen!	**1047** *Let's work!* is — — —.

114

wir wollen **arbeiten**	1048 We will come back to modal verbs a little later.

Agreement of Adjectives – Strong Declension

1049
Up to now we have only met adjectives used after the verb *to be*. Adjectives used in this way do not change. *The father is old* (**alt**) is — — — —.

der Vater ist alt

1050
The mother is old is — — — —.

die Mutter ist alt

1051
The pictures are old is **die Bilder** — —.

sind alt

1052
When adjectives are used attributively however (i.e. in front of a noun) they change in accordance with the number gender and case of the noun. **Alter Mann** is an example of an adjective used —.

attributively

1053
Think back to determinatives (defining words). You remember that there was one group of determinatives (**der, dieser, jener, welcher, solcher, jeder**) which we called the **der**-group because in every case they show the same endings as —.

der (or **der, die,**
das)

1054
The agreement of an adjective depends upon whether there is a determinative before it, and if so whether it belongs to the **der**-group or the **ein**-group. This will be repeated later on.

	1055
	Let us take first an adjective with **no** determinative before it, e.g. *good cheese*. The adjective in German then has the same ending as **der** would have in the same case and gender. The nominative is **dER Käse**, so *good cheese* is — —.
guter Käse	**1056**
	I have the cheese is — — — —.
ich habe den Käse	**1057**
	So *I have good cheese* is — — — —.
ich habe guten Käse	**1058**
	A piece of the cheese is **ein Stück** — —.
des Käses	**1059**
	So you would expect *a piece of good cheese* to be **ein Stück** — —.
gutes Käses	**1060**
	However in modern German they feel that the **s** on the noun is a sufficient sign of the genitive, and prefer to say **ein Stück guteN Käses**. *A piece of old cheese* is therefore — — — —.
ein Stück alten Käses	**1061**
	With the cheese is — — —.
mit dem Käse	**1062**
	With good cheese is — — —.
mit gutem Käse	**1063**
	The milk is **diE Milch**. *Cold* is **kalt**. *Cold milk* is — —.
kalte Milch	**1064**
	The nominative and accusative are *the same/different* with feminine nouns.
the same	**1065**
	I take (**nehme**) *cold milk* is therefore — — — —.

116

	1066
ich nehme kalte Milch	*Of the milk* (genitive) is — —.
	1067
der Milch	*Of cold milk* (genitive) is — —.
	1068
kalter Milch	*A glass* (**Glas**, neut.) *of cold milk is* — — — —.
	1069
ein Glas kalter Milch	*To the milk* (dative) is — —.
	1070
der Milch	So *to cold milk* is — —.
	1071
kalter Milch	*In cold milk* is — — —.
	1072
in kalter Milch	*The grass* is — —.
	1073
das Gras	You remember that in the determinatives like **dieser, jener** etc., the nominative neuter singular is **dieses, jenes** etc., so that the **as** of **das** has changed to —.
	1074
es	*Green* is **grün**. *Green grass* is — —.
	1075
grünes Gras	The nominative and accusative of neuter nouns are *the same/different*.
	1076
the same	So *He sees green grass* is — — — —.
	1077
er sieht grünes Gras	Except in the nominative and accusative singular all masculine and neuter case endings are *the same/different*.
	1078
the same	*Of the grass* (genitive) is — —.

117

	1079
des Grases	Following the same pattern, *of green grass* (genitive) would be — —.
	1080
grünes Grases	But you saw with **ein Stück alten Käses** that in modern German it is usual to change a genitive **s** on an adjective to —, . . .
	1081
n	. . . so *the heap* (**der Haufen**) *of green grass* is — — — —.
	1082
der Haufen grünen Grases	*To the grass* (dat.) is — —.
	1083
dem Gras(e)	So *to green grass* (dat.) is — —.
	1084
grünem Gras(e)	*On green grass* is **auf** — —.
	1085
grünem Gras(e)	You remember that in the plural there are *some/no* distinctions of gender.
	1086
no	*The birds* is — **Vögel.**
	1087
die	**Schön** = *fine, beautiful. Fine birds* is — —.
	1088
schöne Vögel	In the plural there is *some/no* difference between nominative and accusative.
	1089
no	So *He sees fine birds* is — — — —.
	1090
er sieht schöne Vögel	*Of the birds* (gen.) is — —.
	1091
der Vögel	*Of fine birds* (gen.) is — —.

118

schöner Vögel	1092 *A picture of fine birds* is — — — —.
ein Bild schöner Vögel	1093 *To the birds* (dat.) is — —.
den Vögeln	1094 *To fine birds* (dat.) is — —.
schönen Vögeln	1095 *With fine birds* is — — —.
mit schönen Vögeln	1096 Here is a table to sum up the strong declension of adjectives (i.e. when there is no determinative before the adjective).

Sing.	Masc.	Fem.	Neut	Pl. (all genders).
Nom.	**gutER** ⎰	**gutE** ⎰	**gutES** ⎰	**gutE** ⎰
Acc.	**gutEN** ⎱	**gutE** ⎱	**gutES** ⎱	**gutE** ⎱
Gen.	**gutEN**	**gutER**	**gutEN**	**gutER**
Dat.	**gutEM**	**gutER**	**gutEM**	**gutEN**

It will be clear that the endings are those of a **der**-type determinative (except for the masc. and neut. genitive singular).

Modal Verbs, continued

1097
You remember that with modal verbs the singular of the present tense (e.g. **können – ich kann**) usually shows a change of — from the infinitive. . . .

vowel	1098 . . . and that the vowel in the plural of the present tense is *the same as/different from* that of the infinitive.
the same as	1099 The 1st and 3rd persons of the singular of the present tense are *the same/different*.

119

the same	**1100** If a modal verb is followed by another verb (e.g. **ich kann gehen**) that other verb must be in the —.
infinitive	**1101** **Mögen** is another modal verb meaning *to like*. *I like* is **ich mag.** *He likes* is — —.
er mag	**1102** *I like to run* is — — —.
ich mag laufen	**1103** *He likes her* is — — —.
er mag sie	**1104** *You like* (fam. sing.) is — —.
du magst	**1105** *We like* (remember what you know about the plural of modal verbs) is — —.
wir mögen	**1106** *We don't like it* is — — — —.
wir mögen es nicht	**1107** *You like* (fam. pl.) is — —.
ihr mögt	**1108** *You like to eat* (fam. pl.) is — — —.
ihr mögt essen	**1109** *They like* is — —.
sie mögen	**1110** *You like to work* (polite) is — — —.
Sie mögen arbeiten	**1111** **Mögen** is occasionally used to mean *may*. So *That may well be* is **Das — wohl sein.**
mag	**1112** **Dürfen**, another modal verb, means *to be allowed*. The 1st pers. sing. is **ich darf.** *I am allowed to swim* is — — —.

120

ich darf schwimmen	1113 *He is allowed to come* is — — —.
er darf kommen	1114 *You are allowed to speak* (fam. sing.) is — — —.
du darfst sprechen	1115 *We are allowed* (remember vowel change) is — —.
wir dürfen	1116 *You are allowed to go out* (**ausgehen**) (fam. pl.) is — — —.
ihr dürft ausgehen	1117 *They are allowed* is — —.
sie dürfen	1118 *You are allowed to help* (polite) is — — —.
Sie dürfen helfen	1119 **Sollen** (*to be required to, ought to*) is the last of the modal verbs. The first pers. sing. is **ich soll** so you notice that in this case there is no change of —.
vowel	1120 *I am required to go* or *I am to go* is — — —.
ich soll gehen	1121 *He is (required) to travel* is — — —.
er soll fahren	1122 **Sollen** is also sometimes used for *to be said to*. So *he is said to travel* is also — — —.
er soll fahren	1123 *We are required to stand* is — — —.
wir sollen stehen	1124 *You are to ask* (fam. pl.) is — — —.
ihr sollt fragen	1125 *They are said to arrive* is — — **ankommen.**
sie sollen	

More About The Infinitive

1126

In a main sentence if there is an infinitive it must go at the end, e.g. **ich muß es tun.** The German for *I can see it* is therefore — — — —.

ich kann es sehen

1127

I can see the man is — — — — — —.

ich kann den Mann sehen

1128

The length of the sentence makes no difference – the infinitive must still come at the —.

end

1129

Do you want to come home with me? is **Wollen Sie mit mir — — —?**

nach Hause kommen

1130

In a *main* sentence the infinitive must go at the —.

end

1131

The infinitive must go at the end in a — sentence.

main

1132

To explain the word order in a dependent sentence we must first make clear what is meant by the converse of an infinitive, namely a FINITE VERB.

1133

A finite verb is a verb which is directly connected with a subject, so that we can say to what person, tense, etc. it belongs. In the sentence *I am tired* the verb *am* is a — verb.

finite

1134

In the sentence *I am tired* the verb *am* is finite because it belongs to the subject, —.

I	**1135** In the sentence *We go to bed at eight,* the verb *go is/is not* a finite verb.
is	**1136** In the sentence *We go to bed at eight* the verb *go* is finite because it has a —.
subject	**1137** In the sentence *I go to bed to sleep* the verb *to sleep is/is not* a finite verb.
is not	**1138** The verb *to sleep* is not a finite verb because it does not (and cannot) belong to a subject. You cannot say 'I to sleep', and that is why a verb in this form is called an *in—ive.*
infinitive	**1139** In the sentence *He speaks of being tired,* the verb *speaks is/is not* finite.
is	**1140** In the same sentence. *He speaks of being tired,* the verb *being is/is not* a finite verb.
is not	**1141** The verb *being* is not a finite verb because it does not belong to a —. (You cannot say 'he being'.)
subject	**1142** Of course the subject may sometimes be understood rather than expressed; for example, with an imperative such as *Go out!* the subject is *you* (understood) so the imperative *go is/is not* a finite verb.
is	**1143** In the sentence *You have gone* the verb *have is/is not* a finite verb.

is	**1144** In the same sentence, *You have gone,* the verb *gone* is/*is not* a finite verb.
is not	**1145** *Gone* is not a finite verb because it has no —. (You cannot say 'You gone'.)
subject	**1146** You must not forget how to distinguish between a main and a dependent sentence. In the complex sentence *You must go before he finds you,* the words *You must go* form the — sentence.
main	**1147** In the complex sentence *You should look before you leap,* the words . . . *before you leap* are the *main/dependent* sentence.
dependent	**1148** *You should look* is the main sentence because it *is/is not* complete in itself.
is	**1149** *Before you leap* is the dependent sentence because it *needs/does not need* another sentence to make complete sense.
needs	**1150** In the complex sentence **Die Katze schläft, nachdem sie eine Maus fängt**, the sentence . . . **nachdem sie eine Maus fängt** is a *main/dependent* sentence.
dependent	**1151** **Die Katze schläft, nachdem sie eine Maus fängt.** Here, **fängt** *is/is not* a finite verb.
is	**1152** The last word in the dependent sentence . . . **nachdem sie eine Maus fängt** is the — —.

124

finite verb	**1153** In the complex sentence **Ich frage, ob Sie es tun wollen** (*I ask whether you are willing to do it*) the main sentence is — —.
ich frage	**1154** In the dependent sentence **ob Sie es tun wollen,** the last word is the — —.
finite verb	**1155** In the same dependent sentence **ob Sie es tun wollen** the next to last word is the —.
infinitive	**1156** Here is the sentence again: **Ich frage, ob Sie es tun wollen.** If there is an infinitive as well as a finite verb in a dependent sentence, which word comes last? *The infinitive/the finite verb.*
the finite verb	**1157** *We must go home* is **Wir müssen — — —.**
nach Hause gehen	**1158** *We ask whether we must go home* is **Wir fragen, ob wir — — — —.**
nach Hause gehen müssen	**1159** *I am allowed to do it* is **ich darf — —.**
es tun	**1160** *I say that I am allowed to do it* is **ich sage, daß ich — — —.**
es tun darf	**1161** *You can see the lady* is **Sie können — — —.**
die Dame sehen	**1162** *You go before you can see the lady* is **Sie gehen, bevor Sie — — — —.**

125

die Dame sehen können	**1163** *My son likes to throw a ball* (**Ball,** masc.) is **Mein Sohn mag — — —.**
einen Ball werfen	**1164** *My son goes out today because he likes to throw a ball* is **Mein Sohn geht heute aus, weil er — — — —.**
einen Ball werfen mag	**1165** If you learn the above sentence by heart it will help you to remember several things about word order. **Mein Sohn geht heute aus, weil er einen Ball werfen mag.** Write it out.
Mein Sohn geht heute aus, weil er einen Ball werfen mag	**1166** *My son goes out today because he likes to throw a ball.* Finite verb at end of dependent sentence. **Mein Sohn geht heute aus, weil er einen Ball werfen —.**
mag	**1167** *My son goes out today because he likes to throw a ball.* Infinitive just before finite verb at end of sentence. **Mein Sohn geht heute aus, weil er einen Ball — —.**
werfen mag	**1168** *My son goes out today because he likes to throw a ball.* Punctuation between main and dependent sentences. **Meine Sohn geht heute aus — — — —.**
,weil er einen Ball werfen mag	**1169** *My son goes out today because he likes to throw a ball.* Separable verb (**ausgehen**) – prefix at end of main sentence. **Mein Sohn — — —, — — — — — —.**
geht heute aus, weil er einen Ball werfen mag	**1170** *My son goes out today because he likes to throw a ball — — — — —, — — — — — —.*

126

Mein Sohn geht heute aus, weil er einen Ball werfen mag	# Declension of Adjectives after 'Der'-type Determinatives

<table>
<tr>
<td style="vertical-align:top; width:25%">

der

der

e

en

nominative

</td>
<td style="vertical-align:top">

1171

You remember that there are two types of determinative (defining word). One type (**der, dieser, jener, welcher, solcher, jeder**) we have referred to as the —-type.

1172

We have called them the **der**-type because in all cases and genders they behave like —.

1173

If an adjective is preceded by a **der**-type determinative there are only two endings which the adjective can have. Consider these examples – **der gute Mann, die gute Frau, das gute Mädchen.** One of the endings for an adjective after a **der**-type determinative is the letter —.

1174

Consider the following random examples: **den guten Mann, die guten Männer, der guten Frau, dem guten Mädchen.** The other possible ending for an adjective after a **der**-type determinative is the letters —.

1175

When is **e** the correct ending? Look at these examples: **Der alte Mann ist hier. Die gute Frau schläft. Das schöne Mädchen arbeitet.** After a **der**-type determinative **e** is the correct ending for an adjective in the — case singular.

1176

But that is not all. Look at these further examples. **Ich sehe den alten Mann. Ich sehe die gutE Frau. Ich sehe das schönE Mädchen.** In two of these examples **e** is still the correct ending, although we are now using the — case singular.

</td>
</tr>
</table>

127

accusative

1177

	Masc.	Fem.	Neut.
Nom.	**der gutE Mann**	**die gutE Frau**	**das gutE Mädchen**
[Acc.	**den gutEN Mann]**	**die gutE Frau**	**das gutE Mädchen**

After a **der**-type determinative e is the correct ending for the adjective in the nominative and accusative sing. except for the — gender in the — case.

masculine
accusative

1178

The reason for this exception is that the masc. acc. sing. is the only case in which the accusative sing. differs from the — sing.

nominative

1179

That is, the accusative case for feminine and neuter *is/is not* the same as the nominative.

is

1180

You could express it another way by saying that after a **der**-type determinative e is the correct ending for an adjective in the nominative singular and the two accusatives which are *the same as/different from* the nominative singular.

the same as

1181

In all other cases, singular and plural, after a **der**-type determinative the adjective ends in the letters —.

en

1182

Der gut— Mann schläft.

gutE

1183

Die alt— Frau ißt.

altE

1184

Das schön— Mädchen arbeitet.

128

schönE	1185 In the sentence **Sie fängt die flinke Maus** the form of **die Maus** is *the same as/different from* the nominative.
the same as	1186 It is therefore **Sie fängt die flink— Maus.**
flinkE	1187 In the sentence **Wir sehen das Gras**, the form of **das Gras** is *the same as/different from* the nominative.
the same as	1188 It is therefore **wir sehen das grün— Gras.**
grünE	1189 In the sentence **ich sehe den Lehrer** the form of **den Lehrer** is *the same as/different from* the nominative.
different from	1190 **Hier ist das Haus der alt— Frau.**
altEN	1191 **Das ist der Ball des gut— Kindes.**
gutEN	1192 **Wir sind in dem still— Haus(e).**
stillEN	1193 **Du sprichst mit der schön— Dame.**
schönEN	1194 The rule about the letter **e** as the correct ending for an adjective after a **der**-type determinative in the nominative (and the accusative if it is identical) e.g. **der gutE Mann, die gutE Frau,** etc., applies only to the nominative *singular/plural.*
singular	1195 We must therefore say with a plural adjective, e.g. **Die flink— Mäuse laufen.**
flinkEN	1196 **Hier sind die Bücher der intelligent— Schülerinnen.**

intelligentEN	1197 **Der Hund läuft nach den schwarz— Katzen.**
schwarzEN	1198 You can sum up this rule about adjectives quite simply by saying that after a **der**-type determinative in the nominative singular (and the accusative if it is identical) (e.g. **der gute Mann, das gute Haus,** etc.) the adjective must end in — . . .
e	1199 . . . but that if there is any change from the form of the nominative singular (e.g. **den guten Mann, des alten Hauses,** etc.) the adjective must end in —.
en	1200 (You can omit this item if you like). Old English used to decline its adjectives very much as German does and we still have a trace of an old dative plural in the expression 'in oldEN days'.
	1201 So far, we have only had examples of adjectives used after **der** itself. The position is just the same with the other **der**-type determinatives such as **dieser** etc. **Dieser gut— Mann schläft.**
gutE	1202 **Jenes schön— Mädchen geht heute nicht aus.**
schönE	1203 **Er spricht mit jedem alt— Hund(e).**
altEN	1204 **Solche intelligent— Schüler arbeiten.** (Think carefully whether this is singular or plural).
intelligentEN	1205 **Alle** (= *all*) **müd— Hunde schlafen ein.**
müdEN	1206 **Mit welchen alt— Lehrern sprecht ihr?**

altEN	1207
	In the above examples you have met all the **der**-type determinatives, i.e. the ones which make an adjective end in — or —.
E or EN	1208
	You should now learn the list. Apart from **der** itself there are six: **dieser, jeder, jener, solcher, welcher, alle.** Notice that **alle** has a different ending from the others because, as it means *all*, it is normally used in the —.
plural	1209
	We shall now fade out the **der**-type determinatives one at a time until you know them all. Here, first, is the complete list again: **Dieser, jeder, jener, solcher, welcher, alle.** When you think you are familiar with them go to next item.
	1210
	The six **der**-type determinatives are —, **jeder, jener, solcher, welcher, alle.**
dieser	1211
	The six **der**-type determinatives are —, —, **jener, solcher, welcher, alle.**
dieser, jeder	1212
	The six **der**-type determinatives are —, —, —, **solcher, welcher, alle.**
dieser, jeder, jener	1213
	The six **der**-type determinatives are —, —, —, —, **welcher, alle.**
dieser, jeder, jener, solcher	1214
	The six **der**-type determinatives are —, —, —, —, —, **alle.**
dieser, jeder, jener, solcher, welcher	1215
	Write out the six **der**-type determinatives.

dieser, jeder, jener, solcher, welcher, alle

e or **en**

e

en

1216
The **der**-type determinatives are the words which make an adjective end in — or —.

1217
After a **der**-type determinative in the nominative singular an adjective must end in —.

1218
If there is any change from the form of the nominative singular the adjective must end in —.

1219
Here is a table to sum up the declension of adjectives preceded by a **der**-type determinative:

Sing.	Masc.	Fem.	Neut.
Nom.	**der gutE**	**die gutE**	**das gutE**
Acc.	**den gutEN**		
Gen.	**des gutEN**	**der gutEN**	**des gutEN**
Dat.	**dem gutEN**	**der gutEN**	**dem gutEN**

Pl. (all genders).

Nom.	**die gutEN**
Acc.	
Gen.	**der gutEN**
Dat.	**den gutEN**

The only possible ending above the line is **E**; the only possible ending below the line is **EN**. Go to next section.

Word Order: Separable Verbs in Dependent Sentences

1220
You remember that in a main sentence the prefix of a separable verb goes to the — of the sentence.

end	**1221** For example, using **ankommen** – *He arrives with them* (**mit ihnen**) is — — — — —.
er kommt mit ihnen an	**1222** However, in a dependent sentence it is the — which must go at the end.
verb (or finite verb)	**1223** What happens then to the prefix? This example will show: **Er bleibt zu Hause, wenn er mit ihnen ANKOMMT.** The prefix therefore again becomes joined to the —.
verb	**1224** **Er geht heute nicht aus.** Incorporate in the following sentence: **Er schwimmt nicht, weil er — — —.**
heute nicht ausgeht	**1225** Do the same with the following sentences: **Du machst die Tür zu. – Es ist nicht kalt, wenn du — — —.**
die Tür zumachst	**1226** Do the same here: **Sie schläft vor zehn Uhr ein. – Sie wird nicht müde, da sie — — — —.**
vor 10 Uhr einschläft	

Relative Pronouns

	1227 *Next door lives a man. The man has seven cats.* We can join these sentences together, omitting the second reference to *man* by using instead a relative pronoun – *Next door lives a man — has seven cats.*
who	**1228** Instead of *This is the ball; I found the ball*, we can say *This is the ball — I found.*

133

which	**1229** There is a third form of relative pronoun in English: *This is the house — Jack built.*
that	**1230** In each of the above examples we have used a relative pronoun instead of using a — twice over.
noun	**1231** A relative pronoun is so called because it relates back to a — in the first part of the sentence.
noun	**1232** In the sentence *Next door lives a **man** who has seven cats,* the relative pronoun *who* relates back to the noun —.
man	**1233** In the sentence *This is the house that Jack built,* the relative pronoun *that* relates back to the noun —.
house	**1234** The noun to which a relative pronoun relates back is called the ANTECEDENT (which means 'something going before'). In the sentence *This is the ball which I found,* the antecedent of the relative pronoun *which* is the noun —.
ball	**1235** The noun to which a relative pronoun relates back is called the —.
antecedent	**1236** *These are the men who* is/are *going abroad.*
are	**1237** *There is the girl who* plays/play *tennis so well.*
plays	**1238** In the sentence *These are the men who are going abroad* the word *who* is *singular/plural.*
plural	**1239** In the sentence *There is the girl who plays tennis so well* the word *who* is *singular/plural.*

singular	**1240** Here are the two examples again: *These are the* men *who* are *going abroad.* *This is the* girl *who* plays *tennis so well.* A relative pronoun, whilst not itself changing in form, is singular or plural according to its antecedent, so that we can say that it *must/need not* agree with its antecedent in number (i.e. in being singular or plural).
must agree	**1241** *I see a woman* who/whom *knows me.*
who	**1242** *I see a woman . . . who knows me.* Here, *woman* is the *subject/object* of its sentence.
object	**1243** *I see a woman . . . who knows me.* Here, *who* is the *subject/object* of its sentence.
subject	**1244** *I see a woman . . . who knows me.* Here, *woman* is the object of its sentence; *who* is the subject of its sentence. A relative pronoun *must/need not* agree with its antecedent in case.
need not agree	**1245** The case of a relative pronoun, in fact, depends upon the part it plays in its own —.
sentence	**1246** In German **der, die, das** are used as relative pronouns. The *gender* of the relative pronoun will of course be the same as the — of the antecedent.
gender	**1247** Here is an example: **Ist das ein Mann, der spricht? – Nein, es ist eine Frau, — spricht.**
die	**1248** **Das ist ein Mädchen, — schwimmt.**

das	1249 **Das ist ein Mädchen** (*That is a girl*) is a *main/dependent* sentence.
main	1250 . . . **das schwimmt** (. . . *who is swimming*) is a *main/dependent* sentence.
dependent	1251 The last word in a dependent sentence must be the —.
verb (or finite verb)	1252 The punctuation mark which must separate a main sentence from a dependent sentence is a —.
comma	1253 *The cat which sits in front of me* (**vor mir**) *is old* is **Die Katze, — — — —, ist alt.**
die vor mir sitzt	1254 *It is a car which is standing near the house.* (**neben dem Haus**) is **Es ist ein Wagen, — — — — —.**
der neben dem Haus steht	1255 The accusative singular of the relative pronoun is the same as that of the definite article, namely — (masc.), — (fem.) and — (neut.).
den, die, das	1256 *Is it a Frenchman whom I see in the town?* (**in der Stadt**) is **Ist es ein Franzose, — — — — — —.**
den ich in der Stadt sehe?	1257 *That is a knife that he is taking* (**nimmt**) *home* (**nach Hause**) is **Das ist ein Messer** (neut.), **— — — — —.**
das er nach Hause nimmt	1258 The genitive singular of the relative pronoun is slightly different from the definite article. For masculine and neuter it is **dessen**. *That is the boy whose father does not work* is **Das ist der Junge, — Vater nicht arbeitet.**

dessen	**1259** Notice that **dessen** is used just like *whose* in English – that is, we say *whose father* not *whose the father*. *Whose father is* — —.
dessen Vater	**1260** *There stands the girl whose book I have* is **Dort steht das Mädchen,** — — — —.
dessen Buch ich habe	**1261** The feminine genitive singular of the relative pronoun is **deren**. *That is the schoolgirl whose mother is coming today* is **Das ist die Schülerin,** — — — —.
deren Mutter heute kommt	**1262** The genitive singular forms of the relative pronoun are — (masc.) — (fem.) — (neut.).
dessen, deren, dessen	**1263** The dative sing. forms of the relative pronoun are the same as those of the definite article, namely — (masc.), — — (fem.) — (neut.)
dem, der, dem	**1264** *Here is a boy to whom I give a book.* **Hier ist ein Junge,** — — — — —.
dem ich ein Buch gebe	**1265** *It is my mother with whom you are speaking* (using **du**) is **Es ist meine Mutter, mit** — — — —.
(mit) der du sprichst	**1266** *Is it your house on which I see a bird?* (**Vogel,** masc.) is **Ist es Ihr Haus, auf** — — — — —?
(auf) dem ich einen Vogel sehe	**1267** Nominative and accusative plural of the relative pronoun are the same as the definite article, namely —.
die	**1268** *Those are the woods which stand there* (**dort**) is **Das sind die Wälder,** — — —.

die dort stehen

1269

Those are my pencils which you have there (polite) is **Das sind meine Bleistifte, — — — —.**

die Sie dort haben

1270

The genitive plural of the relative pronoun is **deren.** *Here come the girls whose books he steals* (**stiehlt**) is **Hier kommen die Mädchen, — — — —.**

deren Bücher er stiehlt

1271

The dative plural of the relative pronoun is **denen.** *Are those the boys with whom you* (**du**) *go out* is **Sind das die Jungen, mit — — —?**

denen du ausgehst

1272

These are the girls to whom I give the milk is **Dies sind die Mädchen, — — — —.**

denen ich die Milch gebe

1273

In the singular the relative pronoun differs from the definite article in the — case.

genitive

1274

The forms of the relative pronoun in the genitive singular are — (masc.), — (fem.), — (neut.).

dessen, deren, dessen

1275

In the plural the relative pronoun differs from the definite article in the — and — cases.

genitive and dative

1276

The genitive plural of the relative pronoun is —.

deren

1277

The dative plural of the relative pronoun is —.

denen

1278

Instead of the various forms of **der, die, das** for the relative pronoun it is possible to use **welcher, welche, welches** which you have already met as an interrogative adjective, and which has no unexpected case forms. *A man whom I see* (using **welcher**) is **ein Mann, — — —.**

138

welchen ich sehe	1279 *A boy with whom I speak* (using **welcher**) is **ein Junge, mit — — —.** 1280
(mit) welchem ich spreche	**Welcher, welche, welches** has no genitive forms, so **dessen** or **deren** are used instead. 1281 Instead of using a preposition + a relative pronoun in referring to a *thing* it is possible to use the prefix **wo** + the preposition. Thus, instead of saying **das Haus, vor dem ein Wagen steht,** you can say **das Haus —vor ein Wagen steht.** 1282
wovor	Instead of saying **die Stadt, von der ich fahre,** you can say **die Stadt, — ich fahre.** 1283
wovon	If the preposition begins with a vowel you must add, not **wo-** but **wor-**. Thus, instead of **der Stuhl, auf dem ich sitze,** you can say **der Stuhl, — ich sitze.** 1284
worauf	You can compare this of course with the addition of *where* to a preposition in English in the same circumstances, for example, *the tree whereof I commanded thee that thou shouldest not eat.* 1285 Here is a table to sum up the various cases of the relative pronoun. Differences from the definite article are shown by capitals:

Sing.	Masc.	Fem.	Neut.	Pl. (all genders).
Nom.	der	die	das	die
Acc.	den			
Gen.	desSEN	derEN	desSEN	derEN
Dat.	dem	der	dem	denEN

When you are sure that you know all this, go to next section.

Declension of Adjectives after 'Ein'-Type Determinatives (Mixed Declension)

1286

When there is no determinative (defining word) before an adjective you know that the endings of the adjective must normally be the same as those of the — article.

definite

1287

When there is a determinative of the **der**-type before an adjective the adjective must end in either — or —.

e, en

1288

Apart from the **der**-type determinative there is still the —-type of determinative.

ein

1289

The difference between **der Mann** and **ein Mann** is that **der** shows a special masculine ending, whereas **ein** shows (*no such/some other*) special ending.

no such

1290

The difference between **das Haus** and **ein Haus** is that **das** shows a special neuter ending, whereas **ein** shows *no such/some other* special ending.

no such

1291

In all the cases except **der** (masc. nom. sing.) and **das** (neut. nom. and acc. sing.) the endings of **ein, eine, ein** and **der, die, das** are *identical/different*.

identical

1292

It follows that the endings of the adjectives used after those parts of **ein** and **der** which are identical will also be identical: **Ich sehe den guten Mann; ich sehe einen — Mann.**

guten

1293

Das Haus des guten Mannes; das Haus eines — Mannes.

140

	1294
guten	Mit der guten Frau; mit einer — Frau.
	1295
guten	The only special cases we need consider therefore are those in which the endings of **ein** differ from those of **der**. Let us take first the masc. nom. sing. *The man is — —* and *a man is — —*.
	1296
der Mann ein Mann	**Der Mann** shows conclusively that **Mann** is a masculine noun in the nominative case. **Ein Mann** *does/does not*.
	1297
does not	Since **ein Mann** does not show a distinctive nominative masculine singular ending, **er**, the adjective must show it instead – **Ein gut— Mann arbeitet.**
	1298
gutER	Similarly with the neuter nominative singular, e.g. **ein Haus**. Since the word **ein** does not show a distinctive neuter ending, **es**, the adjective must show it instead – **Ein gut— Haus.**
	1299
gutes	The neuter accusative singular is *the same as/different from* the nominative singular.
	1300
the same as	**Ich sehe ein schön— Haus.**
	1301
schönes	The cases in which the endings of **ein, eine, ein** and **der, die, das** are not identical are the masculine — singular and the — nominative and accusative singular.
	1302
nominative, neuter	In this and the following six items expressions with **der die, das** are given side by side with the corresponding expressions with **ein, eine, ein**. Sometimes they are identical, sometimes different. **DiE gute Frau.** **EinE gut— Frau.**

gutE	**1303** **Der gute Mann.** **Ein gut— Mann.**
gutER	**1304** **DEN guten Jungen.** **EinEN gut— Jungen.**
gutEN	**1305** **DES guten Herrn.** **EinES gut— Herrn.**
gutEN	**1306** **Das gute Haus.** **Ein gut— Haus.**
gutES	**1307** **DER guten Frau.** **EinER gut— Frau.**
gutEN	**1308** **DEM guten Jungen.** **EinEM gut— Jungen.**
gutEN	**1309** So far, we have dealt only with **ein** of the **ein**-type determinatives. The other members of this group are easy to remember; they are **kein** and the possessive adjectives (**mein, dein, sein, ihr, unser, euer, ihr, Ihr**). All of these behave just like —.
ein	**1310** The **ein**-type determinatives are **ein, kein** and the — —.
possessive adjectives	**1311** The **ein**-type determinatives are —, — and the — —.
ein, kein and the possessive adjectives	**1312** *No old man sleeps* (**schläft**) is — — — —.
Kein alter Mann schläft	**1313** *I see my old house* is **ich sehe** — — —.
mein altes Haus	**1314** Remember, we are dealing with the **ein**-type determinatives. **Ein** itself (which means *one* or *a*) has no plural, but **kein** and the possessive adjectives of course *do/do not* have a plural.

	1315
do have	*These men* is **diesE Männer**; *no men* is **keinE Männer**. In the plural, therefore, the endings of the **der**-type and **ein**-type determinatives are *the same/different*.
	1316
the same	As both types of determinative have the same endings in the plural the adjectives which follow them will have the same endings as one another. *The good men* is **diE gutEN Männer**; *no good men* is **keinE — Männer**.
	1317
guten	*Our good men* (nom. or acc.) is — — —.
	1318
unsere guten Männer	*Of your good houses* (polite) is — — —.
	1319
Ihrer guten Häuser	The logic behind the declension of adjectives in German is that number, gender and case are required to be identified beyond doubt by the presence either in the determinative or the adjective of an ending of the kind shown by a — -type determinative.
	1320
der	If the determinative itself does not show endings of the **der**-type, such an ending must be shown by the —.
	1321
adjective	Here is a table to sum up the declension of adjectives preceded by an **ein**-type determinative:

	Masc. Sing.	Fem. Sing.	Neut. Sing.	Pl. (all genders)
Nom.	**kein gutER**	⎰ **keine gutE**	⎰ **kein gutES**	⎰ **keine gutEN**
Acc.	**keinen gutEN**	⎱	⎱	⎱
Gen.	**keines gutEN**	**keiner gutEN**	**keines gutEN**	**keiner gutEN**
Dat.	**keinem gutEN**	**keiner gutEN**	**keinem gutEN**	**keinen gutEN**

Above the line the endings of the adjectives are those of a **der**-type determin-

ative; the only possible ending below the line is **EN**.
Go to next section when you know this.

Adjectives from Place-names

1322
In German, adjectives may be made from proper nouns (the names of towns etc.) simply by adding **ER** to the noun. The adjective from **London** is —.

Londoner

1323
The adjective from **Berlin** is —.

Berliner

1324
The adjective from **Hamburg** is —.

Hamburger

1325
Such adjectives are indeclinable – that is, they do not change whatever the case or gender or the determinative with which they are used. *The Berlin Town-hall* is **Das — Rathaus.**

Berliner

1326
You will have noticed that the capital letter of the proper noun *disappears/remains* in the adjective.

remains

1327
In the Hamburg Bank is **in der — Bank.**

Hamburger

Imperfect Tense: Weak Verbs

1328
In English we often form a past tense by adding *ed* to a verb. The past tense of *look* is —.

144

looked	**1329** If an English verb forms its past tense by adding *ed*, we say it is a *weak* verb. *Look* is a — verb.
weak	**1330** *Speak is/is not* a weak verb.
is not	**1331** *Walk is/is not* a weak verb.
is	**1332** German, too, has weak verbs; these form their past tense by replacing the **(e)n** of the infinitive by **te. Machen** (*to make*) is a weak verb; its past tense is —.
machte	**1333** This tense is usually called the IMPERFECT tense to distinguish it from other past tenses. **Machte** is in the — tense.
imperfect	**1334** There are several ways of translating the German imperfect tense into English. Often it corresponds to the English Past Definite (e.g. *I looked, I walked*). One translation for **ich machte** would therefore be *I —*.
made	**1335** The imperfect is also used for interrupted or incomplete actions (e.g. *I was looking*). Another translation of **ich machte** would therefore be *I — —*.
was making	**1336** The imperfect is also used for habitual actions in the past (e.g. *I used to look*). A further translation for **ich machte** would therefore be *I — — —*.
used to make	**1337** The name of the tense used in German to describe the actions *I made, I was making* and *I used to make* is the — tense.

145

imperfect	**1338** The German for *I made, I was making* and *I used to make* is **ich** —.
machte	**1339** **Ich machte** means *I —, I — —* and *I — — —*.
made, was making, used to make	**1340** Some infinitives end in **n** only, not **en**. In such cases only the **n** is removed before adding **te** to form the imperfect. The imperfect of **klingeln** (*to ring*) is **ich** —.
klingelte	**1341** The German for *I made, I was making* and *I used to make* is — —.
ich machte	**1342** *I rang, I was ringing, I used to ring* are — —.
ich klingelte	**1343** The 2nd pers. sing. (fam. sing.) of the imperfect is made by adding **st** to the imperfect stem (e.g., **klingelte – du klingeltest**). The 2nd pers. sing. imperfect of **machen** is **du** —.
machtest	**1344** *You were ringing* (fam. sing.) is — —.
du klingeltest	**1345** The 1st pers. sing. of the imperfect is formed by adding the letters — when the (e)n of the infinitive has been removed.
te	**1346** The 3rd pers. sing. of the imperfect is the same as the 1st pers. sing. *He made* is —.
er machte	**1347** *She used to make* is — —.
sie machte	**1348** The 1st and 3rd persons sing. of the imperfect are *the same/different*.

	1349
the same	*It rang* is — —.
	1350
es klingelte	1st, 2nd and 3rd pers. sing. of the imperfect of **machen** are **ich —, du —, er —.**
	1351
machte, machtest, machte	The 1st pers. plural of the imperfect is formed by adding **n** to the imperfect stem. *We made* is — —.
	1352
wir machten	*We were ringing* is — —.
	1353
wir klingelten	2nd pers. pl. (fam. pl.) of the imperfect is formed by adding **t** to the imperfect stem. *You made* (fam. pl.) is — —.
	1354
ihr machtet	*We made* is — —.
	1355
wir machten	3rd pers. pl. of the imperfect is the same as the 1st pers. pl. *They made* is — —.
	1356
sie machten	*You made* (polite) is — —.
	1357
Sie machten	The verb in the 1st and 3rd persons plural of the imperfect is *the same/different.*
	1358
the same	*You rang* (fam. pl.) is — —.
	1359
ihr klingeltet	1st, 2nd and 3rd persons pl. of the imperfect of **machen** are — —, — — and — —.
	1360
wir machten, ihr machtet, sie machten	1st, 2nd and 3rd persons sing. of the imperfect of **machen** are — —, — — and — —.

147

ich machte, du machtest, er machte	**1361** When the **e(n)** of the infinitive has been removed the stem may end in **d, t,** or some other consonant after which **te** cannot be pronounced. In such a case **ete** must be added to form the imperfect. **Enden** = *to end. It ended* is — —.
es endete	**1362** **Regnen** = *to rain. It was raining* is — —.
es regnete	**1363** **Rechnen** = *to reckon. We reckoned* is — —.
wir rechneten	**1364** **Hören** = *to hear. I heard* is — —.
ich hörte	**1365** **Sagen** = *to say. You were saying* (polite) is — —.
Sie sagten	**1366** **Warten** = *to wait. She waited* is — —.
sie wartete	**1367** **Du machtest** means *you* —, or — — or — — —.
made, were making, used to make	**1368** **Arbeiten** = *to work. They used to work* is — —.
sie arbeiteten	**1369** **Wohnen** = *to dwell* (live). *We lived* is **wir** —.
wohnten	**1370** **Sie klingelte** means *she* — or — — or — — —.
rang, was ringing, used to ring	**1371** **Rauchen** = *to smoke. You smoked* (fam. pl.) is — —.
ihr rauchtet	**1372** **Holen** = *to fetch. They fetched* is — —.
sie holten	**1373** **Lächeln** = *to smile. They smiled* is — —.
sie lächelten	

148

Imperfect Tense: Strong Verbs

1374

Some English verbs do not form their past tense by adding *ed*. The past tense of *speak* is not *speaked* but —.

spoke

1375

Verbs which form their past tense by changing an internal vowel (e.g. *sing–sang*) are called *strong* verbs. *Speak* is a — verb.

strong

1376

Help is a *strong/weak* verb.

weak

1377

German strong verbs, like English, form their past tense (imperfect) by changing the vowel of the infinitive stem – e.g. **sprEchen – ich sprAch. Sprechen** is a — verb.

strong

1378

Ich sprach means — —.

I spoke

1379

I spoke is — —.

ich sprach

1380

The personal endings of strong and weak verbs are the same. **Ich machte** has no personal ending, so **ich sprach** has — personal ending.

no

1381

There is a personal ending on **du machteST**, so that the German for *you spoke* is — —.

du sprachst

1382

The imperfect of **singen** (*to sing*) is **sang**. *I sang* is — —.

ich sang

1383

You sang (fam. sing.) is — —.

du sangst

1384

1st and 3rd persons sing. of the imperfect are always the same. *He spoke* is — —.

149

er sprach	1385 1st, 2nd and 3rd persons sing. of **singen** are — —, — —, — —.
ich sang, du sangst, er sang	1386 1st, 2nd and 3rd persons sing. of **sprechen** are — —, — —, — —.
ich sprach, du sprachst, er sprach	1387 1st pers. plural of the imperfect of all verbs ends in **en**. *We sang* is — —.
wir sangen	1388 2nd pers. plural of the imperfect of all verbs ends in **t**. *You sang* (fam. pl.) is — —.
ihr sangt	1389 1st and 3rd persons plural of all verbs are the same. *They sang* is — —.
sie sangen	1390 *You sang* (polite) is — —.
Sie sangen	1391 1st, 2nd and 3rd persons plural of the imperfect of **sprechen** are — —, — —, — —.
wir sprachen, ihr spracht, sie sprachen	1392 There is no rule to tell you how the vowels change in the various verbs, but you will notice certain patterns. **i** in the infinitive stem often changes to **a. Finden** = *to find*. *I found* is — —.
ich fand	1393 **ei** often changes to **ie. Bleiben** (vowels pronounced rather like English *eye*) means *to stay. You stayed* (fam. sing.) is — —.
du bliebst (vowels pronounced like English *ee*)	1394 If the English verb resembles the German verb the vowel change is often the same: *to sEe* is **sEhen**; *he sAw* is — — (the German has no consonant change).

150

	1395
er sah	Similarly *to begIn* is **begInnen**; *We begAn* is — —.
	1396
wir begannen	Sometimes in slightly irregular strong verbs there may be a change affecting the consonant as well. (You noticed a change of this kind with the English verb *see*). **Kommen** gives **kam**. *They came* is — —.
	1397
sie kamen	1st, 2nd and 3rd persons sing. imp. of **finden** are — —, — —, — —.
	1398
ich fand, du fandst (fandest), er fand	1st, 2nd and 3rd persons plural imp. of **bleiben** (*to stay*) are — —, — —, — —.
	1399
wir blieben, ihr bliebt, sie blieben	*I spoke* is — —.
	1400
ich sprach	*He sang* is — —.
	1401
er sang	3rd pers. sing. of the imperfect is the same as the — — —.
	1402
first person singular	*You began* (polite) is — —.
	1403
Sie begannen	*You found* (fam. sing.) is — —.
	1404
du fandst (or **fandest**)	3rd pers. plural of the imperfect is the same as the — — —.
	1405
first person plural	*We stayed* (using **bleiben**) is — —.
	1406
wir blieben	*You saw* (fam. pl.) is — —.
ihr saht	

The Imperfect Tense - Verbs
which are both Weak and Strong (Mixed)

1407

A few verbs are both weak and strong ('mixed'). As they are weak the imperfect stem ends in the letters —.

te

1408

. . . and as they are strong there is a change of — in the imperfect.

vowel

1409

Such verbs are nearly all similar in form: **brennen** (*to burn*) has imperfect **brannte. Kennen** (*to know* (a person not a fact)) has imperfect —.

kannte

1410

Senden (*to send*) has imperfect —.

sandte (sometimes **sendete**)

1411

Wenden (to turn) has imperfect —. (You may find it interesting to know that English *went* comes from this verb).

wandte (sometimes **wendete**)

1412

Bringen (*to bring*) is rather more irregular and has imperfect **brachte.** (Have you noticed how often in English there is a silent *gh* where in German there is a **ch**? – *Brought* – **brachte**; *night* – **Nacht**; *through* (and its older form *thorough*) – **durch**, etc.). This *gh* of course used to be pronounced just like German **ch**, and in Scotland sometimes still is.)

1413

They brought is — —.

sie brachten

1414

Somewhat similarly the imperfect of **denken** (*to think*) is **dachte.** *You thought* (fam. sing.) (notice the silent *gh* again) is — —.

152

du dachtest	1415 The vowel of all these verbs which are both weak and strong (mixed) changes in the imperfect to —.
a	1416 *We brought* is — —.
wir brachten	1417 *They thought* is — —.

sie dachten	## Test on Imperfect of Strong, Weak and Mixed Verbs
	1418 In this and the next nine items change the verb which is in capitals in each sentence into the imperfect: **Der Doktor RAUCHT zwei Zigaretten** (*two cigarettes*).
rauchte	1419 **Ich KOMME gern** (*gladly*) **ins Haus.**
kam	1420 **Ich MACHE einen guten Spaziergang.**
machte	1421 **Ihr DENKT an eure Mutter.**
dachtet	1422 **SPRECHEN Sie mit dem Lehrer?**
Sprachen	1423 **Es KLINGELT an der Haustür** (*front door*).
klingelte	1424 **Wir BRINGEN unserer Mutter ein Messer.**
brachten	1425 **Die Klasse SINGT nicht heute.**
sang	1426 **Du BLEIBST zu Hause.**
bliebst	1427 **Jenen Mann KENNE ich nicht.**

kannte	# Reflexive Verbs
	### 1428
	A REFLEXIVE verb is one in which the doer performs the action to himself (or, if you like, the action is *reflected* upon the subject). *I wash myself* is an example of a — verb.
	### 1429
reflexive	English verbs when used reflexively make use of the suffix -*self* attached to the possessive adjective – e.g. *I hurt my*—.
	### 1430
myself	However, we are not very particular about using reflexive pronouns in English and we often do not use the reflexive pronoun even when we mean the verb reflexively. We say *I wash* when we mean *I wash* —.
	### 1431
myself	This process of shedding reflexive pronouns is still continuing in English. Quite recently newspapers have begun to write such things as *He adjusted to the situation* instead of *He adjusted* — . . .
	### 1432
himself	There are however still a few verbs in English where the reflexive pronoun must still be used. We could not omit it, for instance, in the sentence *I resign — to the position.*
	### 1433
myself	. . . or in the sentence *He expresses — well in writing.*
	### 1434
himself	In German however as in most other languages, if a verb is used in a *reflexive* sense the — pronoun must be used.
	### 1435
reflexive	The German for *to wash oneself* is **sich waschen.** Here the word which means *oneself* is —.

sich	1436 **Waschen** is one of those verbs which show a vowel change by adding an Umlaut in the 2nd and 3rd persons of the present tense. *He washes* (not 'himself') is — —.
er wäscht	1437 Except in the 3rd person there is no special reflexive form of German pronouns. *I wash myself* (= *me*) is **ich wasche** —.
mich	1438 *You wash yourself* (= *you*) (fam. sing.) is **du wäschst** —.
dich	1439 The 3rd person reflexive pronoun is **sich**. It has only one form for singular and plural and all genders (compare French 'se'). You have already met it in the infinitive (**sich waschen**) where it means —.
oneself	1440 *He washes himself* is — — —.
er wäscht sich	1441 *She washes herself* is — — —.
sie wäscht sich	1442 *It washes itself* is — — —.
es wäscht sich	1443 The only special reflexive form of pronoun is in the *1st/2nd/3rd* person.
3rd person	1444 *We wash ourselves* is — — —.
wir waschen uns	1445 *You wash yourselves* (fam. pl.) is — — —.
ihr wascht euch	1446 *They wash themselves* (remember that the 3rd person reflexive pronoun is both singular and plural) is — — —.

sie waschen sich	1447 You know that the polite way of saying *you* is really *1st/2nd/3rd* person plural.
3rd person	1448 The reflexive pronoun for the polite form of address does not have a capital letter. *You wash yourselves* (or *yourself*) (polite) is — — —.
Sie waschen sich	1449 **Ich wasche —.**
mich	1450 **Du wäschst —.**
dich	1451 **Er (sie, es) wäscht —.**
sich	1452 With a finite verb the reflexive pronoun comes *before/after* the verb.
after	1453 But you noticed **sich waschen.** Here the infinitive comes after the pronoun because, as you know, an infinitive likes to come at the —.
end	1454 **Wir waschen —.**
uns	1455 **Ihr wascht —.**
euch	1456 **Sie (sie) waschen —.**

sich	1457
	Here is a table to sum up reflexive verbs:
	   ich wasche MICH **wir waschen UNS**
	   du wäschst DICH **ihr wascht EUCH**
	   er, sie, es wäscht SICH **sie (Sie) waschen SICH**
	Go to next item when you know this.

	1458
	The reflexive pronoun can be used as direct object (accusative), as in the sentence *He washes — with soap.*
himself	1459 . . . or it can be the indirect object (dative) as in the sentence *He often talks — himself.*
to	1460 In the verb **sich waschen** the reflexive pronoun is in the — case.
accusative	1461 In sentences such as *I wash my hands* the Germans (rather like the French) prefer not to use a possessive adjective but to insert a dative pronoun instead, i.e. to say *I wash the hands — myself.*
to (or for)	1462 In the sentence *I wash the hands to myself* the noun *hands* is of course the direct object and must be in the — case.
accusative	1463 . . . while the reflexive pronoun (*to myself*) is of course in the — case.
dative	1464 As you already know, there is no special reflexive form of pronoun except in the *1st/2nd/3rd* person.
3rd person	1465 The dative of the ordinary 1st person singular pronoun (= *to me*) is —.
mir	1466 *I wash my hands* (= *the hands to myself*) is therefore **ich wasche — die Hände.**
mir	1467 *I wash my hands* is — — — — —.

157

ich wasche mir die Hände	**1468** The dative of the 2nd person singular pronoun (= *to you*) is —.
dir	**1469** *You wash your hands* is **du wäschst — die Hände.**
dir	**1470** *You wash your hands* (fam. sing.) is — — — —.
du wäschst dir die Hände	**1471** The dative of the 3rd person reflexive pronoun is the same as the accusative which you already know, namely —.
sich	**1472** *He washes his hands* (*the hands to himself*) is **er wäscht — die Hände.**
sich	**1473** *She washes her hands* is — — — — —.
sie wäscht sich die Hände	**1474** You may remember that in the 1st and 2nd persons plural the dative of the pronoun (*to us, to you*) does not differ from the accusative. *We wash our hands* (*the hands to us*) is **Wir waschen — die Hände.**
uns	**1475** *We wash our hands* is — — — — —.
wir waschen uns die Hände	**1476** *You wash your hands* (fam. pl.) is **ihr wascht — die Hände**
euch	**1477** *You wash your hands* (fam. pl.) is — — — — —.
ihr wascht euch die Hände	**1478** Similarly the dative form of the 3rd person reflexive pronoun, as you already know, is the same as the —.
accusative	**1479** *They wash their hands* is — — — — —.

sie waschen sich die Hände	**1480** *You wash your hands* (polite) is — — — — —.
Sie waschen sich die Hände	**1481** This same construction is used with most expressions involving parts of the body. *I comb my hair* is **ich kämme** — **das Haar.**

mir	**1482**
	Here is a table to sum up the reflexive verbs which have the reflexive pronoun in the dative:
	
	ich kämme MIR das wir kämmen UNS das
	   Haar Haar
	du kämmst DIR das ihr kämmt EUCH das
	   Haar Haar
	er, sie, es kämmt SICH sie (Sie) kämmen SICH
	   das Haar das Haar.
	
	Go to next section when you know this.

Perfect Tense: Weak Verbs

	1483 The perfect tense is the tense which in English requires the PAST PARTICIPLE of the verb, together with the AUXILIARY (or 'helping') verb *to have*. The perfect tense of *to be* is *I have* —.
been	**1484** The *past participle* of the verb *to be* is —.
been	**1485** *Been* is the past part— of the verb *to be*.
participle	**1486** *Been* is the past — of the verb *to be*.
participle	**1487** *Been* is the — — of the verb *to be*.

past participle	**1488** To form the perfect tense the past participle needs the help of an *auxiliary* verb. In the sentence *I have been* the auxiliary verb is —.
have	**1489** In *I have been* the verb *have* is the auxil— verb.
auxiliary	**1490** In *I have been* the verb *have* is the aux— verb.
auxiliary	**1491** In *I have been* the verb *have* is the — verb.
auxiliary	**1492** Notice that a past participle is not a finite verb; you cannot (or should not) say 'I been' but *I — been*
have	**1493** The finite verb in the sentence *I have been* is the verb —.
have	**1494** The PERFECT tense is so called because it deals with completed (or 'perfected') actions. If you have been interrupted in doing something you do not use the perfect to describe it, but the imperfect, e.g. if you are interrupted in writing a letter you do not say 'I have written' but *I WAS writ—*.
writing	**1495** But when the writing is completed ('perfected') you say *I have —*.
written	**1496** The German perfect tense is made up on the same lines as the English perfect – with the past — and an auxiliary ('helping') verb.
participle	**1497** The German perfect tense is made up of the past participle and an — verb.

160

auxiliary	1498 *I have made* is **ich habe gemacht. Gemacht** is the past —.
participle	1499 **Gemacht** is the — —.
past participle	1500 **Ich habe gemacht.** The auxiliary verb is —.
habe	1501 **Ich habe gemacht. Habe** is the — verb.
auxiliary [it is also the *finite* verb]	1502 Notice that the past participle of **machen** (**gemacht**) begins with the prefix —.
ge-	1503 Most past participles in German have the prefix —.
ge-	1504 Notice that the past participle of **machen** (**gemacht**) apart from beginning with the prefix **ge-**, ends in the letter —.
t	1505 You remember from your study of the imperfect that **machen** is a *weak/strong* verb.
weak	1506 The past participle of **machen** is —.
gemacht	1507 The past participle of weak verbs ends in the letter —.
t	1508 Most past participles begin with the letters —.
ge-	1509 The past participle of most weak verbs is made by adding the prefix **ge-** and substituting for the (**e**)**n** of the infinitive the letter —.
t	1510 The past participle of **hören** (*to hear*) is —.

gehört	1511 The past participle of **sagen** (*to say*) is —.
gesagt	1512 The past participle of *wohnen* (*to live, dwell*) is —.
gewohnt	1513 If the infinitive stem ends in **d** or **t** the letters **et** must be added to form the past participle, as otherwise the word could not be properly pronounced. The past participle of **arbeiten** is —.
gearbeitet	1514 The past participle of **enden** (*to end*) is —.
geendet	1515 The specimen sentence was **Ich habe gemacht.** The auxiliary verb is of course the — tense of **haben.**
present	1516 *You have made* (fam. sing.) is — — —.
du hast gemacht	1517 *He has made* is — — —.
er hat gemacht	1518 *We have heard* (using **hören**) is — — —.
wir haben gehört	1519 *He has said* (using **sagen**) is — — —.
er hat gesagt	1520 *You have lived* (*dwelt*) (fam. pl.) (using **wohnen**) is — — —.
ihr habt gewohnt	1521 *They have worked* is — — —.
sie haben gearbeitet	1522 Strong verbs form their perfect tense in the same way as weak verbs, but the past participle is differently made.

162

Word Order: Perfect Tense

1523
Remember that the past participle *is/is not* a finite verb.

is not

1524
In a main sentence the position of the past participle, like that of the infinitive, is at the — of the sentence.

end

1525
I have made it is — — — —.

**ich habe es
gemacht**

1526
I have heard you (**dich**) (using **hören**) is — — — —.

**ich habe dich
gehört**

1527
I have fetched my car (using **holen**) is — — — — —.

**ich habe meinen
Wagen geholt**

1528
I have lived at home (using **wohnen**) is — — — — —.

**ich habe zu Hause
gewohnt**

1529
In a *main* sentence the position of a past participle is at the —.

end

1530
But in a *dependent* sentence the word which must go at the end is the finite —.

verb

1531
No other words change their order, e.g., **Ich habe es gemacht,** but **Ich komme, wenn ich es gemacht —.**

habe

1532
In a dependent sentence with verb in the perfect tense the last word is the — —.

finite verb (or
auxiliary verb)

1533
In a dependent sentence with verb in the perfect tense, e.g. **Ich komme, wenn ich es gemacht habe** the next to the last word is the — —.

past participle	**1534** In this and the next three items complete the dependent sentence using the words shown in brackets at the beginning: (**Ich habe es gemacht**). **Ich sage, daß** (= *that*, conjunction) **ich — — —.**
es gemacht habe	**1535** (**Ich habe dich gehört**). **Ich spreche, weil ich — — —.**
dich gehört habe	**1536** (**Ich habe meinen Wagen geholt**). **Ich komme, nachdem ich — — — —.**
meinen Wagen geholt habe	**1537** (**Ich habe zu Hause gewohnt**). **Sie fragen, ob ich — — — —.**
zu Hause gewohnt habe	

Strong Verbs: Formation of Past Participle

	1538 We mentioned that strong verbs form their past participles differently from weak verbs, e.g. **sprechen-gesprochen.** The past participle still begins with the letters —.
ge-	**1539** **Sprechen-gesprochen.** The past participle ends in the letter —.
n	**1540** **Sprechen-gesprochen.** You will notice that in addition in the formation of the past participle there has been a change of — in the stem.
vowel	**1541** The past participle of all strong verbs ends in —.
n	**1542** **Tragen** = *to carry*. The past participle is **getragen.** With this verb therefore there *is/is not* a change of vowel in the stem.

is not	**1543** **Sprechen-gesprochen; tragen-getragen.** The past participle of all strong verbs ends in **n**, and in addition there *may/must not* be a change of vowel in the stem.
may	**1544** As with the imperfect, the only thing to do is to learn the past participle of each strong verb. Go to next section.

Strong Verbs: 'Sprechen' Group (I-A-O)

	1545 Whereas weak verbs form their various tenses according to regular patterns and therefore present no difficulty, strong verbs are more of a law unto themselves, as there may be more or less unexpected changes of — in the stem.
vowel	**1546** Let us review the types of change we have met in various tenses of strong verbs. Go to next item.
	1547 **Kommen – du kommst, er kommt; Sprechen – du sprichst, er spricht.** There may or may not, therefore, be a change of vowel in the 2nd and 3rd pers. sing. of the — tense.
present	**1548** **Sprechen – ich sprach; kommen – ich kam; bleiben – ich blieb.** From these it appears that there is usually a vowel change in the formation of the — tense.
imperfect	**1549** **Sprechen – gesprochen; tragen – getragen.** There may or may not therefore be a further change of vowel in the — —.

165

past participle	**1550** Here then, using the verb **sprechen** as an example, are the various parts of a strong verb which we must know in order to know its behaviour completely. **SPRECHEN, spricht, sprach, gesprochen.** The word in capitals is the — of the verb.
infinitive	**1551** **Sprechen, SPRICHT, sprach, gesprochen.** The word in capitals is the — person singular of the — tense.
third; present	**1552** **Sprechen, spricht, SPRACH, gesprochen.** The word in capitals is the 1st (or 3rd) person singular of the — tense.
imperfect	**1553** **Sprechen, spricht, sprach, GESPROCHEN.** The word in capitals is the — —.
past participle	**1554** The above, then, are what are called the *principal parts* of a verb. In future when you meet a new strong verb you should learn its principal parts. To make this easier for you we will try to point out certain patterns.
	1555 The patterns become clearer if we classify strong verbs according to the vowel of the 3rd pers. sing. present tense rather than that of the infinitive: thus we would classify **Sprechen, spricht, sprach, gesprochen** as belonging to the group in which the vowel change is **I-a-o** because the vowel of the 3rd pers. sing. pres. tense is —.
i	**1556** **i-a-o. Sprechen, spricht, sprach, gesprochen Beginnen, beginnt,** —, — (*to begin*). (In this case the past participle has no **ge** for a reason which will be explained later).

166

	1557
begann, begonnen	**i-a-o. Beginnen, beginnt, begann, begonnen.**
	Brechen, —, —, — (*to break*).
	1558
bricht, brach,	**i-a-o. Brechen, bricht, brach, gebrochen.**
gebrochen	**Gelten, GILT, —, —** (*to be worth*).
	(Notice the irregularity of the 3rd pers. sing. pres.)
	1559
galt, gegolten	**i-a-o. Gelten, —, —, —.**
	1560
gilt, galt, gegolten	**i-a-o. Gelten, gilt, galt, gegolten.**
	Helfen, —, —, — (*to help*).
	1561
hilft, half,	**i-a-o. Helfen, hilft, half, geholfen.**
geholfen	**Schwimmen, —, —, —** (*to swim*).
	1562
schwimmt,	**i-a-o. Schwimmen, schwimmt, schwamm,**
schwamm,	**geschwommen.**
geschwommen	**Sterben, —, —, —** (*to die*).
	1563
stirbt, starb,	**i-a-o. Sterben, stirbt, starb, gestorben.**
gestorben	**Treffen —, TRAF, —** (*to meet*).
	(Note the slight irregularity in the consonant of the imperfect of this verb).
	1564
trifft, getroffen	**i-a-o. Treffen, —, —, —.**
	1565
trifft, traf,	**i-a-o. Treffen, trifft, traf, getroffen.**
getroffen	**Werfen, —, —, —** (*to throw*).
	1566
wirft, warf,	**i-a-o. Werfen, wirft, warf, geworfen.**
geworfen	**Nehmen, n—mmt, n—hm, ge—mmen** (*to take*).
	(Notice the slight irregularities in present tense and past participle.)

nImmt, nAhm,	**1567** i-a-o. Nehmen, **NIMMT**, —, **GENOMMEN.**
nahm	**1568** i-a-o. Nehmen, —, —, —.
nimmt, nahm, genommen	## Perfect Tense With 'Sein'
	1569 Consider the following examples of the perfect tense in English: 'I am come that ye might have life.' 'Be gone, dull care!' 'Now is Christ risen!' In all these cases the perfect tense has been made, not with the verb *to have* as auxiliary, but with the verb — —.
to be	**1570** German still uses the auxiliary verb **sein** instead of **haben** to make the perfect tense of verbs signifying a change of place or state. **Reisen** = *to travel. I have travelled* (change of place) is **ich — gereist.**
bin	**1571** *We have travelled* is — — —.
wir sind gereist	**1572** *Dying* (**sterben, stirbt, starb, gestorben**) is a change of state. *He has died* is — — —.
er ist gestorben	**1573** *They have died* is — — —.
sie sind gestorben	**1574** *Coming* (**kommen, kommt, kam, gekommen**) is a change of place. *You have come* (fam. sing.) is — — —.
du bist gekommen	**1575** *It has come* is — — —.

168

es ist gekommen	**1576** (You can omit this item if you like). Perhaps you know the old song 'Summer is icumen in'. You may have thought this means 'is a-coming', but in fact it is the perfect tense – 'has come'. The prefix *i*- (or *y*-) in front of a past participle corresponded in Old English to the German **ge-**. Milton uses the past participle 'yclept' ('called') and Spenser uses 'yclad' ('clad').
	1577 **Eilen** (*to hurry*) is another verb representing a change of place. *I have hurried* is — — —. (Note: The **ge-** is always pronounced separately and never forms a diphthong with any other vowel.)
ich bin geeilt	**1578** *We have hurried* is — — —.
wir sind geeilt	**1579** **Wandern** (*to walk*) is another weak verb representing a change of position. *I have walked* is — — —.
ich bin gewandert	**1580** *You have walked* (polite) is — — —.
Sie sind gewandert	**1581** More examples of verbs requiring **sein** will be given in the following sections, but you will not go very far wrong if you rely on the principle that verbs of change of place or state require **sein**.
	1582 If you have learnt French, do not imagine that German reflexive verbs take **sein**. No transitive verb (i.e. verb capable of having an object) can take **sein**. *I have washed myself* is **Ich — mich gewaschen.**
habe	

Strong Works: 'Singen' Group (I-A-U)

1583

i.a.u. This group of strong verbs contains several verbs showing the same vowel changes as English. They have no vowel change in the present tense. We may take **singen** as typical. **Singen, —, sang, gesungen** (*to sing*).

singt	**1584** **i-a-u. Singen, —, —, —.**
singt, sang, **gesungen**	**1585** **i-a-u. Singen, singt, sang, gesungen.** **Finden, —, —, —** (*to find*).
findet, fand, **gefunden**	**1586** **i-a-u. Finden, findet, fand, gefunden.** **Sinken, —, —, —** (*to sink*).
sinkt, sank, **gesunken**	**1587** *Sinking* is a change of place. *I have sunk* is — — —.
ich bin gesunken	**1588** **i-a-u. Sinken, sinkt, sank, gesunken.** **Springen, —, —, —** (*to jump*).
springt, sprang, **gesprungen**	**1589** *Jumping* is a change of place. *I have jumped* is — — —.
ich bin **gesprungen**	**1590** **i-a-u. Springen, springt, sprang, gesprungen.** **Trinken, —, —, —** (*to drink*).
trink, trank, **getrunken**	**1591** **i-a-u. Trinken, trinkt, trank, getrunken.** **Zwingen, —, —, —** (*to compel*).

170

zwingt, zwang, gezwungen	## Inseparable Verbs
	1592
	You have already met separable verbs, consisting of a simple verb + a separable prefix which in a main sentence is removed from the verb and put at the — of the sentence.
	1593
end	There are also a number of verb prefixes which are not separable. One of these is **be-**, which you have already met in the verb **beginnen** (*to begin*). *I begin it* is — — —.
	1594
ich beginne es	Other inseparable prefixes are **er-, emp-, ent-, ge-, ver-**. Inseparable prefixes are never stressed, e.g. **erwárten** (*to expect*). Mark the stress in **ich vergesse** (*I forget*). **Ich —**.
	1595
vergésse	There is not much difficulty in distinguishing separable from inseparable verbs; the separable prefixes are mostly recognizable as independent words, whereas the inseparable prefixes are not. Thus **zumachen** (*to close*) is *separable/inseparable*.
	1596
separable	Inseparable prefixes (e.g. **ich beginne**) are *stressed/unstressed*.
	1597
unstressed	Inseparable verbs are specially mentioned as a separate class because they do not add **ge-** in forming the past participle. The past participle of **werfen** is —.
	1598
geworfen	. . . but the past participle of **verwerfen** (*to reject*) is —.
	1599
verworfen	The past participle of **warten** (*to wait*) is —.

171

gewartet	1600 ... but the past participle of **erwarten** ('to expect') is —.

erwartet	## Strong Verbs: 'Geben' Group (I-A-E)
	1601 **Geben** (*to give*) is a typical member of the next group of strong verbs, which again mostly show a vowel change in the present tense: **i-a-e. Geben, —, gab, gegeben.**
gibt	1602 **i-a-e. Geben, —, —, —.**
gibt, gab, gegeben	1603 **i-a-e. Geben, gibt, gab, gegeben.** **Fressen, —, —, —** (*to eat* – referring to animals only).
frißt, fraß, gefressen	1604 **i-a-e. Fressen, frißt, fraß, gefressen.** **Messen, —, —, —** (*to measure*).
mißt, maß, gemessen	1605 **i-a-e. Messen, mißt, maß, gemessen.** **Bitten, —, baT, gebeTen** (*to request*). (Notice the consonant irregularity).
bittet	1606 **i-a-e. Bitten, —, —, gebeten.**
bittet, bat	1607 **i-a-e. Bitten, —, —, —.**
bittet, bat, gebeten	1608 It will have struck you that **Bitte!** (*Please!*) comes from this verb. **Bitte!** is really short for **ich bitte**, so that this expression really means *I* —!

172

request	1609
	i-a-e. Geben, gibt, gab, gegeben.
	Essen, —, —, geGessen (*to eat* – of human beings).
	(Note the irregularity of consonant).
ißt, aß	1610
	i-a-e. Essen, —, —, —.
ißt, aß, gegessen	1611
	i-a-e. Geben, gibt, gab, gegeben.
	Treten, triTT, —, — (*to step*).
	(Notice the consonant irregularity).
trat, getreten	1612
	i-a-e. Treten, —, —, —.
tritt, trat,	1613
getreten	*Stepping* may represent a change of place and when it does the perfect tense of **treten** must be made with **sein.** *I have stepped into the house* is **Ich — in das Haus —.**
bin (in das Haus)	1614
getreten	**i-a-e. Geben, gibt, gab, gegeben.**
	Sitzen, —, saß, geseSSen (*to be sitting*).
	(Note the consonant irregularities).
sitzt	1615
	i-a-e. Sitzen, —, —, gesessen.
sitzt, saß	1616
	i-a-e. Sitzen, —, —, —.
sitzt, saß,	1617
gesessen	To be sitting is *not* a change of place or state. *I have been sitting* is — — —.
ich habe gesessen	

Adverbs

1618

Most German adjectives can be used without change as adverbs: **Gut** = *good*; *well* = —.

173

	1619
gut	**Schnell** = *quick. Quickly* is —.
	1620
schnell	**Langsam** = *slow.* Slowly is —.
	1621
langsam	(You can omit this item if you wish). In English we began to feel the need of a special ending for adverbs to distinguish them from adjectives at the time when we ceased to put case-endings on adjectives. We therefore began to form adverbs by adding the suffix -*like* – originally used for turning nouns into adjectives (*man-like*, etc.). This suffix became condensed into -*ly* but there are parts of England where you can still hear *quick-like* for *quickly.*
	1622
	If there is more than one adverb (or adverbial expression) in a sentence, the order of such expressions is: 1. TIME. 2. MANNER. 3. PLACE. E.g. *I went home* (**nach Hause**) *quickly* (**schnell**) *yesterday* (**gestern**) is **Ich ging** — — — —.
	1623
gestern schnell nach Hause	The order 1. Time. 2. Manner. 3. Place. can be easily remembered by the initials namely, — — —.
	1624
TMP	The initials TMP stand for —, —, —.
	1625
Time, Manner, Place	*He comes to school* (**in die Schule**) *quickly today* (**heute**) is **Er kommt** — — — — —.
	1626
heute schnell in die Schule	*She is travelling home slowly* (**langsam**) *today* is **Sie fährt** — — — —.
heute langsam nach Hause	

174

Strong Verbs: 'Sehen' Group (IE-A-E)

1627

ie-a-e. Sehen is typical of the next group of strong verbs, which again mostly show a vowel change in the present tense. **Sehen, —, sah, gesehen.**

1628

sieht	**ie-a-e. Sehen, —, —, —.**

1629

sieht, sah, gesehen	**ie-a-e. Sehen, sieht, sah, gesehen.**
	Geschehen, —, —, — (*to happen*) (impersonal).

1630

geschieht, geschah, geschehen	*Happening* is a change of state. *It has happened* is — — —.

1631

es ist geschehen	**ie-a-e. Geschehen, geschieht, geschah, geschehen.**
	Lesen, —, —, — (*to read*).

1632

liest, las, gelesen	**ie-a-e. Lesen, liest, las, gelesen.**
	Liegen, —, —, — (*to be lying*).

liegt, lag, gelegen	## Separable Verbs (continued)—Past Participle

1633

Separable verbs have the further peculiarity that in forming the past participle the prefix (or as we should perhaps now call it, the 'infix') **ge** is inserted between the separable prefix and the verb. The past participle of **ankommen** (*to arrive*) is **an—kommen.**

1634

anGEkommen	The past participle of a separable verb is written as *one/two* word(s).

one word	**1635** The past participle of **zumachen** (*to close*) is —.
zugemacht	**1636** *I have closed the door* (**die Tür**) is **Ich habe** — — —.
die Tür **zugemacht**	**1637** The past participle of **ankommen** is —.
angekommen	**1638** Arriving is a change of place. *I have arrived* is — — —.
ich bin **angekommen**	**1639** The past participle of **einschlafen** (*to go to sleep*) is —schlafen.
EINGEschlafen	**1640** Going to sleep is a change of state. *I have gone to sleep* is — — —.

ich bin **eingeschlafen**	## Strong Verbs (continued)– 'Schlafen' Group (Ä-IE-A)
	1641 **ä-ie-a. Schlafen** (*to sleep*) is typical of the next group of strong verbs, which again shows a vowel change in the present tense: **Schlafen, —, schlief, geschlafen.**
schläft	**1642** **ä-ie-a. Schlafen, —, —, —.**
schläft, schlief, **geschlafen**	**1643** **ä-ie-a. Schlafen, schläft, schlief, geschlafen.** **Fallen, —, —, —** (*to fall*).
fällt, fiel, **gefallen**	**1644** *Falling* is a change of place. *I have fallen* is — — —.
ich bin gefallen	**1645** **ä-ie-a. Fallen, fällt, fiel, gefallen.** **Lassen,—, —, —** (*to let, leave*).

läßt, ließ, gelassen	**1646** **ä-ie-a. Lassen, läßt, ließ, gelassen.** **Laufen, —, —, —** (*to run*).
läuft, lief, gelaufen	**1647** Running is a change of place. *I have run* is — — —.
ich bin gelaufen	**1648** **ä-ie-a. Laufen, läuft, lief, gelaufen.** **Halten, hälT, —, —** (*to hold*) (Note the irregularity in the present tense).
hielt, gehalten	**1649** **ä-ie-a. Halten, —, —, —.**
hält, hielt, gehalten	**1650** **ä-i-a.** To this group also belong two verbs, **fangen** and **hangen** (or **hängen**), which have a short **i** (**i** instead of **ie**) in the imperfect: **Schlafen, schläft, schlief, geschlafen.** **Fangen, —, fIng, —** (*to catch*).
fängt, gefangen	**1651** **ä-i-e. Fangen, —, —, —.**
fängt, fing, gefangen	**1652** **ä-i-e. Fangen, fängt, fing, gefangen.** **Hangen, —, —, —** (*to be hanging*).
hängt, hing, gehangen	

'Her' and 'Hin'

	1653 A prefix much used to indicate direction is **her** (*hither*). **Kommen Sie her!** means — —.
come hither (come here)	**1654** **Her** is often used in German together with other separable prefixes in contexts in which all mention of *here* (or *hither*) would be omitted in English, e.g. **Kommen Sie heraus!** means simply *Come —!*

177

out	**1655**
	You can regard **her** as meaning *towards the speaker*. Thus *Come in* (*towards me*) using **einkommen** is **Kommen Sie —ein.**
HERein	**1656**
	Come in (*towards me*) is **Kommen Sie —.**
herein	**1657**
	He's coming out (i.e. *towards me*) (using **auskommen**) is **er kommt —.**
heraus	**1658**
	Hin (*thither* or *away from the speaker*) is the counterpart of **her.** *Go out* (= *away from me*) is **Gehen Sie —aus.**
HINaus	**1659**
	Go in (= *away from me*) (using **eingehen**) is — — —.
gehen Sie hinein!	**1660**
	I'm going out (= *away from where I am now*) is — — —.
ich gehe hinaus	**1661**
	Let's go in (= *away from where we are now*) is **Gehen wir —.**
hinein	**1662**
	If you have any difficulty in distinguishing **hin** and **her** it will perhaps help to memorize the word **hierher** which literally means *Here* (*towards me*). No corresponding compound with **hier** and **hin** exists, as of course you cannot have *Here* (*away from me*).

Strong Verbs (continued)– 'Tragen' Group (Ä-U-A)

1663

ä-u-a. Tragen (*to carry, wear*) is typical of the next group, which also show a vowel change in the present tense. **Tragen, —, trug, getragen.**

178

	1664
trägt	**ä-u-a. Tragen, trägt, trug, getragen.**
	Fahren, —, —, — (*to travel, go by vehicle*).
	1665
fährt, fuhr,	Travelling is a change of place. *I have travelled* is — —
gefahren	—.
	1666
ich bin gefahren	**ä-u-a. Fahren, fährt, fuhr, gefahren.**
	Schlagen, —, —, — (*to strike*).
	1667
schlägt, schlug,	**ä-u-a. Schlagen, schlägt, schlug, geschlagen.**
geschlagen	**Wachsen, —, —, —** (*to grow*).
	1668
wächst, wuchs,	Growing is a change of state. *I have grown* is — — —.
gewachsen	
	1669
ich bin gewachsen	**ä-u-a. Wachsen, wächst, wuchs, gewachsen.**
	Waschen, —, —, — (*to wash*).
wäscht, wusch,	
gewaschen	

Word Order: Position of 'Nicht'

1670

You have now learnt several rules about word order. Thus in the main sentence **Ich kann Sie sehen,** the word **sehen** comes last because it is the —.

1671

infinitive

In the main sentence **Kommst du heute an?**, the word **an** comes last because it is the prefix of a — verb.

1672

separable

In the main sentence **Du hast mich gesehen,** the word **gesehen** comes last because it is the — —.

1673

past participle

In the dependent sentence **Wenn du heute ankommst . . .,** the word **ankommst** comes last because it is the — verb.

179

finite	**1674** If the word **nicht** is present it will normally come last unless there is some other word which must be last in accordance with the rules which you already know. *I don't see her* is — — — —.
ich sehe sie nicht	**1675** Make the following four sentences negative by inserting the word **nicht** in the correct place. **Ich kann Sie sehen.**
Ich kann Sie nicht sehen	**1676** **Kommst du heute an?**
Kommst du heute nicht an?	**1677** **Du hast mich gesehen.**
Du hast mich nicht gesehen	**1678** **Wenn du heute ankommst . . .**
Wenn du heute nicht ankommst	**1679** However, if the negative is to be applied to a particular word, it will precede that word. So *If you don't come TODAY* is **Wenn du — — ankommst.**

nicht heute	## Strong Verbs: 'Beißen' Group (EI-I-I)
	1680 **ei-i-i. Beißen** (*to bite*) is typical of the next group of strong verbs, which show no vowel change in the present tense. **Beißen, —, biß, gebissen.**
beißt	**1681** **ei-i-i. Beißen, —, —, —.**
beißt, biß, gebissen	**1682** **ei-i-i. Beißen, beißt, biß, gebissen.** **Reißen, —, —, —** (*to tear*).

180

reißt, riß, **gerissen**	1683 **ei-i-i. Reißen, reißt, riß, gerissen.** **Reiten, —, riTT, geriTTen** (*to ride on horseback*). (Notice the doubling of the consonant in imperfect and past participle of this verb).
reitet	1684 **ei-i-i. Reiten, —, —, —.**
reitet, ritt, **geritten**	1685 Riding is a change of place. *I have ridden* is — — —.
ich bin geritten	1686 **ei-i-i. Beißen, beißt, biß, gebissen.** **Schneiden, —, schniTT, geschniTTen** (*to cut*). (Notice the irregularities of consonant in this verb).
schneidet	1687 **ei-i-i. Schneiden, —, —, —.**

schneidet, schnitt, **geschnitten**	## Prepositions With Genitive 1688 A few prepositions require the genitive case. They are mostly prepositions which in English include the word *of* and therefore easy to remember. **Während** = *during*, in *the course of. During the morning* (**der Morgen**) is — — —.
während des **Morgens**	1689 *In the course of the night* is — — —.
während der **Nacht**	1690 **Statt** or **anstatt** (*instead of*) also requires the genitive. *Instead of my dog* is — — —.
(an)statt meines **Hundes**	1691 *Instead of the cat* is — — —.

181

(an)statt der Katze	**1692** Another such preposition is **trotz** (*in spite of*). *In spite of the baker* is — — —.
trotz des Bäckers	**1693** *In spite of the news* (**die Nachricht**) is — — —.
trotz der Nachricht	

The Three Auxiliary Verbs

1694
The three AUXILIARY verbs – that is, the verbs used for helping to make other tenses – are **haben, sein** and **werden.** You have not yet met **werden** used in this way.

1695
As you know, **sein** is used with verbs representing a change of place or state to form the — tense.

perfect	**1696** **Sein,** like its counterpart in English, *to be,* is actually an amalgam of various verbs of different origins as you can see by comparing the form of several of the persons of the present tense: **ich** —, **er** —, **ihr** —.
bin, ist, seid	**1697** The imperfect of **sein** is **war.** *I was* is — —.
ich war	**1698** The imperfect tense is regular in itself – that is, it has all the endings which you will expect. *You were* (fam. sing.) is — —.
du warst	**1699** *He was* is — —.
er war	**1700** *We were* is — —.

182

	1701
wir waren	. . . and so on. The past participle of **sein** is **gewesen.** The perfect tense is made with **sein** itself as the auxiliary; *I have been* is **ich bin** —.
	1702
gewesen	*He has been* is — — —.
	1703
er ist gewesen	*They have been* is — — —.
	1704
sie sind gewesen	*She has been* is — — —.
	1705
sie ist gewesen	**Haben,** as you know, is another important auxiliary verb also used to form the — tense of other verbs.
	1706
perfect	You already know the present tense of **haben.** It is an irregular weak verb and its imperfect is **hatte.** *I had* is — —.
	1707
ich hatte	*He had* is — —.
	1708
er hatte	*You had* (fam. pl.) is — —.
	1709
ihr hattet	The past participle is not irregular, so it is —.
	1710
gehabt	The perfect is made using **haben** itself as the auxiliary, so *I have had* is — — —.
	1711
ich habe gehabt	*You have had* (fam. sing.) is — — —.
	1712
du hast gehabt	*You have had* (polite) is — — —.

Sie haben gehabt	**1713** **Werden** (*to become*) is the other important auxiliary verb. The principal parts are **werden, wird, wurde, geworden.** *He becomes* is — —.
er wird	**1714** You will remember that the 2nd pers. sing. present tense is irregular, **du wirst.** *You become tired* is — — —.
du wirst müde	**1715** The imperfect is **wurde.** *I became* is — —.
ich wurde	**1716** *She became* is — —.
sie wurde	**1717** *They became* is — —.
sie wurden	**1718** **Werden, —, —, geworden.**
wird, wurde	**1719** **Werden, —, —, —.**
wird, wurde, geworden	**1720** The perfect tense of **werden** is formed with **sein.** *I have become* is — — —.
ich bin geworden	**1721** *It has become* is — — —.
es ist geworden	**1722** *They have become* is — — —.
sie sind geworden	

Strong Verbs: 'Bleiben' Group (EI-IE-IE)

1723
Bleiben (*to stay*) is typical of the next group of strong verbs, which show no vowel change in the present tense. **Bleiben, —, blieb, geblieben.** (Refer back to introductory section for pronunciation if you need to.)

bleibt	1724 **ei-ie-ie. Bleiben, —, —, —.**
bleibt, blieb, geblieben	1725 It is hard to think of **bleiben** (*to stay*) as representing a change of place or state, but it does require **sein** for its perfect tense. *I have stayed* is — — —.
ich bin geblieben	1726 **ei-ie-ie. Bleiben, bleibt, blieb, geblieben.** **Scheinen, —, —, —.** (*to shine* or *seem*).
scheint, schien, geschienen	1727 A useful expression is *It seems* — —.
es scheint	1728 **ei-ie-ie. Scheinen, scheint, schien, geschienen.** **Schreiben, —, —, —.** (*to write*).
schreibt, schrieb, geschrieben	1729 **ei-ie-ie. Schreiben, schreibt, schrieb, geschrieben.** **Schreien, —, —, —** (*to cry, shout*).
schreit, schrie, geschrieen	1730 **ei-ie-ie. Schreien, schreit, schrie, geschrieen.** **Schweigen, —, —, —.** (*to be silent*).
schweigt, schwieg, geschwiegen	1731 **ei-ie-ie. Schweigen, schweigt, schwieg, geschwiegen.** **Steigen, —, —, —** (*to climb*).
steigt, stieg, gestiegen	1732 *Climbing* is a change of place *I have climbed* is — — —.
ich bin gestiegen	1733 **ei-ie-ie. Steigen, steigt, stieg, gestiegen.** **Treiben, —, —, —** (*to drive, carry on*).
treibt, trieb, getrieben	

Strong Verbs:
'Befehlen' and 'Stehlen' (IE-A-O)

1734

ie-a-o. These two verbs really belong to the **sprechen**-group (**i-a-o**) except that the vowel in the 3rd sing. pres. tense is lengthened to **ie.**

Befehlen (*to command*), —, **befahl, befohlen.**

befiehlt

1735

ie-a-o. Befehlen, —, —, —.

befiehlt, befahl,
befohlen

1736

ie-a-o. Befehlen, befiehlt, befahl, befohlen.
       Stehlen, —, —, — (*to steal*).

stiehlt, stahl,
gestohlen

Future Tense

1737

The future tense in English – *He will be,* etc., is made up up from the infinitive of the verb (without 'to') and an — verb.

1738

auxiliary

The future tense in English is made up with an auxiliary verb and the — (without 'to').

1739

infinitive

The future tense in German is made up in the same way as in English – that is, with the — of the verb together with an — verb.

1740

infinitive, auxiliary

The auxiliary verb used in German to form the future is the present tense of **werden.** *I shall come* is — — **kommen.**

1741

ich werde

I shall come is — — —.

186

ich werde kommen	1742 *You will come* (fam. sing.) is — — —.
du wirst kommen	1743 *We shall go* is — — —.
wir werden gehen	1744 The future of **werden** itself of course is similarly formed *they will become* is — — —.
sie werden werden	1745 As the last component of the future consists of the infinitive, its position in a main sentence is of course at the —.
end	1746 *I shall see you* (**Sie**) is — — — —.
ich werde Sie sehen	1747 *They will come home* (**nach Hause**) *today* (**heute**) is — — — — — —. (Remember the 'TMP' rule for order of adverbial expressions).
sie werden heute nach Hause kommen	

Irregular Verbs: 'Gehen', 'Stehen', 'Heißen'

	1748 The principal parts of **gehen** (*to go*) are **Gehen, geht, ging, gegangen.** *He went* is — —.
er ging	1749 **Gehen, —, —, —.**
geht, ging, gegangen	1750 *We went* is — —.
wir gingen	1751 *You went* (fam. pl.) is — —.

ihr gingt	1752 The past participle of **gehen** is —.
gegangen	1753 As going is a change of place, **gehen** naturally forms its perfect tense with **sein**. *I have gone* is — — —.
ich bin gegangen	1754 *We have gone* is — — —.
wir sind gegangen	1755 Remember that **gehen** normally means going on foot, not in a vehicle (**fahren**). *They have gone on foot* (**zu Fuß**) is — — — — —.
sie sind zu Fuß gegangen	1756 **Stehen** (*to stand*) does not fit into any of the established patterns for strong verbs. The principal parts are **Stehen, steht, stand, gestanden.** *I was standing* is — —.
ich stand	1757 **Stehen, —, —, gestanden.**
steht, stand	1758 **Stehen, —, —, —.**
steht, stand, gestanden	1759 *Standing* is not a change of place or state, so *I have been standing* is — — —.
ich habe gestanden	1760 However, some of the compounds of **stehen** may represent a change of place or state. So for example **aufstehen** (separable) – *to get up*. *I have got up* is — — **aufgestanden.**
ich bin	1761 *I have got up* is — — —.

188

ich bin aufgestanden	1762 In view of the similarity of the imperfect of **stehen** (**ich stand**) to the English present tense, an effort is necessary to remember that *I am standing* is — —.
ich stehe	1763 . . . and that **ich stand** means — — —.
I was standing	1764 **Heißen** (*to be called*, i.e. *named*) shows vowel changes which do not fit into any strong verb pattern. **Heißen, heißt, hieß, geheißen.** Notice that it means *to — called.*
be	1765 *I am called* (present tense) is — —.
ich heiße	1766 You would notice that there is no vowel change in the present tense. **Heißen, —, hieß, geheißen.**
heißt	1767 **Heißen, —, —, —.**
heißt, hieß, geheißen	1768 Do not be confused by the fact that the verb is passive in English (*I am called*) but active in German. **Heißen** requires **haben.** *I have been called* is **ich — geheißen.**
habe	1769 *I have been called* is — — —.
ich habe geheißen	## Strong Verbs: 'Fliegen' Group (IE-O-O)
	1770 **ie-o-o. Fliegen** (*to fly*), is typical of the last group of strong verbs, which show no vowel change in the present tense. **Fliegen, —, flog, geflogen.**
fliegt	1771 **ie-o-o. Fliegen, —, —, —.**

189

fliegt, flog, **geflogen**	**1772** Flying is a change of place. *I have flown* is — — —.
ich bin geflogen	**1773** ie-o-o. **Fliegen, fliegt, flog, geflogen.** **Fließen, —, —, —** (*to flow*).
fließt, floß, **geflossen**	**1774** Flowing is a change of place. *It has flowed* is — — —.
es ist geflossen	**1775** ie-o-o. **Fließen, fließt, floß, geflossen** **Frieren, —, —, —** (*to freeze*).
friert, fror, **gefroren**	**1776** ie-o-o. **Frieren, friert, fror, gefroren.** **Schießen, —, —, —** (*to shoot*).
schießt, schoß, **geschossen**	**1777** ie-o-o. **Schießen, schießt, schoß, geschossen.** **Schließen, —, —, —** (*to shut*).
schließt, schloß, **geschlossen**	**1778** ie-o-o. **Fliegen, fliegt, flog, geflogen.** **Ziehen, —, zoG, gezoGen** (*to pull*). Notice how the **h** of the stem changes to **g** in imperfect and past participle of this verb.
zieht	**1779** ie-o-o. **Ziehen, —, —, —.**
zieht, zog, **gezogen**	

END OF PART I

EXERCISES

In all the following exercises the sentences given should be completely rewritten, making the changes indicated at the head of each exercise. Answers are given on pages 203-214.

I. GENDERS AND DETERMINATIVES (Items 1–106 and 110–149)
Remove the brackets and put the determinative into the correct form.

1. (Der) Haus ist klein.
2. (Dieser) Maus ist nicht schwarz.
3. (Jener) Frau ist alt.
4. (Ein) Hund ist intelligent.
5. (Mancher) Mädchen ist schön.
6. (Mein) Kohle brennt nicht.
7. (Welcher) Gras ist grün?
8. (Kein) Fräulein ist hier.
9. (Ihr) Käse schmeckt nicht gut.
10. (Solcher) Junge ist flink.

II. PRESENT TENSE OF 'SEIN' AND REGULAR VERBS (Items 150–271)
Remove the brackets and put the verbs into the correct form of the present tense.

1. Ich (sein) ein Mann, er (sein) ein Junge.
2. Du (kommen), und ich (stehen) hier.
3. Das Mädchen (tun) nichts, aber wir (arbeiten).
4. Ihr (öffnen) das Fenster, aber es (sein) kalt.
5. Er (arbeiten) nicht, er (schwimmen).
6. Was (machen) Sie dort? Ich (gehen) nach Hause.
7. (Sein) ihr Jungen? Nein, wir (sein) Mädchen.
8. Das Mädchen und die Frau (kommen) nicht, aber ihr (kommen).
9. Was (tun) ich? Ich (machen) einen Spaziergang.
10. (Arbeiten) du? Nein, ich (schwimmen).

EXERCISES

III. PLURALS OF NOUNS AND VERBS (Items 306–332, 343–371, 272–305 and 333–342)

Turn the singular into the plural. Example : Er hat die Katze : sie haben die Katzen

1. Die Frau ist hier.
2. Die Lehrerin spricht Deutsch. (Don't try to make 'Deutsch' plural!)
3. Er sieht die Maus.
4. Du triffst die Mutter. (Remember that the plural of 'du' is 'ihr').
5. Der Wagen steht dort.
6. Sie hat das Messer.
7. Der Mann wird alt.
8. Du gibst das Buch.
9. Der Onkel kommt.
10. Sie sieht die Wand.

IV. NOMINATIVE AND ACCUSATIVE OF PRONOUNS (Items 150–193 and 418–438)

Replace the dashes by the appropriate form of pronoun.

1. Wo ist die Tafel? — ist hier.
2. Siehst du mich? Ja, ich sehe — (du).
3. Treffen Sie Peter heute? Ja, wir treffen — .
4. Ist das der Tisch? Ja, — ist hier.
5. Wo ist der Wein? Ich sehe — nicht.
6. Hast du die Bücher? Ja, ich habe — .
7. Seht ihr uns? Wir sehen — (ihr) nicht.
8. Hat sie das Buch? Ja, sie hat — .
9. Treffen Sie uns? Ja, wir treffen — (Sie).
10. Nehmen Sie Tee? Ja, danke, ich nehme — .

V. PRESENT TENSE OF 'HABEN' AND VERBS WITH IRREGULAR PRESENT TENSE (Items 272–305, 333–342 and 439–448)

Remove the brackets and put the verbs into the correct form of the present tense.

1. (Haben) du ein Haus? Nein, ich (haben) kein Haus.
2. Ich (tragen) ein Buch. Was (tragen) du?
3. Wir (fangen) nichts, aber die Katze (fangen) eine Maus.

4. Er (geben) Margarete und Hans ein Tischlein, und sie (nehmen) es.
5. Was (nehmen) du? Ich (nehmen) nichts.
6. Ich (werden) alt, aber er auch (werden) alt.
7. (Sprechen) er Deutsch? Nein, aber er (lesen) es.
8. Du (laufen) nach Hause, aber du (sehen) nichts.
9. Er (treffen) mich, und Sie (treffen) ihn.
10. Du (lassen) ihn kommen, aber du (sprechen) nicht.

VI. ACCUSATIVE OF NOUNS AND PLURAL OF DETERMINATIVES (Items 460–504)

Fill in the missing portions of words.
1. Er liest d— Buch.
2. Sie hält d— Ball.
3. Siehst du dies— Mann?
4. Nein, ich sehe jen— Frau.
5. Ich habe ein— Katze.
6. Ihr habt ein— Hund.
7. Wir treffen d— Mädchen. (pl.)
8. Ich habe kein— Onkel. (sing.)
9. Sie trifft ihr— Töchter.
10. Sehen Sie jen— Häuser?

VII. PLURALS OF NOUNS AND VERBS (Items 407–417, 449–459 and 505–525)

Turn the singular into the plural in each case.
1. Das Mädchen nimmt Kaffee. (Leave 'Kaffee' in the singular.)
2. Der Junge arbeitet.
3. Du siehst das Geschäft.
4. Hier ist der Sohn.
5. Der Stuhl steht da.
6. Er läßt den Wagen hier.
7. Die Maus stirbt.
8. Die Nacht ist schön.
9. Du wirfst den Ball.
10. Die Frucht schmeckt gut.

EXERCISES

VIII. IMPERATIVES (Items 573–595)

Replace the infinitive in brackets with the correct form of the imperative as shown in each case.

1. (Kommen) mit mir! (fam. sing.)
2. (Machen) einen Spaziergang! (polite.)
3. (Geben) mir jenes Buch! (fam. sing.)
4. (Sprechen) mit ihnen! (fam. pl.)
5. (Sein) still! (fam. sing.)

IX. ACCUSATIVE AND DATIVE OF PRONOUNS AND NOUNS AND SOME PREPOSITIONS REQUIRING DATIVE (Items 526–572, 600–626 and 635–648)

Fill in the missing words or portions of words.

1. Sie zeigt — (ich) ein Buch.
2. Geben Sie dies— Mann das Bild.
3. Herr Braun spricht mit — (sie, pl.)
4. Wir zeigen jen— Frau ihre Katze.
5. Sie wohnt bei ihr— Mutter.
6. Ich spreche nicht mit mein— Töchter—.
7. Wohnen Sie bei — (er)?
8. Jener Mann steht d— Häuser— gegenüber.
9. Zeigen Sie dies— Schülerin— (pl.) ihre Bücher.
10. Was befehlen Sie — (wir)?

X. PREPOSITIONS (Items 627–648 and 709–731)

Fill in the missing words or portions of words.

1. Der Junge kommt aus d— Haus.
2. Herr Braun läuft durch d— Wald.
3. Meine Mutter spricht nicht mit — (ich).
4. Der Vater wohnt bei — (sie, pl.).
5. Er macht einen Spaziergang ohne d— Hund.
6. Um d— Tisch sitzen die Kinder.
7. Für — (er) habe ich nichts.
8. Jener Schüler geht zu d— Geschäft.
9. Der Stuhl ist gegen d— Wand.
10. Die Söhne kommen nach ihr— Mutter.

194

XI. PLURALS OF NOUNS AND VERBS (Items 596–599, 627–634, 691–708 and 732–735)

Turn the singular into the plural in each case.

1. Der Vogel frißt die Nuß.
2. Dieser Wagen fährt schnell.
3. Jener Junge stiehlt eine Gans. (Remember that as in English there is no plural of the indefinite article.)
4. Du befiehlst dem Mädchen.
5. Mein Vater hat ein Büro.
6. Das Gras wächst nicht.
7. Meine Tochter hält das Kind.
8. Der Wald steht hoch.
9. Das Auto trägt einen Schüler.
10. Du schlägst den Bäcker.

XII. POSSESSIVE ADJECTIVES AND OTHER DETERMINATIVES (Items 58–106, 110–149, 493–504 and 736–774)

Complete as necessary.

1. (Mein) Sohn ist mit jen— Schüler.
2. Dies— Katze schläft nicht mit (dein) Hund.
3. Er trägt (unser) Buch aus d— Geschäft.
4. Manch— Mann hat (kein) Vater.
5. Dies— Mädchen lesen (ihr) Bücher.
6. Was machen Sie für (Ihr) Tochter und (Ihr) Sohn?
7. Nehmt ihr (euer) Katze aus (euer) Haus?
8. Wir geben jed— Kind (ein) Ball.
9. Wir haben (unser) Hund aber nicht (unser) Kätzchen (neut.).
10. (Mein) Tochter kommt aus (sein) Haus.

XIII. GENITIVE AND OTHER CASES – STRONG AND WEAK NOUNS (Items 775–823)

Fill in the missing portions of words.

1. Hier ist das Geschäft d— Bäcker—.
2. Wie ist der Name dein— Onkel—?

EXERCISES

3. Er spricht nicht mit d— Jung— (sing.).
4. Wo ist das Haus dies— Frau?
5. Die Wände jen— Häuser sind weiß.
6. Er gibt d— Löwe— (sing.) das Fleisch
7. Das sind die Bleistifte mein— Töchter
8. Wie ist der Name jen— Herr—?
9. Sehen Sie dies— Knab—? (sing.).
10. Wo sind die Häuser jen— Herr—?

XIV. PREPOSITIONS (Items 666–690, 709–731 and 824-853)
Fill in the missing portions of words.
1. Kommen Sie in d— Haus?
2. Die Stadt ist hinter d— Wald.
3. Wir schlafen in d— Nacht.
4. Wir kommen schnell von d— Stadt.
5. Er läuft hinter d— Haus.
6. Hängen Sie bitte dieses Bild an d— Wand.
7. Der Hund geht durch d— Stadt.
8. Das Bild ist an d— Wand.
9. Sie geht zu d— Schule.
10. Der Tisch ist auf d— Gras.

XV. SEPARABLE AND INSEPARABLE VERBS (Items 854–866)
Put the verb into the correct form of the present tense, paying particular attention to word order.
1. Sie (ankommen) mit Ihrem Sohn.
2. Wann (aufstehen) er jeden Morgen?
3. Wir (einschlafen) in der Nacht.
4. Ihr (unterhalten) (= entertain) uns.
5. (Zumachen) Sie die Tür!

XVI. INTERROGATIVE PRONOUNS AND ADVERBS USED INSTEAD OF PRONOUNS (Items 912–952)
Translate into German the words given in brackets . . .
1. (Who) sagt das?
2. (Whom) sehen Sie?

3. (Out of what) läuft die Maus?
4. (With whom) spricht Frau Schmidt?
5. (Whose) Buch ist auf dem Tisch?

... and in the following sentences substitute pronouns or adverbs ('damit' etc.), whichever is appropriate, for the nouns. Examples: Ich sehe den Hund: ich sehe ihn; Ich gehe zu der Stadt: ich gehe dazu.

6. Wir sitzen um den Tisch.
7. Ich spreche mit meiner Mutter.
8. Sie stehen vor der Tafel.
9. Ihr kommt von dem Wald.
10. Was sagst du zu Herrn Bergmann?

XVII. WORD ORDER (INVERSION, ACCUSATIVE AND DATIVE, DEPENDENT SENTENCES) (Items 649–659, 893–911 and 953–1009)

Add the words under heading B to those under heading A so as to make a complete sentence in each case, and altering the word order where necessary.

A.	B.
1. In dem Wald ...	er macht einen Spaziergang.
2. Sehen Sie, daß ...	ich komme in die Stadt.
3. Er zeigt mir ...	es.
4. Der Sohn spricht, und ...	der Vater kommt.
5. Geben Sie einen Bleistift ...	diesem Jungen.
6. Warum fragst du, ob ...	sie kommen aus dem Hause.
7. Er gibt mir ...	einen Bleistift.
8. Mit seinem Hunde ...	er fährt nach England.
9. Ich schwimme, bevor ...	ich gehe nach Hause.
10. Bevor ich nach Hause gehe ...	ich mache einen Spaziergang.

XVIII. AGREEMENT OF ADJECTIVES (STRONG DECLENSION) (Items 1049–1096)

Complete the adjectives as necessary.

1. Komm mit, alt— Freund!
2. Schön— Vögel haben oft schön— Federn (= feathers).
3. Willst du ein Glas kalt— Milch?

197

4. Er ißt ein Stück gut— Käses.
5. Das Kind liegt (= is lying) auf grün— Gras.
6. Der Lehrer mag mit alt— Freunden sprechen.
7. Mein Vater nimmt rot— (= red) Wein.
8. Flink— Mäuse laufen schnell.
9. Grün— Gras wächst im Frühling (= in spring).
10. Die Mutter klein— Kinder muß arbeiten.

XIX. MODAL VERBS (Items 1010–1048 and 1097–1125)
Put the verbs shown in brackets into the correct form of the present tense. . . . .
1. Ich (müssen) mit deiner Mutter sprechen.
2. (Dürfen) du heute nicht ausgehen?
3. Die Mädchen (können) in die Schule gehen.
4. Frau Wagner (können) das Auto nehmen.
5. Seht ihr nicht, daß ich hier sein (wollen)?

. . . and in the following sentences translate the words shown in brackets, using a modal verb in each case.
6. (I am allowed) in den Wald gehen.
7. Meine Mutter (likes) jenen Mann nicht.
8. (She is required) dieses Buch lesen.
9. (Let's) gehen!
10. (They are said) ankommen.

XX. DECLENSION OF ADJECTIVES – WEAK AND STRONG DECLENSIONS
(Items 1049–1096 and 1171–1219)
Complete the adjectives as necessary.
1. Dieser rot— Wein schmeckt gut.
2. Das ist das Haus des klein— Jungen.
3. Alt— Frauen schlafen nicht gut.
4. Geben Sie mir jenes interessant— Buch.
5. Solche intelligent— Schüler sprechen nicht.
6. Wo sind die Bälle der klein— Kinder?
7. Der Hund steht auf dem grün— Gras.
8. Gib mir bitte ein Glas dieser kalt— Milch.

9. Meine Mutter spricht mit den alt— Freunden.
10. Welche groß— Städte liegen am Rhein?

XXI. DECLENSION OF ADJECTIVES – WEAK, STRONG AND MIXED DE-
CLENSIONS (Items 1049–1096, 1171–1219 and 1286–1321)
Complete the adjectives as necessary.
1. Hier ist ein sehr interessant— Buch.
2. Mein alt— Vater liest nicht gut.
3. Geben Sie mir den Namen eines gut— Weins.
4. Dieser jung— Knabe spricht nicht gut.
5. Gut— Wein schmeckt immer (= always) gut.
6. Seine Mutter kommt mit ihren best— Freundinnen.
7. In einem groß— Wald ist es oft sehr schwarz.
8. Die Tür jenes alt— Hauses ist zu.
9. Wo ist euer grün— Ball?
10. Wer spricht mit unserem schwarz— Hund?

XXII. REFLEXIVE VERBS (Items 1428–1482)
Insert the correct form of the reflexive pronoun in place of the dash.
1. Ich wasche — die Hände.
2. Du wäschst — am Abend.
3. Ihr werft — auf den Boden, weil ihr so müde seid.
4. Die Katzen sehen — in dem Spiegel (= mirror).
5. Wenn wir Bücher lesen, unterhalten wir —.
6. Ich kämme — das Haar.
7. Er wäscht — jeden Morgen.
8. Bevor sie ausgeht, kämmt sie — das Haar.
9. Du kannst — in dem Wasser (= water) sehen.
10. Wir ziehen — schnell an. (Sich anziehen = to get dressed.)

XXIII. PERFECT TENSE (Items 1483–1568)
*Put the verbs into the perfect tense. Example: Was machst du dort? Was hast du
dort gemacht?*
1. Jener Schüler sagt nichts.
2. Die Mädchen arbeiten alle sehr gut.

3. Ihr wohnt nicht in der Stadt.

4. Sprichst du zu meiner Mutter?

5. Sie helfen mir jeden Abend.

6. Wir nehmen ein großes Glas Milch.

7. Herr Braun trifft mich vor der Schule.

8. Ich nehme meinen alten Wagen.

9. Tragen Sie die Tafel in die Schule?

10. Wer hört euch?

XXIV. PERFECT TENSE (Items 1483–1591)

Put the verbs into the perfect tense.

1. Der Mai (= May) kommt.

2. Wir waschen uns.

3. Ich eile jeden Morgen in die Schule.

4. Ich trinke ein kleines Glas Wein.

5. Ich finde mein deutsches Buch.

6. Die alte Frau stirbt.

7. Die Lorelei singt ein Lied (= a song).

8. Ich reise nach Deutschland.

9. Wir enden unsere Arbeit.

10. Hans und Margarete wandern in die Stadt.

XXV. IMPERFECT TENSE (Items 1328–1427, 1545–1568, 1583–1591 and 1601–1617)

Put the verbs into the imperfect tense.

1. Ich mache jeden Morgen einen Spaziergang.

2. Er sieht die alte Frau nicht.

3. Wir denken an unsere Mutter.

4. Warum bleibst du nicht zu Hause?

5. Bringen Sie den Hund in das Haus?

6. Hörst du das Mädchen singen? (You cannot change the infinitive.)

7. Ihr kommt in der Nacht nach Hause.

8. Sie nehmen ein großes Glas kalter Milch.

9. Herr Schmidt gibt mir ein altes Buch.

10. Ich sitze in diesem großen Stuhl.

XXVI. WORD ORDER (DEPENDENT SENTENCES, SEPARABLE VERBS IN DEPENDENT SENTENCES, PERFECT TENSE, 'NICHT', ETC.) (Items 953–1009, 1220–1226, 1523-1537 and 1670–1769)

Add the words under heading B to those under heading A so as to make a complete sentence in each case, and altering the word order where necessray.

A.	B.
1. Ich bleibe zu Hause, weil . . .	du gehst heute nicht aus.
2. Wir kommen, wenn . . .	wir haben unseren Wagen geholt.
3. Es ist zu heiß, da . . .	du machst die Tür zu.
4. Diese Mädchen sehe ich . . .	nicht.
5. Den Jungen kann ich auch sehen . . .	nicht.
6. Ich mache nichts, ehe . . .	du kommst heute an.
7. Ich mache nichts, weil . . .	du kommst heute nicht an.
8. Während die Katze eine Maus fängt, . . .	der Hund schläft ein.
9. Du siehst, daß . . .	die Katze hat eine Maus gefangen.
10. Weil ihr so müde seid, . . .	ihr arbeitet nicht.

XXVII. PREPOSITIONS (ALL CASES) (Items 666–690, 709–731, 824–853, 867–892, 1688–1693)

Fill in the missing words or portions of words.

1. Der Hund läuft zwischen d— Häuser.
2. Ich gehe mit der Katze statt d— Hund— spazieren.
3. Der Schüler kommt vor d— Lehrer.
4. Ich hänge das Bild über d— Tür.
5. Das Mädchen steht zwischen d— Haus und d— Schule.
6. Meine Mutter kommt während d— Morgen— .
7. Mein Vater wohnt bei — (ich).
8. Ich kaufe das Buch für d— Schüler (sing.).
9. Trotz d— Nachricht, geht er in die Stadt.
10. Vor zwei Tag— ist meine Mutter nach Hause gekommen.

XXVIII. THE VERBS 'HABEN', 'SEIN' AND 'WERDEN' (Items 1694–1722)

Put the verbs into (a) the present, (b) the imperfect, (c) the perfect tenses.

1. Jene Frau (sein) nicht alt.
2. Ich (haben) einen Vater aber keine Mutter.

3. Das Gras (werden) grün.
4. Warum (haben) diese Kinder keinen Ball?
5. (Werden) du im Winter nicht kalt?
6. Ihr (sein) nicht so groß wie ich.
7. Ich (werden) Lehrer.
8. Was (haben) du in der Hand?
9. Warum (sein) wir heute so müde?
10. Ihr (werden) sehr stark.

XXIX. FUTURE TENSE (Items 1737–1747)

Put the verbs into the future tense.

1. Wann kommst du heute an?
2. Er spricht nicht mit der Lehrerin.
3. Ihr seid müde.
4. Wir fahren heute nach England.
5. Ich werde Lehrer.

XXX. STRONG VERBS (Up to item 1779)

Put the verbs into (a) the imperfect, (b) the perfect tenses.

1. Ich gehe mit meinem Hund spazieren.
2. Wir schreiben unserer Mutter einen langen Brief (= a long letter).
3. Warum stehen Sie hinter dem Tisch?
4. Das Buch liegt auf dem Stuhl.
5. Er heißt Doktor Faust.
6. Der Vogel fliegt über das Haus.
7. Was geschieht nach der Schule?
8. Du schließt die Tür nicht.
9. Ihr fahrt jeden Januar nach Deutschland.
10. Ich denke an meinen schwarzen Kater.

ANSWERS TO THE EXERCISES ON PAGES 191 TO 202
OF PART 1

Where the exercise calls for a change in a single word, only that word is given. Otherwise the whole sentence is reproduced.

I.   GENDERS AND DETERMINATIVES

1. Das
2. Diese
3. Jene
4. Ein
5. Manches
6. Meine
7. Welches
8. Kein
9. Ihr
10. Solcher

II.   PRESENT TENSE OF "SEIN" AND REGULAR VERBS

1. Ich bin ein Mann, er ist ein Junge.
2. Du kommst, und ich stehe hier.
3. Das Mädchen tut nichts, aber wir arbeiten.
4. Ihr öffnet das Fenster, aber es ist kalt.
5. Er arbeitet nicht, er schwimmt.
6. Was machen Sie dort? Ich gehe nach Hause.
7. Seid ihr Jungen? Nein, wir sind Mädchen.
8. Das Mädchen und die Frau kommen nicht, aber ihr kommt.
9. Was tue ich? Ich mache einen Spaziergang.
10. Arbeitest du? Nein, ich schwimme.

ANSWERS
III.   PLURALS OF NOUNS AND VERBS
   1. Die Frauen sind hier.
   2. Die Lehrerinnen sprechen Deutsch.
   3. Sie sehen die Mäuse.
   4. Ihr trefft die Mütter.
   5. Die Wagen stehen dort.
   6. Sie haben die Messer.
   7. Die Männer werden alt.
   8. Ihr gebt die Bücher.
   9. Die Onkel kommen.
  10. Sie sehen die Wände.

IV.   NOMINATIVE AND ACCUSATIVE OF PRONOUNS
   1. sie
   2. dich
   3. ihn
   4. er
   5. ihn
   6. sie
   7. euch
   8. es
   9. Sie
  10. ihn

V.   PRESENT TENSE OF "HABEN" AND VERBS WITH IRREGULAR
             PRESENT TENSE
   1. Hast du ein Haus? Nein, ich habe kein Haus.
   2. Ich trage ein Buch. Was trägst du?
   3. Wir fangen nichts, aber die Katze fängt eine Maus.
   4. Er gibt Margarete und Hans ein Tischlein, und sie nehmen es.
   5. Was nimmst du? Ich nehme nichts.
   6. Ich werde alt, aber er auch wird alt.
   7. Spricht er Deutsch? Nein, aber er liest es.
   8. Du läufst nach Hause, aber du siehst nichts.

9. Er trifft mich, und Sie treffen ihn.
10. Du läßt ihn kommen, aber du sprichst nicht.

VI.   ACCUSATIVE OF NOUNS AND PLURAL OF DETERMINATIVES
1. das
2. den
3. diesen
4. jene
5. eine
6. einen
7. die
8. keinen
9. ihre
10. jene

VII.   PLURALS OF NOUNS AND VERBS
1. Die Mädchen nehmen Kaffee.
2. Die Jungen arbeiten.
3. Ihr seht die Geschäfte.
4. Hier sind die Söhne.
5. Die Stühle stehen da.
6. Sie lassen die Wagen hier.
7. Die Mäuse sterben.
8. Die Nächte sind schön.
9. Ihr werft die Bälle.
10. Die Früchte schmecken gut.

VIII.   IMPERATIVES
1. Komme *or* komm'.
2. Machen Sie.
3. Gib.
4. Sprecht.
5. Sei.

ANSWERS

IX.   ACCUSATIVE AND DATIVE OF PRONOUNS AND NOUNS AND SOME
                    PREPOSITIONS REQUIRING DATIVE

1. mir
2. diesem
3. ihnen
4. jener
5. ihrer
6. meinen Töchtern
7. ihm
8. den Häusern
9. diesen Schülerinnen
10. uns

X.   PREPOSITIONS

1. dem
2. den
3. mir
4. ihnen
5. den
6. den
7. ihn
8. dem
9. die
10. ihrer

XI.   PLURALS OF NOUNS AND VERBS

1. Die Vögel fressen die Nüsse
2. Diese Wagen fahren schnell
3. Jene Jungen stehlen Gänse
4. Ihr befehlt den Mädchen
5. Unsere Väter haben Büros
6. Die Gräser wachsen nicht
7. Unsere Töchter halten die Kinder
8. Die Wälder stehen hoch

9. Die Autos tragen Schüler
10. Ihr schlagt die Bäcker

XII.   POSSESSIVE ADJECTIVES AND OTHER DETERMINATIVES
  1. Mein Sohn ist mit jenem Schüler.
  2. Diese Katze schläft nicht mit deinem Hund.
  3. Er trägt unser Buch aus dem Geschäft.
  4. Mancher Mann hat keinen Vater.
  5. Diese Mädchen lesen ihre Bücher.
  6. Was machen Sie für Ihre Tochter und Ihren Sohn?
  7. Nehmt ihr eure Katze aus eurem Haus?
  8. Wir geben jedem Kind einen Ball.
  9. Wir haben unseren Hund aber nicht unser Kätzchen.
 10. Meine Tochter kommt aus seinem Haus.

XIII.   GENITIVE AND OTHER CASES—STRONG AND WEAK NOUNS
  1. Hier ist das Geschäft des Bäckers.
  2. Wie ist der Name deines Onkels?
  3. Er spricht nicht mit dem Jungen.
  4. Wo ist das Haus dieser Frau?
  5. Die Wände jener Häuser sind wieß.
  6. Er gibt dem Löwen das Fleisch.
  7. Das sind die Bleistifte meiner Töchter.
  8. Wie ist der Name jenes Herrn?
  9. Sehen Sie diesen Knaben?
 10. Wo sind die Häuser jenes Herrn [sing.] or jener Herren [plural].

XIV.   PREPOSITIONS
  1. das
  2. dem
  3. der
  4. der
  5. das
  6. die

ANSWERS

   7. die

   8. der

   9. der

  10. dem

XV.   SEPARABLE AND INSEPARABLE VERBS

   1. Sie kommen mit Ihrem Sohn an.

   2. Wann steht er jeden Morgen auf?

   3. Wir schlafen in der Nacht ein.

   4. Ihr unterhaltet uns.

   5. Machen Sie die Tür zu!

XVI.   INTERROGATIVE PRONOUNS AND ADVERBS USED INSTEAD OF
             PRONOUNS

   1. Wer sagt das?

   2. Wen sehen Sie?

   3. Woraus läuft die Maus?

   4. Mit wem spricht Frau Schmidt?

   5. Wessen Buch ist auf dem Tisch?

   6. Wir sitzen darum.

   7. Ich spreche mit ihr.

   8. Sie stehen davor.

   9. Ihr kommt davon.

  10. Was sagst du zu ihm?

XVII.   WORD ORDER—INVERSION, ACCUSATIVE AND DATIVE,
             DEPENDENT SENTENCES

   1. In dem Wald macht er einen Spaziergang.

   2. Sehen Sie, daß ich in die Stadt komme?

   3. Er zeigt es mir.

   4. Der Sohn spricht, und der Vater kommt.

   5. Geben Sie diesem Jungen einen Bleistift.

   6. Warum fragst du, ob sie aus dem Hause kommen?

   7. Er gibt mir einen Bleistift.

   8. Mit seinem Hunde fährt er nach England.

9. Ich schwimme, bevor ich nach Hause gehe.
10. Bevor ich nach Hause gehe, mache ich einen Spaziergang.

XVIII.   AGREEMENT OF ADJECTIVES (STRONG DECLENSION)
1. Komm mit, alter Freund!
2. Schöne Vögel haben oft schöne Federn.
3. Willst du ein Glas kalter Milch?
4. Er ißt ein Stück guten Käses.
5. Das Kind liegt auf grünem Gras.
6. Der Lehrer mag mit alten Freunden sprechen.
7. Mein Vater nimmt roten Wein.
8. Flinke Mäuse laufen schnell.
9. Grünes Gras wächst im Frühling.
10. Die Mutter kleiner Kinder muß arbeiten.

XIX.   MODAL VERBS
1. Ich muß mit deiner Mutter sprechen.
2. Darfst du heute nicht ausgehen?
3. Die Mädchen können in die Schule gehen.
4. Frau Wagner kann das Auto nehmen.
5. Seht ihr nicht, daß ich hier sein will?
6. Ich darf in den Wald gehen.
7. Meine Mutter mag jenen Mann nicht.
8. Sie soll dieses Buch lesen.
9. Wir wollen gehen!
10. Sie sollen ankommen.

XX.   DECLENSION OF ADJECTIVES—WEAK AND STRONG DECLENSIONS
1. rote
2. kleinen
3. Alte
4. interessante
5. intelligenten
6. kleinen
7. grünen

ANSWERS
8. kalten
9. alten
10. großen

XXI. DECLENSION OF ADJECTIVES—WEAK, STRONG AND MIXED DECLENSIONS

1. interessantes
2. alter
3. guten
4. junge
5. Guter
6. besten
7. großen
8. alten
9. grüner
10. schwarzen

XXII. REFLEXIVE VERBS

1. mir
2. dich
3. euch
4. sich
5. uns
6. mir
7. sich
8. sich
9. dich
10. uns

XXIII. PERFECT TENSE

1. Jener Schüler hat nichts gesagt.
2. Die Mädchen haben alle sehr gut gearbeitet.
3. Ihr habt nicht in der Stadt gewohnt.
4. Hast du zu meiner Mutter gesprochen?

5. Sie haben mir jeden Abend geholfen.
6. Wir haben ein großes Glas Milch genommen.
7. Herr Braun hat mich vor der Schule getroffen.
8. Ich habe meinen alten Wagen genommen.
9. Haben Sie die Tafel in die Schule getragen?
10. Wer hat euch gehört?

XXIV. PERFECT TENSE
1. Der Mai ist gekommen.
2. Wir haben uns gewaschen.
3. Ich bin jeden Morgen in die Schule geeilt.
4. Ich habe ein kleines Glas Wein getrunken.
5. Ich habe mein deutsches Buch gefunden.
6. Die alte Frau ist gestorben.
7. Die Lorelei hat ein Lied gesungen.
8. Ich bin nach Deutschland gereist.
9. Wir haben unsere Arbeit geendet.
10. Hans und Margarete sind in die Stadt gewandert.

XXV. IMPERFECT TENSE
1. machte
2. sah
3. dachten
4. bliebst
5. Brachten
6. Hörtest
7. kamt
8. nahmen
9. gab
10. saß

XXVI. WORD ORDER (DEPENDENT SENTENCES, SEPARABLE VERBS IN DEPENDENT SENTENCES, PERFECT TENSE, "NICHT", ETC.

211

ANSWERS

1. Ich bleibe zu Hause, weil du heute nicht ausgehst.
2. Wir kommen, wenn wir unseren Wagen geholt haben.
3. Es ist zu heiß, da du die Tür zumachst.
4. Diese Mädchen sehe ich nicht.
5. Den Jungen kann ich auch nicht sehen.
6. Ich mache nichts, ehe du heute ankommst.
7. Ich mache nichts, weil du heute nicht ankommst.
8. Während die Katze eine Maus fängt, schläft der Hund ein.
9. Du siehst, daß die Katze eine Maus gefangen hat.
10. Weil ihr so müde seid, arbeitet ihr nicht.

XXVII.   PREPOSITIONS (ALL CASES)
1. die
2. des Hundes [or dem Hunde]
3. den
4. die
5. dem Hause und der Schule
6. des Morgens
7. mir
8. den
9. der
10. Tagen

XXVIII.   THE VERBS HABEN, SEIN, AND WERDEN
1. (a) Jene Frau ist nicht alt.
   (b) Jene Frau war nicht alt.
   (c) Jene Frau ist nicht alt geworden.
2. (a) Ich habe einen Vater aber keine Mutter
   (b) Ich hatte einen Vater aber keine Mutter
   (c) Ich habe einen Vater aber keine Mutter gehabt
3. (a) Das Gras wird grün
   (b) Das Gras wurde grün
   (c) Das Gras ist grün geworden
4. (a) Warum haben diese Kinder keinen Ball?
   (b) Warum hatten diese Kinder keinen Ball?

(c) Warum haben diese Kinder keinen Ball gehabt?
5. (a) Wirst du im Winter nicht kalt?
   (b) Wurdest du im Winter nicht kalt?
   (c) Bist du im Winter nicht kalt geworden?
6. (a) Ihr seid nicht so groß wie ich
   (b) Ihr wart nicht so groß wie ich
   (c) Ihr seid nicht so groß wie ich gewesen
7. (a) Ich werde Lehrer
   (b) Ich wurde Lehrer
   (c) Ich bin Lehrer geworden
8. (a) Was hast du in der Hand?
   (b) Was hattest du in der Hand?
   (c) Was hast du in der Hand gehabt?
9. (a) Warum sind wir heute so müde?
   (b) Warum waren wir heute so müde?
   (c) Warum sind wir heute so müde gewesen?
10. Ihr werdet sehr stark
    (b) Ihr wurdet sehr stark
    (c) Ihr seid sehr stark geworden

XXIX.   FUTURE TENSE
1. Wann wirst du heute ankommen?
2. Er wird nicht mit der Lehrerin sprechen
3. Ihr werdet müde sein
4. Wir werden heute nach England fahren
5. Ich werde Lehrer werden

XXX.   STRONG VERBS
1. (a) Ich ging mit meinem Hund spazieren
   (b) Ich bin mit meinem Hund spazieren gegangen
2. (a) Wir schrieben unserer Mutter einen langen Brief
   (b) Wir haben unserer Mutter einen langen Brief geschrieben
3. (a) Warum standen Sie hinter dem Tisch?
   (b) Warum haben Sie hinter dem Tisch gestanden?
4. (a) Das Buch lag auf dem Stuhl

(b) Das Buch hat auf dem Stuhl gelegen

5. (a) Er hieß Doktor Faust

(b) Er hat Doktor Faust geheißen

6. (a) Der Vogel fliegt über das Haus

(b) Der Vogel ist über das Haus geflogen

7. (a) Was geschieht nach der Schule?

(b) Was ist nach der Schule geschehen?

8. (a) Du schlossest die Tür nicht

(b) Du hast die Tür nicht geschlossen

9. (a) Ihr fuhrt jeden Januar nach Deutschland

(b) Ihr seid jeden Januar nach Deutschland gefahren

10. (a) Ich dachte an meinen schwarzen Kater

(b) Ich habe an meinen schwarzen Kater gedacht

GERMAN-ENGLISH

NOTES. (1) Plurals of nouns are shown in brackets but **-(e)n** endings of regular feminine nouns in the plural are not shown.

(2) In the case of weak nouns the genitive singular ending is also shown in brackets, before the plural.

(3) The numerical reference is to the item in which the meaning is first given.

der **Abend** (-e), evening 416
aber, but 268
alle, all 1205
alt, old 1049
an (Acc. or Dat.), on, on to 845, 846
ankommen (sep.), to arrive 856
anstatt (Gen.), instead of 1690
arbeiten, to work 228
auf (Acc. or Dat.), on, on to 839, 840
aufstehen (sep.), to get up 858
aus (Dat.), out of 636
ausgehen (sep.), to go out 854
das **Auto** (-s), motor-car 732

der **Bäcker** (-), baker 350
der **Ball** (-e), ball 449
die **Bank,** bank 1327
befehlen (insep.), to command 627
beginnen (insep., strong), to begin 1395

bei (Dat.), at the house of 639
beißen (strong), to bite 1680
bevor (conj.), before 985
das **Bild** (-er), picture 604
bin, am 150
bist (you) are 153
bitten (strong), to request 1605
bleiben (strong), to stay 1393
der **Bleistift** (-e), pencil 415
der **Boden** (-), floor, ground 361
braun, brown 51
brechen (strong), to break 514
brennen (mixed), to burn 106
bringen (strong), to bring 1412
das **Buch** (-er), book 27
das **Büro** (-s), office 733

da (adv.), there 933
da (conj.), as, since 988
da-, dar- (see 926–45)
die **Dame,** lady 23
daß (conj.), that 1534
dein, your 742

215

denken (mixed), to think 1414
denn (conj.), for 999
dieser, this 65–71
dort (adv.), there 270
du, you (fam. sing.) 153
durch (Acc.), through 709
dürfen (mixed), to be allowed
  1112

ehe (conj.), before 987
eilen, to hurry 1577
ein, a, an, one 111
einschlafen (sep., strong), to go
  to sleep 860
enden, to end 1361
er, he 159
erwarten (insep.), to expect 1594
es, it 162
essen (strong), to eat 596
euer, your (fam. pl.) 758

fahren (strong), to travel 691
fallen (strong), to fall 289
fangen (strong), to catch 285
finden (strong), to find 1392
das Fleisch, meat 819
fliegen (strong), to fly 1770
fließen (strong), to flow 1773
flink, lively 97
fragen (Acc.), to ask 979
der Franzose (-n, -n), Frenchman 812
die Frau, woman 22
das Fräulein (-), young lady, Miss 93
fressen (strong), to eat (of animals)
  598

frieren (strong), to freeze 1775
froh, glad 57
die Frucht (-̈e), fruit 508
für (prep.) (Acc.), for 712
Fuß, zu, on foot 1002

die Gans (-̈e), goose 703
geben (strong), to give 294
gegen (Acc.), against 715
gegenüber (Dat.), opposite 641
gehen (strong), to go (on foot)
  224
gelten (strong), to be worth 520
gern, gladly 1419
das Geschäft (-e), business 417
geschehen (strong), to happen
  630
das Glas (-̈er), glass 1068
das Gras (-̈er), grass 84
groß, big 47
grün, green 48
gut, good, well 46, 1618

das Haar (-e), hair 1481
halten (strong), to hold 698
die Hand (-̈e), hand 329
hangen (or hängen) (strong), to be
  hanging 1650, 1652
hängt, hangs 846
der Haufen (-), heap 1081
das Haus (-̈er), house 26
Hause, nach, home(wards) 269
Hause, zu, at home 683
die Haustür, front door 1423
heißen (strong), to be called 1764

der **Held** (-en, -en) hero 818

helfen (strong), to help 292

her, hither, to here, towards the speaker 1653

der **Herr** (-n, -en), gentleman, lord, Mr. 821

heute, today 855

hin, thither, to there, away from the speaker 1658

hinter (Acc. or Dat.), behind 849

holen, to fetch 1372

hören, to hear 1364

der **Hund** (-e), dog 92

ich, I 150

ihr (pronoun) you (fam. pl.) 167

ihr (poss. adj.), (1) her 751 (2) their 135

in (Acc. or Dat.), in, into 832, 834

die **Insel,** island 506

intelligent, intelligent 99

interessant, interesting 98

ist, is 46

jeder, each 76

jener (adj.), that 73

jetzt, now 271

der **Junge** (-n, -n), boy 21

kalt, cold 1063

kämmen, to comb 1481

der **Käse** (-), cheese 82

der **Kater** (-), tom-cat 35

die **Katze,** cat 36

kein, no, not any 129

kennen (mixed), to know (be acquainted with) 1409

das **Kind** (-er), child 366

die **Klasse,** class 637

klein, small 53

klingeln, to ring 256

der **Knabe** (-n, -n), boy 817

die **Kohle,** coal 83

kommen (strong), to come 199

können (mixed), to be able, can 1014

der **Korrespondent** (-en, -en), correspondent 820

die **Kuh** (ːe), cow 509

lächeln, to smile 1373

langsam, slow(ly) 1620

lassen (strong), to leave, let 445

laufen (strong), to run 443

lesen (strong), to read 341

liegen (strong), to be lying 1632

der **Löffel** (-), spoon 345

der **Löwe** (-n, -n), lion 819

machen, to make 235

das **Mädchen** (-), girl 37

mancher, many a 85

der **Mann** (ːer), man 19

das **Männlein** (-), little man 57

die **Maus** (ːe), mouse 91

mein, my 132

der **Mensch** (-en, -en), human being 810

messen (strong), to measure 1604

das **Messer** (-), knife 351

die **Milch,** milk 1063
  mit (Dat.), with 644
  mögen (mixed), to like 1101, may 1111
  müde, tired 971
  müssen (mixed), must 1031
die **Mutter** (-̈), mother 323

  nach (Dat.) after 653, to, towards 667
  nachdem (conj.), after 990
die **Nachricht,** piece of news 663
die **Nacht** (-̈e), night 510
der **Name** (-ns, -n), name
  neben (Acc. or Dat.), near 869
  nehmen (strong), to take 297
  neun, nine 858
  nicht, not 52
  nichts, nothing 267
die **Nummer,** number 326

  oder, or 262
  offen (adj.), open 55
  öffnen, to open 221
  ohne (Acc.), without 718
der **Onkel** (-), uncle 344

der **Präsident** (-en, -en), president 820

das **Rathaus** (-̈er), town hall 1326
  rauchen, to smoke 1371
  rechnen, to reckon 1363
  regnen, to rain 1362
  reisen, to travel 1570
  reißen (strong), to tear 1682

reiten (strong), to ride on horseback 1683

sagen, to say 1365
scheinen (strong), to seem, shine 1726
schießen (strong), to shoot 1776
schlafen (strong), to sleep 440
schlagen (strong), to strike 694
schließen (strong), to shut 1777
schmecken, to taste 101
schmutzig, dirty 56
schneiden (strong), to cut 1686
schnell, quick(ly) 1619
schön, beautiful 49
schreiben (strong), to write 1728
schreien (strong), to shout, cry 1729
der **Schüler** (-), schoolboy 317
die **Schülerin** (-nen), schoolgirl 317
schwarz, black 54
schweigen (strong), to be silent 1730
schwimmen (strong), to swim 236
sehen (strong), to see 339
sehr, very 103
sein (poss. adj.), his, its 745
sein (verb), to be 205
seit (prep.) (Dat.), since 675
senden (mixed), to send 1410
sie, she, her, they, them 160, 175
Sie, you 180
sind, are 164, 175
singen (strong), to sing 1382

sinken (strong), to sink 1586
sitzen (strong), to be sitting 1614
der Sohn (¨e), son 450
sollen, to be required, ought to, to have to, am to 1119
sondern, but, on the contrary 1001
der Spaziergang (¨e), walk (for pleasure) 266
sprechen (strong), to speak 333
springen (strong), to jump 1588
die Stadt (¨e), town 670
stark, strong 50
statt (Gen.), instead of 1690
stehen (strong), to stand 213
stehlen (strong), to steal 629
steigen (strong), to climb 1731
sterben (strong), to die 516
still, quiet 590
das Stück (-e), piece, 1058
der Student (-en, -en), student 820
der Stuhl (¨e), chair 451

die Tafel, board 325
die Tante, aunt 630
teuer, expensive 100
der Tisch (-e), table 32
das Tischlein (-), little table 42
die Tochter (¨), daughter 324
tragen (strong), to wear, carry 279
treffen (strong), to meet 336
treiben (strong), to drive, carry on 1733
treten (strong), to step 1611

trinken (strong), to drink 1590
trotz (Gen.), in spite of 1692
tun (strong), to do 211
die Tür, door 505

über (Acc. or Dat.), over 871
übersetzen (insep.), to translate 865
die Uhr, clock 725
um (Acc.), around, at (with time) 722, 725
und, and 658
unser, our 755
unter (Acc. or Dat.), under 873, among 875
unterhalten (insep.) (strong), to entertain 862
unterhalten (sep.) (strong), to hold under 861

der Vater (¨), father 360
vergessen (insep.), to forget 1594
verwerfen (insep.), to reject 1598
das Viertel (-), quarter 346
der Vogel (¨), bird 359
von (Dat.), from, of 677, 663
vor (Acc. or Dat.), in front of 876, ago 878
vorlesen (sep.) (strong), to read aloud 898
vorsichtig, careful 591

wachsen (strong), to grow 696
der Wagen (-), car, cart 347
während (conj.), while 992

219

während (prep.) (Gen.), during, in the course of 1688

der **Wald** (⁻ er), forest 371

die **Wand** (⁻ e), wall 33

wandern, to walk 1579

warten, to wait 1366

was?, what? 264

waschen, (sich) (strong), to wash (oneself) 1435

weil, because 994

der **Wein** (-e), wine 105

welcher?, which? 88

welcher (rel. pro.), who, which, that 1278

wenden (π ixed), to turn 1411

wenn, if, when, whenever 972

wer?, who? 916

werden (strong), to become 301

werfen (strong), to throw 518

wir, we 164

wo, where 947

wo, wor- (see 946–52)

wohnen, to dwell, live 1369

wollen, to want, wish, be willing 1037

zeigen, to show 551

ziehen (strong), to pull 1778

die **Zigarette,** cigarette 1418

zittern, to tremble 255

zu (Dat.), to, too 681

zumachen (sep.), to shut 1418

zwei, two 1418

zwingen (strong), to compel 1591

zwischen (Acc. or Dat.), between 879

a, **ein** 111
able, to be, **können** (irr.) 1014
after (conj.) **nachdem** 990
after (prep.) **nach** (Dat.) 653
against, **gegen** (Acc.) 715
ago, **vor** (Dat.) 878
all, **alle** 1205
allowed, to be, **dürfen** (irr.) 1112
am, **bin** 150
am to, **sollen** (irr.) 1119–20
among, **unter** (Acc. or Dat.) 875
an, **ein** 111
and, **und** 658
around, **um** (Acc.) 722
to arrive, **ankommen** (sep., strong) 856
as (conj.), **da** 988
to ask, **fragen** (Acc.) 979
asleep, to fall, **einschlafen** (sep., strong) 860
at (with time), **um** (Acc.) 725
aunt, **die Tante** 640
away, **hin-** 1658

baker, **der Bäcker** (-) 350
ball, **der Ball** (¨e) 449
bank, **die Bank** 1327
to be, **sein** (irr.) 205
beautiful, **schön** 49
because, **weil** 994
to become, **werden** (strong) 301
before (conj.), **bevor** 985, **ehe** 987
to begin, **beginnen** (strong) 1395

behind, **hinter** (Acc. or Dat.) 849
between, **zwischen** (Acc. or Dat.) 879
big, **groß** 47
bird, **der Vogel** (¨) 359
to bite, **beißen** (strong) 1680
black, **schwarz** 54
board, **die Tafel** 325
book, **das Buch** (¨er) 27
boy, **der Junge** (-n, -n) 21, der **Knabe** (-n, -n) 817
to break, **brechen** (strong) 514
to bring, **bringen** (mixed) 1412
brown, **braun** 51
to burn, **brennen** (mixed) 106
business, **das Geschäft** (-e) 417
but, **aber** 268, (on the contrary), **sondern** 1001

called, to be, **heißen** (strong) 1764
can (verb), **können** (irr.) 1014
car, **der Wagen** (-) 347, **das Auto** (-s) 732
careful, **vorsichtig** 591
to carry, **tragen** (strong) 279
to carry on, **treiben** (strong) 1733
cart, **der Wagen** (-) 347
cat, **die Katze** 36, (tom-cat), **der Kater** (-) 35
to catch, **fangen** (strong) 285
chair, **der Stuhl** (¨e) 451
cheese, **der Käse** (-) 82

child, **das Kind** (-er) 366
cigarette, **die Zigarette** 1418
class, **die Klasse** 637
clock, **die Uhr** 725
coal, **die Kohle** 83
cold, **kalt** 1063
to comb, **kämmen** 1481
to come, **kommen** (strong) 199
to compel, **zwingen** (strong) 1591
  contrary, on the, **sondern** 1001
  correspondent, **der Korrespondent**
    (-en, -en) 820
  cow, **die Kuh** (⁻e) 509
to cry, **schreien** (strong) 1729
to cut, **schneiden** (strong) 1686

  daughter, **die Tochter** (⁻) 324
to die, **sterben** (strong) 516
  dirty, **schmutzig** 56
to do, **tun** (strong) 211
  dog, **der Hund** (-e) 92
  door, **die Tür** 505
to drink, **trinken** (strong) 1590
to drive **treiben** (strong) 1733
  during, **während** (Gen.) 1688
to dwell, **wohnen** 1369

  each, **jeder** 76
to eat (for human beings), **essen**
    (strong) 596, (for animals), **fressen**
    (strong) 598
to end, **enden** 1361
to entertain, **unterhalten** (insep.)
    (strong) 862
  evening, **der Abend** (-e) 416

to expect, **erwarten** 1594
  expensive, **teuer** 100

to fall, **fallen** (strong) 289
to fall asleep, **einschlafen** (sep.)
    (strong) 860
  father, **der Vater** (⁻) 360
to fetch, **holen** 1372
to find, **finden** (strong) 1392
  fine, **schön** 1087
  floor, **der Boden** (⁻) 361
to flow, **fließen** (strong) 1773
to fly, **fliegen** (strong) 1770
  foot, on, **zu Fuß** 1002
  for (conj.), **denn** 999
  for (prep.), **für** (Acc.) 712
  forest, **der Wald** (⁻er) 371
to forget, **vergessen** (insep.) (strong)
    1594
to freeze, **frieren** (strong) 1775
  Frenchman, **der Franzose** (-n, -n)
    812
  from, **von** (Dat.) 677
  front door, **die Haustür** 1423
  front of, in, **vor** (Acc. or Dat.) 876
  fruit, **die Frucht** (⁻e) 508

  gentleman, **der Herr** (-n, -en) 821
to get up, **aufstehen** (sep.) (strong) 858
  girl, **das Mädchen** (-) 37
to give, **geben** (strong) 294
  glad, **froh** 57
  gladly, **gern** 1419
  glass, **das Glas** (⁻er) 1068
to go (on foot), **gehen** (strong) 224

to go out, **ausgehen** (sep.) (strong) 854
good, **gut** 46
goose, **die Gans** (⸚e) 703
grass, **das Gras** (⸚er) 84
green, **grün** 48
ground, **der Boden** (⸚) 361
to grow, **wachsen** (strong) 696

hair, **das Haar** (-e), 1481
hand, **die Hand** (⸚e), 329
hanging, to be, **hangen** (or **hängen**) (strong) 1650, 1652
hangs, **hängt** 846
to happen, **geschehen** (strong) 630
he, **er** 159
heap, **der Haufen** (-) 1081
to hear, **hören** 1364
to help, **helfen** (strong) 292
her (poss. adj.), **ihr** 751
hero, **der Held** (-en, -en) 818
his, **sein** 745
hither, **her** 1653
to hold, **halten** (strong) 698
to hold under, **unterhalten** (sep.) (strong) 861
home, at, **zu Hause** 683
home(wards), **nach Hause** 269
house, **das Haus** (⸚er) 26
house of, at the, **bei** (Dat.) 639
human being, **der Mensch** (-en, -en) 810
to hurry, **eilen** 1577

I, **ich** 150
if, **wenn** 972

in, **in** (Acc. or Dat.) 832, 834
in spite of, **trotz** (Gen.) 1692
instead of, **(an)statt** (Gen.) 1690
intelligent, **intelligent** 99
interesting, **interessant** 98
is, **ist** 46
island, **die Insel** 506
it, **es** (**er, sie**) 162
its, **sein** 745

to jump, **springen** (strong) 1588

knife, **das Messer** (-) 351
to know (be acquainted with), **kennen** (mixed) 1409

lady, **die Dame** 23
to leave, **lassen** (strong) 445
to let, **lassen** (strong) 445
to like, **mögen** (irr.) 1101
lion, **der Löwe** (-n, -n) 819
to live (dwell), **wohnen** 1369
lively, **flink** 97
lord, **der Herr** (-n, -en) 821
lying, to be, **liegen** (strong) 1632

to make, **machen** 235
man, **der Mann** (⸚er) 19
many a, **mancher** 85
may, **mögen** (irr.) 1111
to measure, **messen** (strong) 1604
meat, **das Fleisch** (-e) 819
to meet, **treffen** (strong) 336
milk, **die Milch** 1063
morning, **der Morgen** (-) 348

mother, **die Mutter** (⸚) 323
mouse, **die Maus** (⸚e) 91
Mr., **Herr** (**-n, -en**) 821
must, **müssen** (irr.) 1031
my, **mein** 132

name, **der Name** (**-ns, -n**) 408
near, **neben** (Acc. or Dat.) 869
news (a piece of), **die Nachricht** 663
night, **die Nacht** (⸚e) 510
nine, **neun** 858
no (not a, not any), **kein** 129
not, **nicht** 52
nothing, **nichts** 267
now, **jetzt** 271
number, **die Nummer** 326

o'clock, **Uhr** 725
of, **von** (Dat.) 663
old, **alt** 1049
on, on to, **auf** (Acc. or Dat.) (horizontal) 839, **an** (Acc. or Dat.) (non-horizontal) 845–6
one (the, this, that) (dem. pro.) **der** 107–9
open (adj.), **offen** 55
to open, **öffnen** 221
opposite, **gegenüber** (Dat.) 641
or, **oder** 262
to order (command), **befehlen** (strong) 627
ought to, **sollen** (irr.) 1119
our, **unser** 755
out of, **aus** (Dat.) 636
over, **über** (Acc. or Dat.) 871

pencil, **der Bleistift** (**-e**) 415
picture, **das Bild** (**-er**) 604
piece, **das Stück** (**-e**) 1058
president, **der Präsident** (**-en, -en**) 820
to pull, **ziehen** (strong) 1778

quarter, **das Viertel** (**-**) 346
quick(ly), **schnell** 1619
quiet, **still** 590

to rain, **regnen** 1362
to read, **lesen** (strong) 341
to read aloud, **vorlesen** (sep.) (strong) 898
to reckon, **rechnen** 1363
to reject, **verwerfen** (strong) 1598
to request, **bitten** (strong) 1605
required to, to be, **sollen** (irr.) 1119
to ride on horseback, **reiten** (strong) 1683
to ring, **klingeln** 256
round, **um** (Acc.) 722
to run, **laufen** (strong) 443

to say, **sagen** 1365
schoolboy, **der Schüler** (**-**) 317
schoolgirl, **die Schülerin** (**-nen**) 317
schoolmaster, **der Lehrer** (**-**) 319
schoolmistress, **die Lehrerin** (**-nen**) 319
to see, **sehen** (strong) 339
to seem, **scheinen** (strong) 1726

to send, **senden** (mixed) 1410
she, **sie** 160
to shine, **scheinen** (strong) 1726
to shoot, **schießen** (strong) 1776
to shout, **schreien** (strong) 1729
to show, **zeigen** 551
to shut, **schließen** (strong) 1777, **zumachen** (sep.) 859
silent, to be, **schweigen** (strong) 1730
since (conj.) (as, because), **da** 988
since (prep.), **seit** (Dat.) 675
to sing, **singen** (strong) 1382
to sink, **sinken** (strong) 1586
sitting, to be, **sitzen** (strong) 1614
to sleep, **schlafen** (strong) 440
slow(ly), **langsam** 1620
small, **klein** 53
to smile, **lächeln** 1373
to smoke, **rauchen** 1371
son, **der Sohn** (-̈e) 450
to speak, **sprechen** (strong) 333
spite of, in, **trotz** (Gen.) 1692
spoon, **der Löffel** (-) 345
to stand, **stehen** (strong) 213
to stay, **bleiben** (strong) 1393
to steal, **stehlen** (strong) 629
to step, **treten** (strong) 1611
to strike, **schlagen** (strong) 694
strong, **stark** 50
student, **der Student** (-en, -en) 820
to swim, **schwimmen** (strong) 236

table, **der Tisch** (-e) 32

to take, **nehmen** (strong) 297
to taste, **schmecken** 101
to tear, **reißen** (strong) 1682
that (conj.), **daß** 1534
that (dem. adj.), **jener** 73
their, **ihr** 135
there, **da** 933, **dort** 270
to think, **denken** (irr.) 1414
this (adj.) **dieser** 65
thither, **hin-** 1658
through, **durch** (Acc.) 709
to throw, **werfen** (strong) 518
tired, **müde** 971
to, **nach** (Dat.) 667, **zu** (Dat.) 681
today, **heute** 885
towards, **nach** (Dat.) 667
town, **die Stadt** (-̈e) 670
town-hall, **das Rathaus** (-̈er) 1326
to translate, **übersetzen** (insep.) 865
to travel, **fahren** (strong) 691, **reisen** 1570
to tremble, **zittern** 255
to turn, **wenden** (mixed) 1411
two, **zwei** 1418

uncle, **der Onkel** (-) 344
under, **unter** (Acc. or Dat.) 873

very, **sehr** 103

to wait, **warten** 1366
to walk, **gehen** (strong) 224, **wandern** 1579
walk (noun), **der Spaziergang** (-̈e) 266

wall, **die Wand** (-̈e) 33

to want, **wollen** (irr.) 1037

to wash (oneself), **(sich) waschen** (strong) 1435

we, **wir** 164

to wear, **tragen** (strong) 279

what ?, **was ?** 264

when, **wenn** 972

which, **welcher** 88, 1278

while, **während** 992

who ? **wer ?** 916

who (rel. pro.), **der** 1246, **welcher** 1278

will, **wollen** 1043-'4, **werden** 1740

willing, to be, **wollen** 1037

wine, **der Wein** (-e) 105

with, **mit** (Dat.) 644

without, **ohne** (Acc.) 718

woman, **die Frau** 22

to work, **arbeiten** 228

worth, to be, **gelten** (strong) 520

to write, **schreiben** (strong) 1728

you (Fam. pl.) **ihr** 167, (Fam. sing.) **du** 153, (Pol.), **Sie** 180

young lady, **das Fräulein** (-) 93

your (Fam. pl.) **euer** 742, (Fam. sing.) **dein** 742, (Pol.) **Ihr** 762

Questions 651

Reflexive verbs
  with Accusative pronoun 1428–60, Table 1457
  with Dative pronoun 1459–82, Table 1482, 1582
reisen 1570–1
reißen 1682–3
reiten 1683–5
Relative pronouns 1227–85

scheinen 1726–8
schießen 1776–7
schlafen 440–2, 1641–3
schlagen 694–5, 1666–7
schließen 1777
schneiden 1686–7
schreiben 1728–9
schreien 1729–30
schweigen 1730–1
schwimmen 1561–2
sehen 339–40, 1627–9
sein (poss. adj.) 1309 ff. and see 'Determinatives'
sein (verb) 1694–1704
  as auxiliary 1569–82, 1587, 1589, 1613, 1630, 1638, 1640, 1644, 1647, 1665, 1668, 1685, 1701–4, 1720–2, 1725, 1732, 1753, 1772, 1774
seit 675
senden 1410
Separable verbs 854–66, 1169, 1220–6, 1633–40

Sex, distinguished from Gender 9, 30–38
ship, 9, 30
Simple sentences 953 ff.
singen 1583–5
sinken 1586–8
sitzen 1614–17
Small letters 150
solcher 81–84 and see 'Determinatives'
sollen 1119–25
sondern 1001–3
sprechen 333–5, 1538–56
springen 1588–90
Stadt 705
statt 1690–1
stehen 1756–63
stehlen 629, 1734–6
steigen 1731–3
sterben 516–17, 1562–3, 1572–3
Stress 863–5, 936–7, 949, 1594, 1596
Student 820
Subject 374–406
such 81–84 and see 'Determinatives'

-ten, infinitives ending in 227–9
that, see 'Conjunctions', 'Demonstrative Adjectives' etc.
the, see 'Definite Article'
this 58, 64–71 and see 'Determinatives'
Time, adverbs of 1622–6
Tochter 324
tragen 279–82, 1542–3, 1663–4
treffen 336, 1563–5
treiben 1733
treten 1611–13

231

Part 2

HOW TO SET TO WORK

Have ready writing materials and a card 5 to 6 inches wide.

Set the upper edge of your card to the figure 1.2 on the page opposite.

Read item 1.1. There is a blank between 'the' and 'participle'.

Choose what you think to be the correct word to fill the blank and write it in your notebook.

Next, bring your card down to figure 1.3. The left-hand column shows the correct answer to item 1.1.

If you were correct, read item 1.2, in which the last word is missing. Think of the word and then proceed as before.

If your choice ever proves to be wrong, you must find out what is wrong with it before you go on. If you do not you may get into difficulties.

Do not miss out any items, or you may lose the thread.

This is a way of learning, not a test; there are no trick questions or questions you cannot be expected to answer.

Do not look back at previous items before writing your answers. Some of the benefit of the course will be lost if you do. If you find it difficult to avoid looking back, cut a slot $1\frac{1}{2}$ in. deep and $\frac{1}{2}$ in. across in the edge of a card, about the middle, and use the card upright to cover the left-hand column only. The slot will reveal one answer at a time.

1. Pluperfect Tense

1. 1
The perfect tense is the tense which tells us what someone <u>has</u> done. As you remember from Part 1, it is formed from the present tense of the verb *to have* plus the — participle.

past

1. 2
The perfect of *I do* is *I have* — .

done

1. 3
The perfect of *I go* is *I have* —.

gone

1. 4
The pluperfect tense is the one which tells us what someone <u>had</u> done – that is, one step further back in the past. The name 'pluperfect' comes from the Latin 'plusquam perfectum', meaning *'more than* perfect'. Go to next item.

1. 5
I have gone is present/perfect tense.

perfect

1. 6
I had gone is present/pluperfect tense.

pluperfect

1. 7
I have been is perfect/pluperfect tense.

perfect

1. 8
I had been is perfect/pluperfect tense.

pluperfect

1. 9
You will see that the characteristic sign of the pluperfect tense is the presence of the word *had* as auxiliary verb. The pluperfect of *I come* is *I* — *come*.

235

had	**1. 10** The pluperfect of *I speak* is *I — spoken*.
had	**1. 11** Care may be necessary in distinguishing perfect from pluperfect with the English verb *have* as both the past participle and the past tense of the auxiliary have the same form – *I had —*.
had	**1. 12** *I* have *had* is perfect/pluperfect.
perfect	**1. 13** *I* had *had* is perfect/pluperfect.
pluperfect	**1. 14** The perfect of *I have* is — — —.
I have had	**1. 15** The pluperfect of *I have* is — — —.
I had had	**1. 16** The pluperfect in German is made in the same way as in English, e.g. **ich hatte gemacht** – that is, with the imperfect tense of the auxiliary verb, plus the — participle.
past	**1. 17** **Ich hatte gemacht.** The pluperfect is made with the past participle and the — tense of the auxiliary verb.
imperfect	**1. 18** **Ich hatte gemacht** means — — —.
I had made	**1. 19** *I had made* is **ich hatte** —.
gemacht	**1. 20** *I had made* is — — —.

236

ich hatte gemacht	1. 21 *He had made* is — — —.
er hatte gemacht	1. 22 *We had made* is — — —.
wir hatten gemacht	1. 23 *They had made* is — — —.
sie hatten gemacht	1. 24 You can see that this is really a very straightforward tense. The possibility of confusion which exists in English with the pluperfect of *to have* (*I had had*) does not exist in German because the imperfect of **haben** (**ich hatte**) and the past participle (**gehabt**) are *the same/different*.
different	1. 26 *I had had* is — — —.
ich hatte gehabt	1. 27 Of course the verbs of change of place or state which require **sein** for the perfect require it also for the pluperfect. **Ich hatte gemacht** is *I had made*. *I had gone* (remember it requires **sein**) is **ich** — **gegangen**.
war	1. 28 *He had come* is — — —.
er war ge-kommen	1. 29 *We had become* is — — —.
wir waren geworden	1. 30 *They had been* (remember **sein** requires **sein**) is — — —.
sie waren gewesen	

2. Wissen

2. 1
Wissen (*to know*) is an irregular weak verb. The pattern is rather like that of the modal verbs. The singular persons of the present tense show a vowel change from the infinitive, and 1st and 3rd persons singular are the same. Go to next item.

2. 2
I know is **ich weiß**. As mentioned above, the 3rd person singular is the same. *He knows* is — —.

er weiß

2. 3
The 2nd person singular (**du** form), like some other irregular verbs whose stem ends in **s**, adds not **st** but just **t**. *You know* is **du** —.

weißt

2. 4
1st, 2nd and 3rd persons singular present tense of **wissen** are **ich** —, **du** —, **er** —.

weiß, weißt, weiß

2. 5
The plural persons of the present tense, as usual, go back to the vowel of the infinitive. *We know* is **wir** —.

wissen

2. 6
They know is — —.

sie wissen

2. 7
. . . and the 2nd person plural (familiar plural) is quite regular – **ihr** —.

wißt

2. 8
As **wissen** is a weak verb the imperfect ends in the letters . .

TE

2. 9
. . . and as it is irregular there is a vowel change, from **I** to **U**. *I knew* is **ich** —.

wußte	**2. 10** *He knew* is — —
er wußte	**2. 11** *We knew* is — —.
wir wußten	**2. 12** The past participle is **gewußt.** *I have known* is **ich habe** —.
gewußt	**2. 13** *We have known* is — — —.
wir haben gewußt	**2. 14** You have already met another verb, **kennen,** meaning *to know* but the two verbs are used in different ways. **Kennen** is to know a person or place (*to recognize*). *I know him* is **ich — ihn.**
kenne	**2. 15** *I know Berlin* is — — —.
ich kenne Berlin	**2. 16** **Wissen** is to know facts. *I know that twice two are four* is **ich —, daß zweimal zwei vier sind.**
weiß	**2. 17** *I know what that word means* is **ich —, was jenes Wort bedeutet.**
weiß	**2. 18** **Ich weiß/kenne diese Stadt.**
kenne	**2. 19** **Ich weiß/kenne den Namen dieser Stadt.**
weiß	**2. 20** As a matter of interest you may like to know that **wissen** has many relatives in English – first and most obviously, *wise,* which means —*ing.*

239

knowing	**2. 21** Then we have *witty* (also a form of *knowingness*), the Biblical quotation *Wist ye not that I must be about my Father's business ?*, the old saying *God wot*, and of course our old friend the Anglo-Saxon *Witena gemot*, where *witena* is the genitive plural, meaning *of wise men*. Go to next item.

3. Verbs ending in -IEREN

3. 1
Verbs ending in **-ieren** in the infinitive are all borrowed from French, the ending being in imitation of the French *-er* ending. For this reason the distinctively Teutonic prefix **ge-** is not added for the past participle. Go to next item.

3. 2
Studieren is *to study. I have studied* is — — — (All verbs ending in **-ieren** are weak).

ich habe studiert

3. 3
Regieren is *to reign. The queen has reigned for* 20 *years* is **Die Königin hat 20 Jahre** —.

regiert

4. Infinitive with and without ZU

4. 1
You saw from Part I that in English the infinitive is sometimes used with and sometimes without the word *to*. Thus we say *I must be/to be*.

be

4. 2
On the other hand we say *I have be/to be*.

to be	**4. 3** In general the English modal verbs must be followed by the infinitive without *to* whereas non-modal verbs, even though meaning the same as the corresponding modal verb, require the infinitive with *to*. Thus we say *I can be/to be . . .*
be	**4. 4** . . . but *I am able be/to be.*
to be	**4. 5** The position is roughly the same in German. Modal verbs require to be followed by the infinitive without **zu.** Thus *I want to go* is **ich will —.**
gehen	**4. 6** On the other hand **wünschen,** which also means *to want* is not a modal verb. *I want to go* is **ich wünsche — —.**
zu gehen	**4. 7** The German modal verbs, you will remember, are **können, müssen, mögen, dürfen, wollen** and **sollen.** *I must speak* is — — —.
ich muß sprechen	**4. 8** *We want to come* (using **wollen**) is — — —.
wir wollen kommen	**4. 9** *They like to go* (using **mögen**) is — — —.
sie mögen gehen	**4. 10** *She wishes to come* (using **wünschen** – not a modal verb) is — — — —.
sie wünscht zu kommen	**4. 11** **Zu** is also used with the infinitive to express purpose – *in order to do something* – but in this case the preposition **um** must also be used at the beginning of the phrase. *I come in order to see you* is **ich komme, um** — · —.

241

Sie zu sehen	4. 12 *I go to bed to sleep well* is **ich gehe zu Bett, — gut — —.**
um gut zu schlafen	4. 13 *I went into town to see a friend* (**Freund** m.) is **ich ging in die Stadt, — — — — —.**
um einen Freund zu sehen	4. 14 In addition to the above, certain prepositions which in English are followed by the present participle, are followed in German by the infinitive with **zu.** Thus *without eating* is **ohne zu essen.** *Without coming* is — — —.
ohne zu kommen	4. 15 *Without speaking* is — — —.
ohne zu sprechen	4. 16 *Without seeing her* is — — — —.
ohne sie zu sehen	4. 17 (**An**)**statt** (*instead of*) operates similarly. *Instead of sleeping* is — — —.
(an)statt zu schlafen	

Modal Verbs — Principal Parts

	5. 1 You remember from Part 1, where you studied the present tense of some modal verbs, that our English modal verbs are all defective in some way. You saw that they have no infinitive (and therefore no future). What is more they have no past participle and therefore no — tense.
perfect (or pluperfect)	5. 2 For instance, although in the present tense we can say *He may go* we cannot make the modal verb perfect and say *He has mayed* (*or mighted?*) *to go.* Instead we must say *He may have —.*

242

gone	**5. 3** In other words as we cannot put the finite verb into the perfect we put the infinitive into the — instead.
perfect	**5. 4** Similarly we can say *He must go* but not *He has musted to go.* Instead we have to say *He must — —.*
have gone	**5. 5** If we really need to make the finite verb perfect we must use a non-modal verb, e.g. *be able* instead of *can*, or *have to* instead of *must. I can go*, but *I have been — to go.*
able	**5. 6** *He must go*, but *He has — to go.*
had	**5. 7** The German modal verbs however do have a perfect tense, so these difficulties do not arise. Bear in mind that it is the English rather than the German which is peculiar. Go to next item.
	5. 8 You remember that the modal verbs in German are **dürfen, können, mögen, müssen, sollen** and **wollen**. They are all irregular weak verbs. As they are weak the imperfect stem ends in the letters —
TE	**5. 9** — and as they are irregular there is in most cases a change of vowel as well. The principal parts of **dürfen** (*to be allowed*) are **dürfen, darf, durfte, gedurft** so that the vowel change in the imperfect and past participle consists in the omission of the —.
Umlaut	**5. 10** *I was allowed to speak*, using **dürfen** in the imperfect (and remember that modal verbs do not need **zu** with another verb) is — — —.

ich durfte sprechen

5. 11

I have been allowed to (using the perfect of **dürfen** and inserting **es** in place of the missing infinitive) is
— — **es** —.

ich habe es gedurft

5. 12

The principal parts of **können** are **können, kann, konnte, gekonnt,** so that here too the vowel change in the imperfect and past participle consists in the omission of the —.

Umlaut

5. 13

I was able to see (or *I could see*), using the imperfect of **können,** is — — —.

ich konnte sehen

5. 14

I have been able to (or *I could*), using the perfect of **können** is — — **es** —.

ich habe es gekonnt

5. 15

With **mögen** (*to like,* or very occasionally *may*) the principal parts are **mögen, mag, mochte, gemocht** so that the vowel change in imperfect and past participle consists as before in the omission of the —

Umlaut

5. 16

— but in addition in the imperfect and past participle (**mögen, mag, mochte, gemocht**) the consonant **g** changes to —

CH

5. 17

He liked to go (using the imperfect of **mögen**) is — — —.

er mochte gehen

5. 18

With **müssen** the Umlaut is omitted in the imperfect and past participle (as well as the present which you already know) but there are no other irregularities, so that the principal parts are **müssen, muß,** — —.

mußte, gemußt	**5. 19** *We had to come* (using the imperfect of **müssen**) is — — —.
wir mußten kommen	**5. 20** — and *we have had to,* using the perfect of **müssen,** is — — **es** —.
wir haben es gemußt	**5. 21** **Sollen** (*to be required to*) shows no irregularities of either vowel or consonant in imperfect and past participle, so the principal parts are **sollen, soll,** —, —.
sollte, gesollt	**5. 22** **Wollen** (*to wish to*) also shows no irregularities in imperfect or past participle (again, you are familiar with the present), so the principal parts are **wollen, will,** —, —.
wollte, gewollt	**5. 23** *He was required to do it* (imperfect of **sollen**) is — — — —.
er sollte es tun	**5. 24** *He has been required to* (perfect of **sollen**) is — — **es** —.
er hat es gesollt	**5. 25** *I wanted to speak* (imperfect of **wollen**) is — — —.
ich wollte sprechen	**5. 26** *She has wanted to* (perfect of **wollen**) is — — **es** —.
sie hat es gewollt	

6. Comparison of Adjectives

6. 1

In English we usually express degrees of comparison by altering the form of adjectives. Thus *I am small but you are small— still.*

245

smaller	**6. 2** The form *smaller* is called the <u>comparative</u> form of the adjective. To form the comparative of most simple adjectives we add the letters —.
ER	**6. 3** When we have added the letters *ER* to such an adjective we say it is in the *c* — *ive* form.
comparative	**6. 4** The comparative is used when *two/three/more* things or sets of things are compared.
two	**6. 5** There is another degree of comparison used for comparing one thing with several others. Thus *I am the small— member of the family.*
smallest	**6. 6** The form *smallest* is called the <u>superlative</u> form of the adjective. To make the superlative of most simple adjectives we add the letters —.
EST	**6. 7** When we have added the letters *EST* to such an adjective we say it is in the *s* —— *ive* form.
superlative	**6. 8** The superlative form of *great* is —.
greatest	**6. 9** The comparative form of *great* is —.
greater	**6. 10** When the adjective is in its simple state before the endings *ER* or *EST* are added we say it is in the <u>positive</u> form. Which of the following adjectives is in the positive form? – *New/greater/smallest.*

246

New	**6. 11** The adjective *new* is in the *p* —— *ive* form.
po*siti*ve	**6. 12** Comparison of adjectives in German is rather similar to the English method. **Grüner** is the — form of the adjective **grün** (*green*).
comparative	**6. 13** The comparative of German adjectives is usually formed, like that of English adjectives, by adding the letters . . to the positive form.
ER	**6. 14** The comparative of **klein** (*small*) is —.
kleiner	**6. 15** However, there may be a further change in the comparative form. In the English adjective *old, elder, eldest* there has been a change of —.
vowel	**6. 16** Similarly in German in the word **stärker**, the comparative of **stark** (*strong*), apart from the letters **ER** there has been the addition to the vowel of an —.
Umlaut	**6. 17** Adjectives of one syllable must usually add an Umlaut in the comparative if the vowel can take one. Thus the comparative of **alt** (*old*) is —.
älter	**6. 18** **Kalt** means *cold*. *Colder* is —.
kälter	**6. 19** *Stronger* is —.
stärker	**6. 20** However, if the vowel is the diphthong **AU** no Umlaut is added. **Braun** means *brown*. *Browner* is —.

247

brauner	**6. 21** **Grau** is *gray*. *Grayer* is —.
grauer	**6. 22** No Umlaut is added, either, to adjectives which are not monosyllables. The comparative of **langsam** (*slow*) is —.
langsamer	**6. 23** Adjectives ending in **EL, EN** and **ER** in the positive form drop the **E** of that ending before adding the letters **ER**. The comparative of **edel** (*noble*) is **edler. Teuer** means *dear. Dearer* is —.
teurer	**6. 24** Adjectives ending in **E** in the positive form add **R** only to form the comparative. The comparative of **müde** (*tired*) is —.
müder	**6. 25** When an adjective in the comparative is used before a noun the necessary declension endings must be added after the **ER** of the comparative ending. Thus *a stronger boy* is **ein stärkerer Junge.** *Colder milk* (**Milch,** fem.) is — —.
kältere Milch	**6. 26** *A smaller man* is — — —.
ein kleinerer Mann	**6. 27** The superlative of **schön** (*beautiful*) is **schönst,** so that the superlative is normally formed by adding to the positive form the letters . .
ST	**6. 28** The superlative of **stark** is **stärkst,** so that if an Umlaut is added in the comparative it is *retained/removed* in the superlative.

248

retained	**6. 29** If the positive form of the adjective ends in a vowel, or in **S, Z, D** or **T** the letters **EST** are added to form the superlative. The superlative of **grau** is —.
grauest	**6. 30** The superlative of **alt** is —.
ältest	**6. 31** The superlative form of German adjectives is not normally used without the definite article, so that it is usually found with the appropriate (weak) declension endings. *The strongest man* is — — —.
der stärkste Mann	**6. 32** *The most intelligent girls* is — — —.
die intellig-entesten Mädchen	**6. 33** The word for *than* with comparatives is **als.** *I am older than she* is — — — — —.
ich bin älter als sie	**6. 34** The full meaning of the previous sentence is of course *I am older than she is*. The final pronoun is in the — case in both languages.
nominative	**6. 35** *The woman is older than the man* is **die Frau ist** — — — —.
älter als der Mann	**6. 36** The superlative is normally used with the genitive. Thus *the eldest of the girls* is **das älteste** — —.
der Mädchen	**6. 37** . . . and *the prettiest of the pictures* (**Bild,** neut., pl. **Bilder**) is **das schönste** — —.

249

der Bilder	**6. 38** The superlative may also be used with **von**. Thus *He is the strongest of all* is **Er ist der Stärkste** — —.
von allen	**6. 39** It is also possible to use the superlative with **in**. *The youngest in the school* is **der (die) Jüngste** — — —.
in der Schule	**6. 40** There are other ways of making comparisons apart from those we have dealt with – e.g. where the qualities compared are equal: thus *He is* — *clever* — *I am*.
as as	**6. 41** For this sort of comparison German uses two different words, **so** and **wie**. Thus *I am as strong as you* is **ich bin** — **stark** — **du**.
so wie	**6. 42** *We are as old as they* is **wir sind** — — — —.
so alt wie sie	**6. 43** The form of words is the same in the negative. So *I am not as strong as she* is **ich bin nicht** — — — —.
so stark wie sie	**6. 44** Superlatives are not always used for comparing one thing with others. Thus in the sentence *The weather is best in June* we are comparing the weather with —.
itself	**6. 45** We could have said *The weather is at its best in June*, just as we could say *I am not* — — *best before breakfast*.
at my	**6. 46** In German a similar method must be used for comparing something with itself. Thus *The lion is (at its) strongest at night* is **der Löwe ist nachts am stärksten.** *The weather was coldest yesterday* is **Das Wetter war gestern** — —.

250

am kältesten	**6. 47** The **am** never varies. Thus *She is prettiest* (use **schön**) *in the morning* is **sie ist morgens** — —.
am schönsten	**6. 48** *The milk is dearest* (use **teuer**) *in winter* is **Die Milch ist im Winter** — —.
am teuersten	**6. 49** However long a German adjective is, and no matter what its ending you can always add **(E)R** or **(E)ST** to form comparative or superlative. Thus **tapfer** means *bold. Bolder* is —.
tapferer	**6. 50** To this it may be necessary to add also a declension ending. Thus *a bolder man* is **ein** — **Mann.**
tapfererer	

7. Infinitives used as Nouns

7. 1

In German all infinitives can be used as nouns, (comparable in some ways with our English verbal nouns ending in *-ing*) without any change except that when they become nouns they must be spelt with a *capital/small* letter.

capital	**7. 2** **Gehen** is *to walk. Walking* is **das** —.
Gehen	**7. 3** All such nouns made from infinitives are neuter. **Singen** is *to sing. The singing* is — —.
das Singen	**7. 4** It is customary to use the article with such nouns even where it would not be used in English. *Speaking makes me tired* is — — **macht mich müde.**

das Sprechen	**7. 5** **Wandern** is *to walk* or *travel* (*on foot*). *Travelling is the miller's joy* is — — **ist des Müllers Lust.**
	7. 6
das Wandern	It is interesting to note that in one case the verbal noun has been retained in German although the infinitive from which it came has been lost. This noun is **das Wesen** (*existence* or *being*) and the old infinitive, **wesen,** was the original word for *to be*. Traces of it are still found in various Germanic languages (German **war, gewesen;** Dutch **wezen;** Anglo-Saxon **wesan;** English *was* and the ancient word *wassail* or *wes hail; wes* was the old imperative, so that *wassail* meant *be hale* (*healthy*). Go to next item.

8. Adjectives with Irregular Comparison

	8. 1 Not all English adjectives have a regular comparative and superlative. Thus *good*, —, —.
	8. 2
better, best	Similarly there are German adjectives with irregular comparisons. Thus **gut, besser, der (die, das) beste.** *A better son* is — — — (remember to decline the adjective).
	8. 3
ein besserer Sohn	*The best school* is — — —.
	8. 4
die beste Schule	**Groß, größer, der (die, das) größte.** *The biggest book* is — — —.
	8. 5
das größte Buch	*With the greatest pleasure* (**Freude,** fem.) is — — — —.

252

mit der **größten Freude**	**8. 6** The adjective **hoch** (*high*) loses its **C** when a vowel is added (i.e. in ordinary declension as well as in comparison). *A high table* is **ein — Tisch** (masc.)
hoher	**8. 7** Similarly the comparative of **hoch** (remember it is a monosyllable) is —.
höher	**8. 8** To form the superlative the usual **ST** is added, and as these letters are not vowels the superlative is **höchst**. *The highest table* is — — —.
der höchste **Tisch**	**8. 9** **Nah** (*near*) has a regular comparative —.
näher	**8. 10** . . . but an irregular superlative **der** (**die, das**) **nächste** (compare with English *next* – actually the superlative of *nigh*). *The nearest* (*next*) *town* is — — —.
die nächste **Stadt**	**8. 11** **Viel** (*much*) has comparative **mehr** (*more*), which is indeclinable. *More light* (**Licht,** neut.) is — —.
mehr Licht	**8. 12** The superlative of **viel** is **der** (**die, das**) **meiste** (*most*). *Most girls* is — — —.
die meisten **Mädchen**	**8. 13** Not all English adjectives can form their comparative and superlative by adding *er* and *est*. We cannot say *beautifuller* and *beautifullest*, but only — *beautiful* and — *beautiful*.

more most	**8. 14** You should note especially that comparatives and superlatives <u>cannot</u> be made in this way in German. Thus **mehr hungrig** *does/does not* mean *hungrier*.
does not	**8. 15** **Mehr** can be used with adjectives, but only in the sense of *rather*. Thus **ich bin mehr hungrig als müde** means *I am — hungry — tired* (or *hungry — — tired*).
rather than	**8. 16** In other words, **mehr** can only be used for a comparison between one adjective and another. Go to next section.

9. Comparison of Adverbs

9. 1
You remember that adverbs as a rule have the same form as adjectives. In general therefore comparison of adverbs is similar to comparison of —.

adjectives	**9. 2** However, for the normal superlative of adverbs only the form **am stärksten, am größten** etc. is used. *He travels most slowly* is **er fährt — —.**
am langsamsten	**9. 3** **Ich schwimme gut, du schwimmst besser, aber sie schwimmt — —.**
am besten	**9. 4** *He writes more beautifully than I* is **er schreibt — als ich.**
schöner	**9. 5** *You write most beautifully (of all)* is **Sie schreiben — —.**

254

am schönsten	**9. 6** A slightly different form of the superlative, sometimes called the absolute superlative, is occasionally used. *She speaks most beautifully* (meaning *in the most beautiful way possible*) is **sie spricht aufs schönste.** *He sings in the best way* (*possible*) is **er singt — —.**
aufs beste	**9. 7** The adjectives which have irregular comparisons remain irregular of course when used as adverbs. You have already met **gut** (now, as an adverb, meaning *well*), **—, am —en.**
besser, am besten	**9. 8** ... and **viel, —, — —.**
mehr, am meisten	**9. 9** There are also two adverbs not existing as adjectives, which have irregular comparisons: **bald** (*soon*), **früher, am frühesten.** *You come sooner than I* is **Sie kommen — — —.**
früher als ich	**9. 10** *He comes soonest* is **— — — —.**
er kommt am frühesten	**9. 11** The other adverb previously mentioned is **gern** (*gladly*), **lieber, am liebsten.** This is a very important adverb, frequently used in place of verbs of liking or loving. Thus, for *I like to eat meat* say *I eat meat gladly* – **Ich esse — Fleisch.**
gern	**9. 12** *I like to do it* (*I do it gladly*) is **ich tue es —.**
gern	**9. 13** *He likes to come* is **— — —.**
er kommt gern	**9. 14** *She doesn't like to sing* is **— — — —.**

255

sie singt nicht gern	**9. 15** You may like to know that this adverb is connected with the English verb *yearn*. Go to next item.
	9. 16 Similarly the comparative of **gern** – **lieber** – is used instead of verbs of preferring. *I prefer fish to meat* (say *I eat fish more gladly than meat*) is **ich esse Fisch** — **als Fleisch.**
lieber	**9. 17** *I prefer to come* (say *I come more gladly*) is — — —.
ich komme lieber	**9. 18** *She prefers to sleep* is — — —.
sie schläft lieber	**9. 19** Similarly the superlative **am liebsten** is used to mean *liking to do something best of all. I like to sing best of all* is **ich singe** — —.
am liebsten	**9. 20** *I like to eat bread* (**Brot,** neut.) *best of all* (say *I eat bread most gladly*) is — — — —.
ich esse Brot am liebsten	**9. 21** *I like to swim best of all* is — — — —.
ich schwimme am liebsten	

10. Conditional Tense

10. 1

The conditional tense (*would do* etc.) is formed like the future, by the infinitive plus a part of the auxiliary verb **werden;** thus **ich würde gehen** means *I* — —.

would (should) go	**10. 2** Notice the auxiliary **würde** (actually the imperfect subjunctive which you will learn more about later) and remember the Umlaut. *I would (should) go* is **ich —— gehen.**
würde	**10. 3** *I would (should) go* is — — —.
ich würde gehen	**10. 4** The 2nd person singular of the auxiliary verb is of course formed as usual by adding **ST**. The **E** of the 1st person singular ending is retained throughout. *You would go* is **du — gehen.**
würdest gehen	**10. 5** The 3rd person singular is the same as the 1st person. *He would go* is — — —.
er würde gehen	**10. 6** Remember that in a main sentence the infinitive comes last. *He would go every day* (**jeden Tag**) is **er** — — — —.
würde jeden Tag gehen	**10. 7** 1st and 3rd persons plural of the auxiliary verb end in **N** as usual. *We would (should) go* is — — —.
wir würden gehen	**10. 8** *They would go* is — — —.
sie würden gehen	**10. 9** The 2nd person plural as usual ends in **T**. *You would go* is **ihr** — —.
würdet gehen	**10. 10** The conditional tense therefore is easy but there are one or two pitfalls involved in translation from English as *would* and *should* have several different meanings and do not always introduce the conditional tense. Go to next item.

10. 11

Thus we sometimes use *would* to mean *used to,* as in the sentence *Every day when I was little I would go off to school at 8 o'clock.* Here therefore *would* infers habitual action and the tense is *conditional/imperfect.*

10. 12

imperfect

On other occasions *would* is used as the past tense of the verb *to be willing* (German **wollen**). *I asked him to go but he wouldn't* (= *was not willing*). Here *wouldn't* should be translated by *conditional of* **gehen**/*imperfect of* **wollen.**

10. 13

imperfect of
wollen

With *would* therefore, if there is any doubt ask yourself *Does it mean either 'used to' or 'was willing to' ?* If so, the conditional must not be used. Go to next item.

10. 14

Similarly *should,* which is sometimes used with the 1st person singular and plural to form the conditional, often means *ought to* as in the sentence *I should go but I don't want to.* In this case *should* must be translated by *conditional of* **gehen**/*imperfect of* **sollen.**

imperfect of
sollen

11. There is and There are

11. 1

There are two ways of saying *there is (are)* in German and as these have a different grammatical effect you should be able to distinguish between them. Go to next item.

11. 2

The commonest way is by using **es ist** (*there is*) or **es sind** (*there are*). Thus the German for *There is a girl there* is — — **ein Mädchen da.**

258

es ist	**11. 3** Notice that in the plural whereas the verb changes to **sind** the **es** remains unchanged. Thus *There are two girls there* is — — **zwei Mädchen da.**
es sind	**11. 4** This expression, like all those involving the verb *to be* (in both English and German) is followed by a nominative. Thus *There is a man upstairs* is — — — — **oben.**
es ist ein Mann	**11. 5** . . . and *There is a boy* (use **Junge**) *in this house* is — — — — **in diesem Hause.**
es ist ein Junge	**11. 6** *There are two men upstairs* is — — **zwei Männer oben.**
es sind	**11. 7** Note that with **es ist** (**sind**) the real subject is the noun which follows the verb, and this is the reason why it must be in the — case.
nominative	**11. 8** The **es** is simply a kind of subject substitute used, as it were, to pin the verb in position until the real subject is reached. This is the reason why the **es** *changes/does not change* in the plural.
does not change	**11. 9** For the same reason (i.e. that **es** is only a subject substitute) it disappears altogether in circumstances which would normally cause inversion. Thus *There is a man upstairs* is **es ist ein Mann oben** or **oben** — **ein Mann.**
ist	**11. 10** *There are two men upstairs* is **Es sind zwei Männer oben** or **Oben** — **zwei Männer.**

c

sind	**11. 11** *In this house there is a boy* is **In diesem Hause — — —.**
ist ein Junge	**11. 12** **Es** can be used as a subject substitute with other verbs as well as **sein.** Thus instead of saying **Jemand spricht** (*Someone is speaking*) you could say **Es spricht jemand** and instead of **Jemand kommt** you could say **— —** **jemand.**
es kommt	**11. 13** Similarly instead of **Ein Mann lebt** (*a man lives*) you could say **— — — —.**
es lebt ein Mann	**11. 14** The expression **es ist** (**sind**) can of course be used in every tense. Thus for *There was a girl there* you can say **es — ein Mädchen da.**
war	**11. 15** . . . and for *There were two men upstairs* you can say (remembering that the verb must be plural) **— — —** **— oben.**
es waren **zwei Männer**	**11. 16** *There will be a boy here* is **— — ein Junge hier —.**
es wird . . . **sein**	**11. 17** The other expression for *there is* (*are*) is **es gibt** (from **geben,** *to give*). *There is a house there* is **— —** **ein Haus da.**
es gibt	**11. 18** With this expression however the **es** is the real subject, not a substitute, and this means that the following noun, not being the subject, cannot be in the **—** case . . .

nominative	**11. 19** . . . but in the accusative case. Thus *There is a car there* (use **der Wagen**) is **Es gibt** — — **dort.**
einen Wagen	**11. 20** *There is a river there* (use **der Fluß**) is — — — — **da.**
es gibt **einen Fluß**	**11. 21** Since **es** is here the real subject it cannot be omitted in inversion. So *there is a car there* (beginning with the adverb) is **dort** — — **einen Wagen.**
gibt es	**11. 22** *There is a house here* is **Hier** — — — —.
gibt es ein Haus	**11. 23** For the same reason **es gibt** cannot be made plural. Thus *There are two houses there* is — — **zwei Häuser da.**
es gibt	**11. 24** *There are two cars there* is **Dort** — — — —.
gibt es zwei Wagen	**11. 25** **Es gibt,** like **es ist** (**sind**), can be used in any tense. *There was a house there* (remember the parts of the verb are **geben, gibt, gab, gegeben**) is — — **ein Haus da.**
es gab	**11. 26** *There has been a car there* is — — **einen Wagen dort** —.
es hat . . . gegeben	**11. 27** There is also a slight difference in meaning between **es ist** (**sind**) and **es gibt. Es ist** (**sind**), as you will have understood, is only the verb *to be* in another guise, whereas **es gibt** means *there exists. There is* (= *exists*) *a Queen in England* is — — **eine Königin in England.**
es gibt **gibt**	**11. 28** *There is no such thing* is **So etwas** (literally *that sort of thing*) **ist/gibt es nicht.**

261

12. Future Perfect and Conditional Perfect

12. 1
The future perfect (*will have done*) and conditional perfect (*would have done*) are formed as in English from the past participle + two auxiliary verbs, one for the perfect, *have*, and one for the future or conditional (*will* or *would*) as the case may be. Go to next item.

12. 2
You know that a past participle must go to the end in a main sentence; you have learnt the same thing about an infinitive. If both are present the one which must go last is the infinitive (the reverse order from English). This order is important. *To have made* (**gemacht**) is — —.

gemacht haben

12. 3
All that now remains to form the future perfect is to add the future auxiliary **werden**. *I shall have made* is **ich — gemacht haben.**

werde

12. 4
I shall have made is — — — —.

**ich werde
gemacht haben**

12. 5
The other persons fall into place as a matter of course, just as you learnt for the future. *He will have made* is — — — —.

**er wird
gemacht haben**

12. 6
We shall have made is — — — —.

**wir werden
gemacht haben**

12. 7
The conditional perfect is formed in just the same way, but with **würde** as auxiliary instead of **werde**. *I would (should) have made* is — — — —.

262

ich würde **gemacht haben**	12. 8 *He would have made* is — — — —.
er würde **gemacht haben**	12. 9 Of course the verbs which take **sein** not **haben** to form the perfect continue to do so to form the future perfect and conditional perfect. *To have come* is **gekommen** —.
sein	12. 10 *He will have come* is — — — —.
er wird **gekommen sein**	12. 11 *She would have gone* is — — — —.
sie würde **gegangen sein**	12. 12 . . . and so on. These tenses are very easy if you remember that there are as many words in English as in German and that each word has exactly the same function. The order is different but follows rules which you already know. Go to next item.
	12. 13 In a dependent sentence the word which must come last is the f— verb.
finite	12. 14 In a future perfect or conditional perfect (e.g. **er wird gekommen sein**) the finite verb is the *past participle/part of* **werden**/*infinitive*.
part of **werden**	12. 15 The part of **werden** must therefore come last in a dependent sentence. Thus **sie würde gegangen sein** (main sentence), but **er sagte, daß sie** — — —.
gegangen sein **würde**	

263

13. More about the Definite Article

13. 1
You have already noticed that generally speaking the definite article **der, die, das** is used or omitted in much the same way as in English, not as in French. Thus we say **ich trinke gern Tee** (not **den Tee**), **ich esse Äpfel** (not **die Äpfel**) and so on. However, there are a number of cases where the article is required in German but not in English. Go to next item.

13. 2
Thus nouns used in a general sense usually require the definite article. *Fortune is blind* is **Das Glück ist blind.** *Time presses (time =* **Zeit** f.) is — — **drängt.**

die Zeit

13. 3
We love music (**Musik** f.) is **wir lieben** — —.

die Musik

13. 4
God created Man (use **Mensch** m., and remember that it is weak) is **Gott schuf** — —.

den Menschen

13. 5
Proper nouns preceded by an adjective also require the definite article in German though not in English. *Beautiful Germany* is **Das schöne Deutschland.** *Little Hans* is — — —.

der kleine Hans

13. 6
Poor George (poor = **arm**) is — — **Georg.**

der arme Georg

13. 7
Features of the calendar (days, months, seasons) and the names of meals also require the definite article. *In March* is **im März** (remember that the contraction **im** is equivalent to **in dem**). *In winter* (**Winter** m.) is — —.

264

im Winter	**13. 8** *On Monday* (use **an** with the dative and make a contraction) is — **Montag.**
am	**13. 9** *After supper* (**Abendessen** n.) is — — —.
nach dem Abendessen	**13. 10** The names of countries which are feminine or plural also require the definite article. *Switzerland* is **die Schweiz.** *In Switzerland* is — — —.
in der Schweiz	**13. 11** *The army of Turkey* (**Türkei** f.) is **die Armee** — —.
der Türkei	

14. Modal Verbs in Perfect Tenses

	14. 1 You remember that the modal verbs have past participles like any other verbs: thus *I have wanted it* (using **wollen, will, wollte, gewollt**) is **ich habe es** —.
gewollt	**14. 2** *He has liked it* (using **mögen, mag, mochte, gemocht**) is **er hat es** —.
gemocht	**14. 3** *I have been able to* (**können, kann, konnte, gekonnt**) is **ich habe es** —.
gekonnt	**14. 4** However, consider the following: **Ich habe es gemußt** (*I have had to*) but **Ich habe es tun müssen** (*I have had to do it*). When **müssen** is used with the infinitive of another verb its past participle is replaced by its —.

265

infinitive	**14. 5** The same is true of all the modal verbs. **Ich habe es gedurft** (*I have been allowed to*) (from **dürfen, darf, durfte, gedurft**) but **Ich habe Sie Sehen** — (*I have been allowed to see you*).
dürfen	**14. 6** **Er hat es gesollt** (*He has been required to*) but **er hat gehen** — (*He has been required to go*).
sollen	**14. 7** **Er hat es gewollt** (*He has wanted to*) but **er hat essen** — (*He has wanted to eat*).
wollen	**14. 8** *I have had to do it* (using **müssen**) is — — — — —
ich habe es tun müssen	**14. 9** *We have been able to speak* is — — — —.
wir haben sprechen können	**14. 10** *He has wanted to eat* is — — — —.
er hat essen wollen	**14. 11** *He has liked to play* (using **mögen**) is — — — —.
er hat spielen mögen	**14. 12** The position is of course no different with the pluperfect. *He had wanted to* is **er hatte es** —.
gewollt	**14. 13** *He had wanted to go* is **er** — — —.
hatte gehen wollen	

15. Genitive of Personal Pronouns

15. 1

You remember that in Part 1 you were not given the
Genitive case of the personal pronouns (*of me* etc.)
Note that this is quite different from the possessive pronoun or adjective. We say *in spite of me*; we could not
possibly say *in spite mine* or *in spite my*. Go to next item.

15. 2

The Genitive case of all the personal pronouns ends in
ER. *Of me* is **meiner**. *In spite of me* (*in spite of* =
trotz + Genitive) is — —.

trotz meiner

15. 3

Of you (fam. sing.) is **deiner**. *In spite of you* is — —.

trotz deiner

15. 4

Of him is **seiner**. *Instead of him* (*instead of* = **anstatt**
or just **statt** + Genitive) is — —.

(an)statt seiner

15. 5

As you know, the only differences between masculine
and neuter genders occur in the Nominative and
Accusative cases, and this applies to pronouns as well
as to nouns. *Instead of it* (neut.) is — —.

(an)statt seiner

15. 6

Of her is **ihrer**. *In spite of her* is — —.

trotz ihrer

15. 7

Instead of me is — —.

(an)statt meiner

15. 8

The plural pronouns form their genitive on the same
pattern. *Of us* is **unser**. *In spite of us* is — —.

trotz unser

15. 9

Of you (fam. pl.) is **euer**. *Instead of you* is — —.

(an)statt euer

15. 10

Of them is **ihrer**. *In spite of them* is — —.

trotz ihrer	**15. 11** *In spite of you* (polite pl.) is — —.

trotz Ihrer	**15. 12**
	Here to sum up is the complete list of genitive pronouns:
	    1. Sing. **meiner** Plur. **unser**
	    2. **deiner** **euer**
	    3. m. **seiner**
	         f. **ihrer** } **ihrer**
	Go to next item when you are satisfied you know it.

	15. 13 Several of the prepositions requiring a genitive like to come after their noun or pronoun, notably **halb** or **halber** (*for the sake of*) and **wegen** (*on account of*). *On account of friendship* (**Freundschaft** fem.) is — — —. (As friendship is being used in a general sense the article is required.)
der Freundschaft wegen	**15. 14** When these prepositions are used with a pronoun the two words are written as one and the final **R** of the pronoun is changed to **T**. *On account of me* is **meinetwegen.** *On account of them* is —.
ihretwegen	**15. 15** *For my sake* is **meinethalb.** *For his sake* is —.
seinethalb	**15. 16** In the case of **unser** however the **T** is added to, not substituted for, the **R**. *On account of us* is —.
unsertwegen	**15. 17** In the case of **um . . . willen,** which also means *for the sake of*, the genitive noun or pronoun comes in the middle. *For God's sake* (**Gott** masc.) is — — —.
um Gottes willen	**15. 18** **Um . . . willen** forms a compound with pronouns in the same way as **halber** and **wegen.** *For my sake* is **um meinetwillen.** *For your sake* (polite pl.) is — —.

268

um Ihretwillen	**15. 19** *For our sake* is — —.
um unsertwillen	**15. 20** Sometimes in poetry and stereotyped expressions the **ER** of the genitive pronoun is omitted. Thus *forget-me-not* is **Vergißmeinnicht** (**vergessen** formerly requiring the genitive). Another stereotyped expression meaning *Remember me* (using **gedenken** which similarly takes a genitive) is **gedenke** —.
mein	

16. Possessive Pronouns and the Pronoun Einer

16. 1

In Part 1 you learnt the possessive adjectives but not the possessive pronouns. Let us be clear about the difference. An adjective is used with a noun; a pronoun stands instead of a noun. *His book and mine* (= my book). *Mine* is an *adjective/pronoun*.

16. 2

Mine is a pronoun because it stands for *my* + noun. You could not say *His book and my*. *My* needs a noun in order to help it to make sense. It is therefore an *adjective/pronoun*.

16. 3

Possessive pronouns have two forms but the more usual consists of the possessive adjectives with strong endings (those of **der, die, das**). *This car is mine* is **dieser Wagen ist meiner.** Of course the gender of the pronoun is that of the noun which it replaces and not of the person possessing it. *His house and mine* is **sein Haus und —.**

pronoun

adjective

269

meines (or **meins**)	16. 4 *Our daughter and hers* is **Unsere Tochter und** —.
ihre	16. 5 *Our daughter and his* is **Unsere Tochter und** —.
seine	16. 6 *Their book and ours* is **ihr Buch und** —.
unseres	16. 7 The case of the possessive pronoun will of course be whatever its own function in the sentence requires: *She spoke to her father and I saw mine* is **sie sprach mit ihrem Vater und ich sah** —.
meinen	16. 8 *She saw her father and I spoke to mine* is **sie sah ihren Vater und ich sprach mit** —.
meinem	16. 9 The other form of possessive pronoun (which has exactly the same meaning) is made on the following pattern: **Sein Hut und der meinige, Unser Haus und das seinige** etc. This form therefore includes the — article (rather like French *le mien*).
definite	16. 10 In addition you will notice the **-ige** suffix added to the ordinary possessive adjective. *My book and yours* (fam. sing.) is **mein Buch und das** —.
deinige	16. 11 Thirdly it will come as no surprise to find that the word is declined like a weak adjective since it is preceded by the — —.
definite article	16. 12 *With my book and yours* is **Mit meinem Buch und** (**mit**) — **deinig**—.

<u>dem</u> <u>deinigen</u>	**16. 13** *Out of our house and hers* is **aus unserem Hause und** **(aus)** — —.
dem ihrigen	**16. 14** The suffix **ig** can be omitted, but what remains must still be declined as a weak adjective. Thus for **meine Frau und die seinige** we could have **meine Frau und die** —.
seine	**16. 15** . . . or of course, to go back to the form first given, simply **meine Frau und** —.
seine	**16. 16** You will have noticed that whatever the form of the possessive pronoun it is always possible to identify its number, gender and case, in contrast to the possessive adjective, where, e.g. with **sein Sohn** and **sein Haus** there is no distinction between — and — nominative singular.
masculine neuter	**16. 17** The same need for certainty lies behind a change undergone by **ein** when used as a pronoun; **einer von ihnen kam ins Haus.** Here to show that the pronoun is masc. nom. sing. the ending — has been added.
ER	**16. 18** *It was one of those boys* is **es war — von jenen Knaben.**
einer	**16. 19** A similar addition must be made for the neuter: **das ist — von meinen Häusern.**
eines (or **eins**)	**16. 20** When **kein** is used as a pronoun it too must be given the ending — in the masc. nom. sing . . .

ER	16. 21 ... and the ending .. in the neuter nom. and acc. sing.
ES	16. 22 Thus *none of the boys came* (both the pronoun and the verb are of course singular in both languages) is — **von den Jungen** —.
keiner ... kam	16. 23 *I saw none of my houses* is **ich sah** — **von meinen Häusern.**
keines (or **keins**)	

17. Passive Voice — Present and Past Tenses

	17. 1 The passive voice is the name given to the form of a verb when a person undergoes an action instead of performing it. In the sentence *He is injured* the verb is in the — voice.
passive	17. 2 *He is injured.* In English the passive voice is formed by using a part of the verb *to be* as auxiliary verb, + the — participle.
past	17. 3 *He is injured.* In English the passive voice is formed by using a part of the verb — — as auxiliary verb, + the — —.
to be, past participle	17. 4 *He is injuring.* Here the verb *is/is not* in the passive voice.
is not	17. 5 *He is injuring* is not in the passive voice because, although we have used the auxiliary verb *to be* we have used the present, not the — participle, to go with it.

past	**17.6** The word *passive* comes from the Latin *passus,* meaning *undergone* because the subject of a passive verb (*He is injured etc.*) — the action instead of performing it.
undergoes	**17.7** Where the subject of the verb performs the action instead of undergoing it (e.g. *He is injuring you*) the verb is not said to be in the passive voice but in the active —.
voice	**17.8** *He is injuring you* is in the — voice.
active	**17.9** *He is injured* is in the — —.
passive voice	**17.10** We sometimes use another auxiliary instead of the verb *to be* to form the passive. Thus we can say *He gets injured,* or *He becomes injured,* which mean the same. This is the way the passive is formed in German, namely by using the verb **werden,** which means *to* —.
become	**17.11** The English passive is formed by using an auxiliary verb (*to be, get, become*) + the — participle.
past	**17.12** German similarly uses the auxiliary verb **werden** (*to become*) + the — participle.
past	**17.13** Perhaps at this stage we should revise the principal parts of **werden,** namely **werden, wird, wurde, geworden.** *He becomes* is — —.
er wird	**17.14** *You become* (fam. sing.) is **du** —.

273

wirst	17. 15 *I became* is — —.
ich wurde	17. 16 *He became* is — —.
er wurde	17. 17 *I have become* (remember that **werden** requires **sein** for perfect and pluperfect) is — — —.
ich bin geworden	17. 18 *We had become* is — — —.
wir waren geworden	17. 19 *The mouse is (gets, becomes) eaten* (use **fressen**) is **die Maus — gefressen.**
wird	17. 20 *The mouse is eaten* is **die Maus — —.**
wird gefressen	17. 21 *I am fetched* (using **holen**) is — — —.
ich werde geholt	17. 22 *The book is written* (**schreiben, schreibt, schrieb, geschrieben**) is **das Buch — —.**
wird geschrieben	17. 23 *The balls are thrown* (**werfen, wirft, warf, geworfen**) is **die Bälle — —.**
werden geworfen	17. 24 *The mouse was (= became) eaten* is **die Maus — —.**
wurde gefressen	17. 25 *I was fetched* is — — —.
ich wurde geholt	17. 26 *The book was written* is **das Buch — —.**

wurde gesch-rieben	**17. 27** *The balls were thrown* is **die Bälle** — —.
wurden geworfen	**17. 28** The perfect tense in the passive is easy as long as you remember what you already know about word order and that the perfect of **werden** is made not with **haben** but with —.
sein	**17. 29** *I have become* is — — —.
ich bin geworden	**17. 30** However, when used for making the passive, the past participle of **werden** (normally **geworden**) loses its **ge-**. *I have been* (= *become*) *fetched* is therefore **ich bin geholt** —.
worden	**17. 31** You can see that the purpose of this is to avoid repetition of the syllable **ge-** which will in any case normally be present in the previous word. *The mouse has been eaten* is **die Maus ist gefressen** —.
worden	**17. 32** As regards word order you remember that in a main sentence the past participle comes at the —.
end	**17. 33** . . . or to put it another way, the word which must come at the end in a main sentence is the — —.
past participle	**17. 34** Of course with the perfect passive there are two past participles, one of the principal verb and one of **werden** and you have already noticed that it is the latter which must come last. *The mouse has been eaten* is **die Maus ist gefressen** —.

worden	17. 35 *The mouse has been eaten* is **die Maus ist** — —.
gefressen worden	17. 36 *The mouse has been eaten* is **die Maus** — — —.
ist gefressen worden	17. 37 *The book has been written* is **das Buch** — — —.
ist geschrieben worden	17. 38 *The balls have been thrown* is **die Bälle** — — —.
sind geworfen worden	17. 39 The pluperfect passive introduces no new principle. *I had become* is **ich** — **geworden.**
war	17. 40 *I had been fetched* is **ich** — **geholt worden.**
war	17. 41 *The mouse had been eaten* is **die Maus** — — —.
war gefressen worden	17. 42 *The book had been written* is **das Buch** — — —.
war geschrieben worden	17. 43 *The balls had been thrown* is **die Bälle** — — —.
waren geworfen worden	

18. How to Express Time

18. 1
Time is normally expressed by the accusative. *I was there the whole day* is **ich war** — **ganz** — **Tag dort.**

276

den ganzen	**18. 2** *He works every day* (use **jeder** for *every*) is **er arbeitet — —.**
jeden Tag	**18. 3** *He was here last Monday* (*last* is **letzt** and remember that the days of the week, as they end in **-tag**, are all masculine) is **er war — Montag hier.**
letzten	**18. 4** *I stayed there (for) a month* (**Monat,** masc.) is **ich blieb — — dort.**
einen Monat	**18. 5** Similarly dates given on letters and other documents are in the accusative and the definite article is included. *Tuesday, 2nd April* is **Dienstag, den zweit— April.**
zweiten	**18. 6** *Monday, 23rd August* is **—, — dreiundzwanzigst— August.**
Montag, den dreiundzwan- zigsten August	**18. 7** If figures are used for the day of the month they must be followed either by the letters **EN** to denote the accusative case ending or by a full stop to show that the word is abbreviated, e.g. **den 4. April.** *3rd August* is **— — —.**
den 3. August	**18. 8** However if a date is used as part of the text, not a heading, it takes the ordinary case required by the sentence, e.g. when it is used as the subject: *30th June is my birthday* — **dreißigst— Juni ist mein Geburtstag.**
der dreißigste	**18. 9** **An** with the dative is often used with expressions of time to mean *on* or *in*. *On the previous day* is **— — vorig— Tage.**

an dem vorigen	**18. 10** **An dem** is usually condensed to **am.** *In the morning* is — **Morgen.**
am	**18. 11** *In the afternoon* is — **Nachmittag.**
am	**18. 12** *On 2nd September* is — **zweit**— **September.**
am zweiten	**18. 13** Vague time is put into the genitive. *One day* is **eines Tages.** *One evening* (**Abend,** masc.) is — —.
eines Abends	**18. 14** *One afternoon* is — **Nachmittag**—.
eines Nach- mittags	**18. 15** *In the daytime* (or *by day*) is **des Tages.** Notice that although **Nacht** (*night*) is feminine (so that the true genitive is **der Nacht**) it is treated as masculine for this purpose. *By night* is therefore — —.
des Nachts	**18. 16** Notice that *every day* is not vague but precise time, so that the case used is not genitive but —.
accusative	**18. 17** *Every day* is — —.
jeden Tag	# 19. Adjectives used as Nouns
	19. 1 In English we readily turn adjectives into nouns simply by providing them with a definite article—*the poor, the rich, the humble, the blind* etc. Notice however that all such nouns are *singular/plural.*

278

plural	**19. 2** Presumably we lost the facility to make adjectives into singular nouns when we lost our genders, as it was then no longer possible to distinguish between masculine and feminine adjectives. Go to next item.
	19. 3 German uses adjectives as nouns in both singular and plural. **Fremd** = *foreign*. **Der Fremde** = *the foreigner*. The first thing to notice is that as the adjective has been turned into a noun it now begins with a — letter.
capital	**19. 4** **Fremd, der Fremde, ein Fremder.** The second thing to notice is that although it is now a noun it is still being declined like an —.
adjective	**19. 5** Thus when it is preceded by the definite article it has the weak endings (**E** or **EN** only). *The foreigner is coming* is — — **kommt.**
der Fremde	**19. 6** *I see the foreigner* is **ich sehe** — —.
den Fremden	**19. 7** *The foreigner's book* is **das Buch** — —.
des Fremden	**19. 8** *I speak to the foreigner* is **ich spreche mit** — —.
dem Fremden	**19. 9** *The foreigners* is — —.
die Fremden	**19. 10** With the indefinite article of course the adjective-noun has the endings of the mixed declension (i.e. those of **der, die, das** where **ein** does not show them, and otherwise **EN**). *A foreigner is coming* is — — **kommt.**

279

ein Fremder	19. 11 *A foreigner's book* is **das Buch** — —.
eines Fremden	19. 12 . . . and so on. A singular adjective-noun is not likely to be used without an article but this may well happen in the plural, and then the endings are naturally strong (those of **der, die, das**). *Foreigners are coming* is — **kommen.**
Fremde	19. 13 *The books of foreigners* is **die Bücher** —.
Fremder	19. 14 Many adjectives are used as nouns in this way. **Verwandt** = *related. A relative* is **ein** —.
Verwandter	19. 15 *The relative* is — —.
der Verwandte	19. 16 *My relative's book* is **das Buch** — —.
meines Verwandten	19. 17 **Reisend** means *travelling. A traveller* is — —.
ein Reisender	19. 18 *The traveller* is — —.
der Reisende	19. 19 *Speak to the traveller* is **Sprechen Sie mit** — —.
dem Reisenden	19. 20 *The travellers* is — —.
die Reisenden	19. 21 **Alt** = *old.* **Der Alte** means *the* — —.
old man	19. 22 Naturally these adjective-nouns can also be feminine. **Die Alte** means — — —.

the old woman	19. 23 *An old man is* **ein** —.
Alter	19. 24 *An old woman is* — —.
eine Alte	19. 25 *The old* (remember that in English adjective-nouns are plural) *is* — —.
die Alten	19. 26 Most nouns of nationality (**der Engländer, der Franzose** etc.) are true nouns, but it is important to note that **der Deutsche** (*the German*) is an adjective-noun. *A German is* — —.
ein Deutscher	19. 27 *A German's book is* **das Buch** — —.
eines Deutschen	19. 28 *The Germans is* — —.
die Deutschen	19. 29 Adjective-nouns are also found in the neuter. *Good is* **das Gute** *and Evil is* **das Böse**. *To repay good with evil is* **Gutes mit** — **vergelten**.
Bösem	

20. Passive Voice — Future and Conditional Tenses

20. 1
You remember that the passive is made with **werden** as auxiliary verb + the past participle of the principal verb. *I am caught* (**fangen, fängt, fing, gefangen**) *is* **ich** — —.

281

werde gefangen	**20. 2** You also remember that the future tense (ordinary active voice) is made with **werden** as auxiliary verb + (as in English) the infinitive of the principal verb. *I shall catch* is — — —.
ich werde fangen	**20. 3** In the future passive therefore we find **werden** being used twice. There is nothing difficult about this as long as you remember your rules for word order. *I shall become* is **ich** — —.
werde werden	**20. 4** You remember that both a past participle and an infinitive like to come last in a main sentence. If there are both in the same sentence you can see from the example **gefangen werden** (*to be caught*) that it is the — which comes last.
infinitive	**20. 5** Remember *I shall become* is **ich werde werden.** *I shall be* (= *become*) *caught* is therefore **ich werde** — —.
gefangen werden	**20. 6** *I shall be caught* is — — — —.
ich werde gefangen werden	**20. 7** *He will be caught* is — — — —.
er wird gefangen werden	**20. 8** *We shall be caught* is — — — —.
wir werden gefangen werden	**20. 9** *The mouse will be eaten* is **die Maus** — — —.
wird gefressen werden	**20. 10** The principle is the same for the conditional passive. *I would (should) become* is **ich** — —.

würde werden	20. 11 *I would be (= become) caught is* — — — —.
ich würde gefangen werden	20. 12 *The mouse would be eaten is* **die Maus** — — —.
würde gefressen werden	20. 13 There is no difference of principle in the future perfect and conditional perfect of the passive. Let us build them up step by step as before. *I shall have become* (remember that **werden** is conjugated with **sein**) is **ich werde geworden** —.
sein	20. 14 *I shall have become is* **ich werde** — —.
geworden sein	20. 15 *I shall have become is* — — — —.
ich werde geworden sein	20. 16 *I shall have been (= become) fetched is* **ich werde geholt worden** —.
sein	20. 17 *I shall have been fetched is* **ich werde geholt** — —.
worden sein	20. 18 *I shall have been fetched is* — — — — —.
ich werde geholt worden sein	20. 19 Let us just think about the word order. **Ich werde geholt worden sein.** In a main sentence containing an infinitive and a past participle the word which comes last is the —.
infinitive	20. 20 . . . and of two past participles in a passive construction the one which comes nearer to the end is that of —.
werden	20. 21 *We shall have been caught is* — — — — — .

283

wir werden gefangen worden sein	20. 22 *The mouse will have been eaten* is **die Maus** — — — —.
wird gefressen worden sein	20. 23 The conditional perfect is formed along the same lines. *I would (should) have become* (remember still that **werden** is conjugated with **sein**) is — — — —.
ich würde geworden sein	20. 24 *I would (should) have been (= become) fetched* is **ich** — — — —.
würde geholt worden sein	20. 25 *The mouse would have been eaten* is **die Maus** — — — —.
würde gefressen worden sein	20. 26 If you find the number of words confusing you need only remember that there are as many words in English as in the German version. Write the English meaning of **ich werde gefangen worden sein** (in the same order): *I* — — — —.
shall caught been have	20. 27 You need of course always to remember that **werden** forms its perfect not with **haben** but with —.
sein	20. 28 . . . and as far as word order is concerned, that the infinitive comes —.
last	20. 29 . . . the past participle of **werden** comes (*last/next to the end/next but one to the end*).
next to the end	20. 30 . . . and the past participle of the principal verb comes just *before/after* the past participle of **werden.**
before	

21. Collective Nouns

21.1
Many collective nouns (i.e. singular nouns standing for an accumulation rather than a single object) begin with **GE-** in German. Thus **der Schrei** means *the cry. A lot of crying* is **das —schrei.**

21.2
das Geschrei

Notice that whatever the gender of the original noun, the collective noun resulting from it is likely to be neuter. **Der Bein** = *bone* (or *leg*). *A collection of bones (skeleton)* is — —.

21.3
das Gebein

Der Stein = *stone. The stonework* is — —.

21.4
das Gestein

If the vowel of the original word can take an Umlaut it usually does so and a final **E** may be added. Thus **das Land** is *land; the tract of land* (or *landscape*) is — —.

21.5
das Gelände

Even if the vowel cannot take an Umlaut it may show a change of a similar kind. Thus **der Berg** = *mountain;* **das Gebirge** = — *of mountains.*

21.6
range (or some similar word)

Many such nouns are made from verbs. **Das Gebäck** (from **backen**, *to bake*) means *a collection of —d stuff,* and therefore *cakes.*

21.7
baked

Backen, *to bake* gives **das Gebäck. Packen,** *to pack,* provides a similar word for *luggage* or *baggage* — —.

21.8
das Gepäck

So too **das Gebäude,** from **bauen,** *to build,* means *the —ing.*

285

building ‾‾‾‾‾‾	**21. 9** Even though the original word may be lost the collective word may retain its collective meaning. This is why, as perhaps you have noticed, **das Gemüse** means *the vegetable—*.
vegetables ‐	## 22. Passive Voice — Word Order in Dependent Sentences **22. 1** There is no difficulty about the passive voice in dependent sentences, even with the complicated tenses, if you know well your basic rules for word order. This section simply provides a little practice. Go to next item. **22. 2** **Ich werde gesehen.** Let us make it into a dependent sentence by beginning it with **wenn** . . . *if I am seen* is . . . **wenn ich** — — (finite verb to the end).
gesehen werde	**22. 3** . . . *if I am seen tomorrow morning* (**morgen früh**) is . . . **wenn ich** — — — —.
morgen früh **gesehen werde**	**22. 4** **Ich wurde gesehen** (imperfect). . . . *if I was seen* is . . . **wenn ich** — —.
gesehen wurde	**22. 5** **Ich bin gesehen worden** (perfect). . . . *if I have been seen* is . . . **wenn ich** — — —.
gesehen worden **bin**	**22. 6** **Ich war gesehen worden** (pluperfect). . . . *if I had been seen* is . . . **wenn ich** — — —.

286

gesehen worden war	22. 7 **Ich werde gesehen werden** (future). . . . *if I shall be seen* is . . . **wenn ich — — —**.
gesehen werden werde	22. 8 **Ich würde gesehen werden** (conditional). . . . *if I should be seen* is . . . **wenn ich — — —**.
gesehen werden würde	22. 9 **Ich werde gesehen worden sein** (future perfect). . . . *if I shall have been seen* is . . . **wenn ich — — — —**.
gesehen worden sein werde	22. 10 **Ich würde gesehen worden sein** (conditional perfect). . . . *if I should have been seen* is . . . **wenn ich — — — —**.
gesehen worden sein würde	20. 11 *I wonder whether the mouse would have been eaten* is **ich frage mich, ob die Maus — — — —**.
gefressen worden sein würde	22. 12 Remember that German tenses are formed basically in the same way as English so that the verb should normally have as many components as in English. Translate . . . **wenn ich gesehen worden sein würde** into English, retaining the German word order: . . . *if I — — — —*.
seen been have should (would)	

23. Mixed Nouns

23. 1
Mixed nouns are a small but important group of a dozen masculine nouns which originally ended in **N** but have now dropped it in the nominative singular. You already know **der Name** (once **der Namen**), *the name*. Go to next item.

23. 2
What is your name? is **wie ist Ihr —?**

Name	**23. 3** The missing **N** is replaced in all cases after the nominative singular. *We gave him a name* is **wir gaben ihm einen** —.
Namen	**23. 4** Notice however that these are not weak nouns: the usual strong genitive **S** must be added – but as well as the **N**. *The meaning of the name* is **die Bedeutung** — —.
des Namens	**23. 5** *With a name* is — — —.
mit einem Namen	**23. 6** All mixed nouns form their plural with the **N** alone (no Umlaut). *The names* is — —.
die Namen	**23. 7** To sum up the declension, the missing **N** is replaced in all cases after the — singular.
nominative	**23. 8** . . . but as these are not weak nouns they must in the genitive singular add an — in addition to the replaced **N**.
S	**23. 9** Some of these nouns shed not only **N** but **EN** in the nominative. These nouns of course replace both letters in the other cases. **Der Fels** is *the rock*. *On the rock* is **auf dem** —.
Felsen	**23. 10** *The size of the rock* is **die Größe** — —.
des Felsens	**23. 11** **Der Gedanke,** *the thought,* is a mixed noun. *I have a thought* is **ich habe** — —.
einen Gedanken	**23. 12** *The meaning of the thought* is **die Bedeutung** — —.

288

des Gedankens	**23. 13** Another common mixed noun is **der Wille,** *the will.* *According to my will* is **nach** — —.
meinem Willen	**23. 14** *Strength of will* is **Stärke des** —.
Willens	**23. 15** Several mixed nouns are still occasionally used with the **N** in the nominative singular. Thus for *peace* in addition to **der Friede** we find **der** —.
Frieden	**23. 16** For *rock,* as well as **der Fels** we find — —.
der Felsen	**23. 17** In addition to **der Same** for *seed* we find — —.
der Samen	**23. 18** . . . and for **der Haufe** (*heap*) we now almost always find — —.
der Haufen	**23. 19** Other mixed nouns are **der Buchstabe** (*letter of alpha-* *bet*), **der Drache** (*dragon* or *paper dart*), **der Funke** (*spark*) (the important word **der Rundfunk,** *radio,* comes from this) and **der Glaube** (*faith* or *belief*). Go to next item when you have studied them sufficiently.
	23. 20 There is just one neuter mixed noun—**das Herz** (*heart*). As it is neuter the accusative is of course *different* *from/the same as* the nominative.
the same as	**23. 21** *She has no heart* is **sie hat** — —.
kein Herz	**23. 22** *The heart's blood* is **das Blut** — —.

289

des Herzens	23. 23 *In my heart* is — — —.
in meinem Herzen	23. 24 *The hearts* is — —.
die Herzen	## 24. Adjectives after Indefinite Neuter Pronouns
	24. 1 Adjectives used after the indefinite neuter pronouns **etwas, nichts, viel** and **wenig** must be in the strong neuter form, e.g. *nothing good* – **nichts Gutes.** *Something good* is **etwas** —.
Gutes	24. 2 You will already have noticed that as the adjective is being used as a noun it is spelt with a — letter.
capital	24. 3 *Nothing bad* (use **böse**) is — —.
nichts Böses	24. 4 *Little new* (use **neu**) is **wenig** —.
Neues	24. 5 *Little good* is — —.
wenig Gutes	24. 6 *Much new* is **viel** —.
Neues	24. 7 *Much bad* is — —.
viel Böses	24. 8 The strong declension is followed throughout all the cases. *With something good* is **mit etwas Gutem.** *With nothing bad* is — — —.

mit nichts Bösem	**24. 9** After **alles** (*everything*) which you will remember from Part 1 is a determinative like **der, die, das** requiring the weak declension of adjectives, the adjective is accordingly in the weak form. *Everything bad* is **alles Böse**. *Everything new* is — —.
alles Neue	**24. 10** *All the best !* (= *everything good*) is — —.
alles Gute	**24. 11** Remember that **alles** itself, as a determinative, shows appropriate case endings (those of **das**). *With everything* is — —.
mit allem	**24. 12** The adjective after **alles** follows the weak declension in all cases. *With everything bad* is **mit allem Bösen**. *With everything good* is — — —.

mit allem Guten

25. The Subjunctive Mood

25. 1

All the verbs you have met in German so far and most of those used in everyday English are in a form known as the indicative mood, which means simply the form used for pointing out facts. Thus in sentences such as *He is going*, *That is so*, *I am not the king*, we are dealing with facts and the verb is therefore in the — mood.

25. 2

indicative

However, consider these English examples: *I wish I were you; If I were king, you would be queen; Would that it were true; What if it be so; It was decided that he be instructed to go; So be it*. Here the verbs underlined *are/are not* in the indicative mood.

are not	**25. 3** In the examples above we are not dealing with facts but with wishes or things which are impossible or uncertain – things in the realm of fancy. This is what the subjunctive mood is for. In the sentence *I wish it were summer* the verb *were* is in the *indicative/subjunctive* mood.
subjunctive	**25. 4** Except in conventional phrases such as *God save the Queen, Long live the President, God be praised* and certain kinds of sentences beginning with *if*, the subjunctive is not much used in modern English and it is often possible to avoid it. However in German the subjunctive is frequently used and it is often impossible to avoid it. Go to next item.
	25. 5 As the distinction between indicative and subjunctive in German is one of use rather than meaning it will be advisable for you to learn how to form it before being shown how to use it. Go to next section.

26. Formation of Present Subjunctive

26. 1
The present subjunctive in German is an easy tense to form. The first person singular of the present subjunctive is formed by removing the **N** of the infinitive ending, e.g. **gehen – ich gehe.** The 1st pers. sing. pres. subjunctive of **sagen** is **ich —.**

26. 2
sage | The 1st pers. sing. pres. subjunctive of **kommen** is **ich —.**

komme	26. 3 You will notice that the 1st pers. sing. pres. subjunctive is often the same as the pres. indicative, but this is not always so. The 1st pers. sing. pres. subjunctive of **wollen** is — —.
ich wolle	26. 4 1st pers. sing. pres. subjunctive of **sein** is — —.
ich sei	26. 5 If when the **N** of the infinitive has been removed the verb does not end in **E** one must be added except in the case of **sein.** The 1st pers. sing. pres. subjunctive of **tun** is — —.
ich tue	26. 6 The 2nd pers. sing. pres. subjunctive is formed by adding **ST** to the 1st pers. sing. The 2nd pers. sing. pres. subjunctive of **sagen** is **du** —.
sagest	26. 7 2nd pers. sing. pres. subjunctive of **kommen** is — —.
du kommest	26. 8 2nd pers. sing. pres. subjunctive of **wollen** is — —.
du wollest	26. 9 You will have noticed that as the 2nd person is formed by adding **ST** to the 1st person the verb must end in **EST,** and this **E** cannot be dropped. It is in fact characteristic of the subjunctive throughout. 2nd pers. sing. pres. subjunctive of **tun** is — —.
du tuest	26. 10 The 3rd pers. sing. pres. subjunctive of all verbs is the same as the 1st pers. sing. The 3rd pers. sing. pres. subjunctive of **tun** is **er** —.
tue	26. 11 3rd pers. sing. pres. subjunctive of **sagen** is — —.

er sage	**26. 12** 3rd pers. sing. pres. subjunctive of **kommen** is — —.
er komme	**26. 13** 3rd pers. sing. pres. subjunctive of **wollen** is — —.
er wolle	**26. 14** 1st, 2nd and 3rd pers. sing. pres. subjunctive of **kommen** are — —, — —, — —.
ich komme, du kommest, er komme	**26. 15** The 1st pers. plural of the pres. subjunctive is formed by adding **N** to the 1st pers. sing. The 1st pers. pl. pres. subjunctive of **sagen** is **wir** —.
sagen	**26. 16** The 2nd pers. pl. (familiar pl.) of the pres. subjunctive is formed by adding **T** to the 1st pers. sing. The 2nd pers. pl. pres. subjunctive of **sagen** is **ihr** —.
saget	**26. 17** 2nd pers. pl. pres. subjunctive of **kommen** is — —.
ihr kommet	**26. 18** 2nd pers. pl. pres. subjunctive of **tun** is — —.
ihr tuet	**26. 19** As with the 2nd pers. sing., the ending of the 2nd pers. pl. of the pres. subjunctive always includes the vowel —.
E	**26. 20** The 3rd pers. pl. of the pres. subjunctive (like all tenses of all verbs) is the same as the 1st pers. pl. The 3rd pers. pl. pres. subjunctive of **wollen** is **sie** —.
wollen	**26. 21** 1st, 2nd and 3rd pers. pl. pres. subjunctive of **sprechen** are — —, — —, — —.

wir sprechen,
ihr sprechet,
sie sprechen

26. 22

To go back to the singular, you must notice that although the stem vowel of the present indicative may show a change (e.g. **ich spreche, er spricht**) the stem vowel never changes in the subjunctive. 1st, 2nd and 3rd pers. sing. pres. subjunctive of **sprechen** are — —, — —, — —.

ich spreche,
du sprechest,
er spreche

26. 23

1st, 2nd and 3rd pers. sing. pres. subjunctive of **geben** are — —, — —, — —.

ich gebe, du
gebest, er gebe

26. 24

Let us recapitulate some of the salient features of the present subjunctive. The *1st/2nd/3rd* pers. sing. is always the same as the *1st/2nd/3rd* pers. sing.

1st   3rd

26. 25

All the personal endings (except in the case of **sein**) include the vowel —.

E

26. 26

The verbs which show a change of stem vowel in the 2nd and 3rd pers. sing. pres. indicative (e.g. **ich nehme, er nimmt**) *do/do not* show such a change in the pres. subjunctive.

do not

26. 27

Here to sum up is a table showing the present subjunctive giving in capitals the points to be remembered —.

ich sprechE	wir sprechEn
du sprEchEst	ihr sprechEt
er sprEchE	sie sprechEn

Note the persistence of the letter **E** in the endings. Make sure you know this before going to next item.

295

26. 28
The pres. subjunctive is a very regular tense and the only slight exception, already mentioned, occurs in the verb **sein** which does not add an **E** to form the 1st pers. sing. after the **N** of the infinitive has been removed. 1st pers. sing. pres. subjunctive of **sein** is **ich** —.

26. 29
sei

3rd pers. sing. pres. subjunctive of **sein** is — —.

26. 30
er sei

The other persons of the pres. subjunctive of **sein** are quite regular and therefore have the characteristic **E** in the endings. 2nd pers. sing. pres. subjunctive is **du** —.

26. 31
seiest

1st pers. pl. pres. subjunctive of **sein** is **wir** —.

26. 32
seien

2nd pers. pl. pres. subjunctive of **sein** is **ihr** —.

26. 33
seiet

Here to sum up is a table showing the present subjunctive of **sein** —

ich sei	**wir seien**
du seiest	**ihr seiet**
er sei	**sie seien**

Make sure you know this before going to next item.

---

27. Indirect Speech (1)
(Words spoken in Present Tense)

27. 1
The principal use of the subjunctive is in reporting indirect speech. Note the following example: **Er sagt, daß es regne** (*He says it is raining*). Here the verb — is in the present subjunctive.

296

regne	**27. 2** The complex sentence **Er sagt, daß es regne** consists of a main sentence (**er sagt**) and a dependent sentence (**daß es regne**). In indirect speech the verb which must be in the subjunctive is the verb of the *main/dependent* sentence.
dependent	**27. 3** In indirect speech the verb of the dependent sentence must be in the — mood.
subjunctive	**27. 4** *He says that he is ill* is **Er sagt, daß er krank** —.
sei	**27. 5** *She says that her sister is coming* is **Sie sagt, daß ihre Schwester** —.
komme	**27. 6** *They say that they are tired* is **Sie sagen, daß sie müde** —.
seien	**27. 7** *He says that he is travelling home* is **Er sagt, daß er nach Hause** —.
fahre	**27. 8** In English the conjunction *that* can usually be omitted from indirect speech. Thus instead of *He says that he is ill* we can say *He says* — — —.
he is ill	**27. 9** Similarly **daß** can be omitted in German; but there is one very important consequence: the dependent sentence then ceases to be dependent. In a dependent sentence the word which must come at the end is the —.

verb (finite verb)	**27. 10** If therefore **daß** is omitted the verb will come in the ordinary position for a main sentence (i.e. the second idea). Note however that the verb remains in the subjunctive. **Er sagt, daß er müde sei** could be re-written **Er sagt, er — müde.**
sei	**27. 11** **Sie sagt, daß ihre Schwester heute komme** could be rewritten **sie sagt, ihre Schwester — —.**
komme heute	**27. 12** **Sie sagen, daß sie krank seien** could be rewritten **Sie sagen, sie — —.**
seien krank	**27. 13** **Er sagt, daß er nach Hause fahre** could be rewritten **Er sagt, — — — —.**
er fahre nach Hause	**27. 14** Notice the punctuation. **Er sagt, er fahre nach Hause.** Even though the conjunction **daß** is omitted the two sentences must be separated by a —.
comma	**27. 15** Up to now the examples have all been in the present tense. But notice the following: *He said he was ill* – **Er sagte, er sei krank.** Although the verb of the main sentence is in the imperfect indicative the verb of the indirect statement is in the — subjunctive.
present	**27. 16** To understand this we must think back to what the speaker actually said. The indirect statement was *He said he was ill*. The original direct statement was '*I am/was ill*'.
am	**27. 17** Take another example. *They said they were tired.* The direct statement was 'We *are/were* tired'.

298

are	**27. 18** Compare the direct and indirect speech. **'Meine Schwester kommt.' Sie sagte, daß ihre Schwester komme.** Present indicatives in direct speech therefore become present — in indirect speech.
subjunctives	**27. 19** . . . or you could say that in indirect speech the subjunctive will be in the same tense as that of the verb in direct speech. *He said he was travelling home* (He actually said 'I am travelling') is **Er sagte, er — — —.**
fahre nach Hause	**27. 20** *He said he had a ball* (the actual words were: 'I have a ball') is **Er sagte, er — einen Ball.**
habe	**27. 21** *He asked who was coming* (he actually said: 'Who is coming?') is **Er fragte, wer —.**
komme	**27. 22** In an earlier item we said the English subjunctive was sometimes used to indicate uncertainty. This is really the basis of using the subjunctive in indirect speech in German. **Er sagt, es regne** = *He says it is raining* (*but I don't know whether it is or not*). If therefore we wish to imply that the original statement was correct it would be possible to use the — instead of the subjunctive.
indicative	**27. 23** Thus for *He says it is raining*, implying that the statement is correct, we could say, (instead of **Er sagt, es regne**) **Er sagt, es —.**
regnet	**27. 24** For the same reason, if you are reporting what you yourself say or think, you will normally put the indirect speech into the indicative as you will not wish to cast any doubt on it. *I say that he is there* is **ich sage, daß er dort —.**

27. 25

Again for the same reason the indicative is used after verbs used in the main clause which suggest certainty such as **wissen,** *to know. They know that she is here* is **Sie wissen, daß sie hier —.**

ist

28. Indefinite Pronouns — Man, Jedermann, Jemand, Niemand and Einander

28. 1

The English indefinite pronoun *one* is **man** in German (an earlier form of the noun **Mann**). *One speaks when one can* is **— spricht, wenn — kann.**

man ... man

28. 2

Man exists only in the nominative, the pronoun **ein** being substituted for it in the other cases. *It makes one angry* is **es macht — zornig.**

einen

28. 3

That helps one (remember **helfen, hilft, half, geholfen** takes the dative) is **— — —.**

das hilft einem

28. 4

The possessive adjective for **man** is the ordinary 3rd person sing. masc. form **sein.** *One forgets one's name* is **— vergißt — Namen.**

man ... seinen

28. 5

Jedermann (*everyone*) is declined like a strong masculine noun – that is, it shows a change only in the Genitive. Remember it is singular, as in English. *Everyone comes* is **— —.**

Jedermann kommt

28. 6

He spoke to everyone is **er sprach mit —.**

jedermann	28. 7 *Everyone's book* is — —.
jedermanns Buch	28. 8 **Jemand** (*anyone*) and **niemand** (*no one*) on the other hand, are declined like strong adjectives and therefore show the endings of **der** except in the nominative. *No one is coming* is — —.
niemand kommt	28. 9 *Is anyone there?* is — — **da?**
ist jemand	28. 10 **Ich sehe den Mann.** *I see no one* is — — —.
ich sehe niemanden	28. 11 **Er spricht mit dem Jungen.** *Is he speaking to anyone?* is **Spricht er mit —?**
jemandem	28. 12 **Des Vaters Buch.** *No one's book* is — —.
niemand(e)s Buch	28. 13 In practice the accusative and dative endings (**EN** and **EM**) are now often omitted but it is best to know the full form, which is always used in dictionaries as a convenient way of showing whether verbs require accusative or dative etc. Go to next item.
	28. 14 **Einander** means *one another* and need not keep us long as it is invariable. *They see one another* is **sie sehen —.**
einander	28. 15 *They speak to one another* is **sie sprechen mit —.**
einander	28. 16 **Miteinander** is written as one word. *They play with one another* is **sie spielen —.**

miteinander	**28. 17** **Einander** is less used than the corresponding English expression as normally the ordinary reflexive pronoun is considered sufficient. *We see one another* (= *ourselves*) is therefore normally — — —.
wir sehen uns	**28. 18** Similarly *they help one another* is — — —.
sie helfen sich	

29. Wohin and Woher

	29. 1 The exact meaning of **wo** (*where*) is *in what place*. You can therefore say *Where* (= *in what place*) *is he?* — — **ist er?**
wo	**29. 2** In English you can say *Where are you going?* but you could not say *In what place are you going?* **Wo** therefore *can/cannot* be used in such a case.
cannot	**29. 3** If *where* means *to what place?* (or *whither?*) the word **wohin** must be used. (You will remember **hin** and **her** from Part 1). *Where are you going?* is therefore — **gehen Sie.**
wohin	**29. 4** *Where is she going?* is — — —.
wohin geht sie?	**29. 5** Similarly *where from?* (*whence?*) is **woher.** *Where do you come from?* is — **kommen Sie?**
woher	**29. 6** *Where does he come from?* is — — —.

302

woher kommt er?	**29. 7** **Hin** and **her** are very often split off from the **wo** and sent to the end of the sentence. Thus instead of **Wohin geht sie?** you will often find **Wo geht sie —?**
hin	**29. 8** . . . and instead of **Woher kommen Sie?** you will find — — — —.

30. The Perfect Subjunctive

wo kommen Sie her?	**30. 1** You remember that the perfect tense (which we must now call the perfect indicative) of a verb is formed by using its past participle together with the present indicative of an auxiliary verb (usually **haben**). *He has said* is — — —.
er hat gesagt	**30. 2** *I have spoken* (**gesprochen**) is — — —.
ich habe gesprochen	**30. 3** *We have made* is — — —.
wir haben gemacht	**30. 4** There is no difficulty about forming the perfect subjunctive and perhaps you have already guessed that it is formed by using the past participle as before together with, not the present indicative, but the present — of the auxiliary verb (**haben** or **sein**).
subjunctive	**30. 5** The first pers. sing. perf. subjunctive of **sagen** is **ich —** —.
habe gesagt	**30. 6** The first pers. pl. perf. subjunctive of **sprechen** is **wir —** —.

303

haben gesprochen	30. 7 The 3rd pers. sing. perf. subjunctive of **machen** (remember that you will want the present subjunctive of **haben**) is **er** — —.
habe gemacht	30. 8 Of course you remember that verbs involving a change of place or state form their perfect with —, not **haben**.
sein	30. 9 *I have come* (ordinary perfect indicative) is **ich** — **gekommen**.
bin	30. 10 *He has come* (indicative again) is — — —.
er ist gekommen	30. 11 . . . and *we have gone* (**gegangen**) is — — —.
wir sind gegangen	30. 12 Naturally the perfect subjunctive of these verbs is formed in the same way but by using the present — of **sein** instead of the present indicative.
subjunctive	30. 13 1st pers. sing. perf. subjunctive of **kommen** is **er** — —.
sei gekommen	30. 14 3rd pers. sing. perf. subjunctive of **gehen** is **er** — —.
sei gegangen	30. 15 3rd pers. pl. perf. subjunctive of **sein** (remember that **sein** forms its perfect with **sein**) is **sie** — **gewesen**.
seien	30. 16 Here to sum up is the full perfect subjunctive of a verb conjugated with **haben**:

30. 16 (continued)

1 Sing.	**ich habe getragen**	Plur.	**wir haben getragen**
2	**du habest getragen**		**ihr habet getragen**
3	**er habe getragen**		**sie haben getragen**

Go to next item when you are satisfied that you know it.

30. 17
And here is the full perfect subjunctive of a verb
conjugated with **sein:**

1 Sing.	**ich sei geworden**	Plur.	**wir seien geworden**
2	**du seiest geworden**		**ihr seiet geworden**
3	**er sei geworden**		**sie seien geworden**

Go to next section when you are satisfied that you know it.

31. Demonstrative Pronouns —
Derjenige, Diejenige, Dasjenige

31. 1
Derjenige corresponds to the English demonstrative
pronoun *the one*. **Derjenige, der mir das sagte, ist tot**
can be translated as — — *who told me that is dead.*

the one

31. 2
Derjenige although it may look a little frightening, is
really quite simple; it is two words in one – the definite
article + the adjective **jenig-** (connected with **jener**).
You already know well the declension of the definite
article, and the second part of the word is declined as a
weak adjective – naturally, since it follows the definite
article. The **jenig-** part can therefore have only two
possible endings, — or —.

31. 3
E   EN

The feminine nominative singular of **derjenige** (write it
in two parts till you feel quite at home with it) is — —.

31. 4
die jenige

. . . and the neuter nominative singular is — —.

31. 5
das jenige

The masculine accusative singular is **denjenigen.** *I saw
the one who told me that* is **ich sah —, der mir das
sagte.**

305

denjenigen	**31. 6** The dative masc. sing. (remember to decline the **jenig-** portion as a weak adjective) is —.
demjenigen	**31. 7** *I spoke to the one who told me that* is **ich sprach mit —, der mir das sagte.**
demjenigen	**31. 8** You should now feel at home with the rest of the declension. The nominative plural is —.
diejenigen	**31. 9** . . . and the genitive plural is —.
derjenigen	**31. 10** **Derjenige** etc. is normally used in only two ways – first before a relative pronoun; then it means *the one(s), that, those* etc. Thus *This book is the one I gave you* is **Dieses Buch ist —, das ich Ihnen gab.**
dasjenige	**31. 11** *These ladies are the ones who work at school* is **Diese Damen sind —, die in der Schule arbeiten.**
diejenigen	**31. 12** *I came with this man and with the ones who live with him* is **ich kam mit diesem Mann und mit —, die bei ihm wohnen.**
denjenigen	**31. 13** The second use of **derjenige** is in circumstances where in English we use a genitive without expressing the following noun – *My hat and my wife's (hat)* – **Mein Hut und derjenige meiner Frau.** Here too it really means *the one,* since of course we could say *My hat and — — of my wife.*
the one	**31. 14** Naturally the demonstrative pronoun takes the gender of the noun for which it stands. *This book and my father's* (= *the one of my father*) is **dieses Buch und — — —.**

dasjenige meines Vaters	**31. 15** *He spoke to my wife and the master's (wife)* is **Er sprach mit meiner Frau und** (mit) — — —.
derjenigen des Lehrers	**31. 16** It is often possible to use just **der** etc. instead of **derjenige** etc., so instead of **Mein Hut und derjenige meiner Frau** you could say **Mein Hut und** — — —.
der meiner Frau	**31. 17** However it is often preferable to use **derjenige** to avoid the occurrence of such duplications as **der, der, die, die** etc. Go to next section.

32. <u>Was</u> as a Relative Pronoun

32. 1

In Part 1 you met **der, die, das** and **welcher, welche, welches** as relative pronouns. After neuter type indefinite pronouns **alles, das, etwas, nichts** and **vieles** however, only **was** may be used as a relative pronoun. *Nothing (that) you have is mine* is —, — **Sie haben, ist meins.**

Nichts, was

32. 2

Notice that the relative pronoun (*that* or *which*), although it may be omitted in English, cannot be omitted in German. *All (that) I say is wrong* is —, — — —, **ist falsch.**

Alles, was ich sage

32. 3

Here is something (that) I found is **Hier ist** —, — — —.

etwas, was ich fand

32. 4

What (= *that which*) *he says is right* is — — — —, **ist richtig.**

Das, was er sagt	**32. 5** In the last case however it is possible to omit the **das** and to say it as we do in English: *What he says is right* is — — —, **ist richtig.**
Was er sagt	**32. 6** **Was** must also be used instead of **das** or **welches** when the antecedent (the word or words to which the relative pronoun refers; see Part 1 if you have forgotten) is not a single word but a whole sentence: *it is raining, which pleases him* is **es regnet, — ihn freut.**
was	**32. 7** (You can compare this last use of **was** with the use of *ce qui* or *ce que* in French in similar circumstances.) *She isn't coming, which is a thousand pities* is — — —, — **ewig schade ist.**
Sie kommt nicht, was	# 33. Indirect Speech (2) — Words Spoken in a Past Tense
	33. 1 You remember that where words are spoken in the present indicative in direct speech, e.g. **'Ich komme'**, they are normally reported in the present — in indirect speech – **Er sagte, daß er komme.**
subjunctive	**33. 2** *She said he was there* (the actual words being 'He is there') is **sie sagte, daß er — —.**
dort sei	**33. 3** *They said he had money* is **sie sagten, daß er Geld —.**
habe	**33. 4** We still have to deal with the case where words are spoken in a past tense, e.g. *He said he had begun.* Here the actual words were '*I — —*'.

308

have begun	**33. 5** Similarly with *They said she had been ill.* Here the words spoken were '*She — — —*'.
has been ill	**33. 6** In the last two cases (*He said he had begun* and *They said she had been ill*) the verb of the indirect statement, having been spoken in the perfect indicative, is reported in the perfect — in German.
subjunctive	**33. 7** '*He has begun*' (perfect indicative) is '*— — **begonnen**'.
er hat	**33. 8** *He said he had begun* is therefore **Er sagte, er — —**. (Remember you can omit the **daß** and put the verb in the ordinary place for a main sentence.)
habe begonnen	**33. 9** '*She has been ill*' is '**sie — krank gewesen**'.
ist	**33. 10** *They said she had been ill* is **sie sagten, sie — — —**.
sei krank gewesen	**33. 11** *They have come* is **sie — —**.
sind gekommen	**33. 12** *He said they had come* is **er sagte, sie — —**.
seien gekommen	**33. 13** All the above examples deal with words spoken in the perfect indicative, but in fact the perfect subjunctive is normally used for reporting words spoken in any past tense. Thus '*I began*' in indirect speech is *He said he had begun* and in German **er sagte, er — —**.

309

habe begonnen	**33. 14** Similarly '*I came*' in direct speech is *He said he had come* and in German **er sagte, er — —.**
sei gekommen	**33. 15** Let us sum up the rules for reporting of direct speech so far. Words spoken in the <u>present</u> indicative are reported in the present —.
subjunctive	**33. 16** Words spoken in the present indicative are reported in the — —.
present subjunctive	**33. 17** Words spoken in a past tense are reported in the perfect —.
subjunctive	**33. 18** Words spoken in a past tense are reported in the — —.
perfect subjunctive past	**33. 19** The words which are reported in the perfect subjunctive in German are those spoken in a — tense.

34. Past Participles — Two Special Uses

34. 1
You are already familiar with the normal use of past participles – that is, with an auxiliary verb to form perfect and pluperfect tenses. *I have made* is **ich habe —.**

gemacht

34. 2
A special use of the past participle is to form commands, especially of a military nature. **Stillstehen** means *to stand still*, or *at attention*. **Stillgestanden,** therefore corresponds to the military command —.

310

Attention!	**34. 3** **Abmarschieren** (separable, like all verbs prefixed by **ab**) means *to march off*. The command *March off!* (remember what you know about past participles of verbs ending in **-ieren**) would therefore be —.
Abmarschiert	**34. 4** Presumably the rationale behind this use of the past participle is that obedience will be instantaneous, so that the action will already be in the past before the command has died away! Go to next item.
	34. 5 A further special use of the past participle is after the verb **kommen,** where it corresponds to the English present participle (-*ing* form). **Er kommt gelaufen** (**laufen** = *to run*) therefore means *He comes* —.
running	**34. 6** *To jump* = **springen, springt, sprang, gesprungen.** *He comes jumping* is **er kommt** —.
gesprungen	**34. 7** **Reiten, reitet, ritt, geritten** is *to ride on horseback.* *He came riding* is — — —.
er kam geritten	**34. 8** Whilst dealing with past participles we should mention also that in literature it is not uncommon for writers to omit the auxiliary verb from perfect and pluperfect tenses in dependent sentences, so that instead of **sie hörten, daß er gegangen war** you might find simply **sie hörten, daß er** —.
gegangen	**34. 9** Instead of **sie sagten, daß alles besser gewesen sei** you might find **sie sagten, daß alles besser** —.
gewesen	

35. Formation of Imperfect Subjunctive

35.1

The formation of the imperfect subjunctive does not offer many problems. For weak verbs it is identical with the imperfect indicative in all persons. 1st pers. sing. imperfect subjunctive of **machen** is therefore **ich —**.

machte

35.2

The 3rd pers. sing. imp. subjunctive of **arbeiten** is **er —**.

arbeitete

35.3

. . . and so on. Strong and irregular verbs form the 1st pers. sing. imp. subjunctive from the imperfect indicative by adding an Umlaut if possible and a final **E**. Thus **sein . . . war . . . ich wäre. Kommen . . . kam . . . ich —**.

käme

35.4

The 1st pers. sing. imp. subjunctive of strong and irregular verbs is formed from the — indicative by adding an Umlaut if possible and a final **E**.

imperfect

35.5

The 1st pers. sing. imp. subjunctive of strong and irregular verbs is formed from the imperfect indicative by adding an — if possible and a final **E**.

Umlaut

35.6

The 1st pers. sing. imp. subjunctive of strong and irregular verbs is formed from the imperfect indicative by adding an Umlaut if possible and a final —.

E

35.7

Haben . . . ich hatte. Imp. subjunctive: **ich —**.

hätte

35.8

Geben . . . ich gab. Imp. subjunctive: **ich —**.

312

gäbe	**35. 9**
	Fahren . . . ich fuhr. Imp. subjunctive: **ich** —.
führe	**35. 10**
	The remaining persons of the imp. subjunctive are formed by adding the personal endings to the 1st pers. sing. **Ich wäre, du wäreST.** 2nd pers. sing. imp. subjunctive of **haben** is **du** —.
hättest	**35. 11**
	2nd pers. sing. imp. subjunctive of **geben** is **du**—.
gäbest	**35. 12**
	2nd pers. sing. imp. subjunctive of **fahren** is **du** —.
führest	**35. 13**
	3rd pers. sing. imp. subjunctive is the same as the 1st pers. sing. **Ich wäre . . . er** —.
wäre	**35. 14**
	Ich hätte . . . er —.
hätte	**35. 15**
	3rd pers. sing. imp. subjunctive of **geben** is **er** —.
gäbe	**35. 16**
	3rd pers. sing. imp. subjunctive of **schreiben** is **er** —.
schriebe	**35. 17**
	3rd pers. sing. imp. subjunctive of **fahren** is **er** —.
führe	**35. 18**
	1st and 3rd pers. pl. imp. subjunctive end as usual in **N.** 1st pers. pl. imp. subjunctive of **sein** is **wir** —.
wären	**35. 19**
	1st pers. pl. imp. subjunctive of **haben** is **wir** —.
hätten	**35. 20**
	3rd pers. pl. imp. subjunctive of **kommen** is **sie** —.
kämen	**35. 21**
	3rd pers. pl. imp. subjunctive of **geben** is **sie** —.

gäben	**35. 22** 2nd pers. pl. (fam. pl.) of the imp. subjunctive ends as usual in **T** — e.g. **ihr wäret**. 2nd pers. pl. imp. subjunctive of **haben** is **ihr** —.
hättet	**35. 23** 2nd pers. pl. imp. subjunctive of **fahren** is **ihr** —.
führet	**35. 24** Here, to sum up, is the complete table of the imp. subjunctive of the strong verb **tragen, trägt, trug, getragen:** 1 Sing. **ich trügE** Pl. **wir trügEN** 2 **du trügEST** **ihr trügET** 3 **er trügE** **sie trügEN** Notice, as in the present subjunctive, the presence in all endings of the characteristic vowel —.
E	

36. Formation and Use of Future Subjunctive

	36. 1 There are no difficulties about the future subjunctive. You will remember that the future indicative of a verb is made by using its infinitive together with the present indicative of **werden**. *I shall go* is — — —.
ich werde gehen	**36. 2** *He will come* is — — —.
er wird kommen	**36. 3** You have probably guessed that the future subjunctive is formed by using the infinitive as before together with the present — of **werden.**
subjunctive	**36. 4** Present subjunctives you remember are formed by removing the **N** of the infinitive. 1st pers. sing. pres. subjunctive of **werden** is — —.

314

ich werde	36. 5 3rd pers. sing. pres. subjunctive of **werden** is **er** —.
werde	36. 6 1st pers. sing. <u>future</u> subjunctive of **gehen** is therefore **ich — gehen.**
werde	36. 7 3rd pers. sing. future subjunctive of **gehen** is — — —.
er werde gehen	36. 8 2nd pers. sing. future subjunctive of **kommen** is **du** — —
werdest kommen	36. 9 It is probably unnecessary to go in detail through the whole tense. Here it is in full: 1 Sing. **ich werde gehen** Plur. **wir werden gehen** 2 **du werdest gehen** **ihr werdet gehen** 3 **er werde gehen** **sie werden gehen** Go to next item when you are sure that you know it.
	36. 10 The principal use of the future subjunctive is in indirect speech to report something originally said in the — indicative.
future	36. 11 Thus *He said he would come*. Here the actual words were '*I — —*'.
shall come	36. 12 *He said he would come* is **er sagte, er — kommen.**
werde	36. 13 *They said she would go*. They actually said "*She — —*".
will go	36. 14 *They said she would go* is **sie sagten, sie — —.**
werde gehen	36. 15 *You said you would work* is **du sagtest, du — —.**
werdest arbeiten	

37. Expressions of Quantity

37. 1

With expressions of quantity such as *a glass of wine* (**Wein** masc.) the word *of* is not translated in any way and both nouns have the same case. *A glass of wine* is therefore **ein Glas —.**

37. 2

A glass of wine is — — —.

Wein

37. 3

Die Flasche = *the bottle. A bottle of wine* is — — —.

ein Glas Wein

37. 4

Das Wasser = *the water. A bottle of water* is — — —.

eine Flasche Wein

37. 5

The position is the same if the adjective **voll** is used, e.g. **ein Glas voll Wasser.** *A bottle full of wine* is — — — —.

eine Flasche Wasser

37. 6

A glass full of milk (**Milch** fem.) is — — — —.

eine Flasche voll Wein

37. 7

Sometimes in phrases of this kind the adjective has the form **voller – Eine Flasche voller Wasser.** The **ER** is not a declension ending and the adjective is invariable. *A glass full of wine* would thus be — — — —.

ein Glas voll Milch

37. 8

However, if there is an adjective with the second noun e.g. *a bottle of sour wine* the noun and adjective will usually go into the genitive: **eine Flasche sauren Weins.** *A glass of good wine* is — — — —. (If you have forgotten what you learnt about the genitive case of strong adjectives look back to items 1058–1068 of Part I.)

ein Glas voller Wein

ein Glas **guten Weins**	**37. 9** *A glass of good milk* (remember it is **die Milch**) is — — — —.
ein Glas **guter Milch**	**37. 10** The position is the same with **voll**. *A bottle full of old* *wine* is **eine Flasche voll** — —.

alten Weins

38. Formation of Pluperfect Subjunctive

38. 1

The pluperfect subjunctive, like the other subjunctives of compound tenses, is easy. You remember that the pluperfect indicative of a verb is formed by using its past participle together with the imperfect indicative of the auxiliary verb (**haben** or **sein**). *I had spoken* is — — —.

ich hatte
gesprochen

38. 2

She had made is — — —.

sie hatte gemacht

38. 3

We had gone (remember this is a verb of change of position) is — — —.

wir waren
gegangen

38. 4

They had come is — — —.

sie waren
gekommen

38. 5

As you will expect, the pluperfect subjunctive is formed by using the past participle as before, together with the imperfect — of the auxiliary verb.

subjunctive

38. 6

You already know the imperfect subjunctive of **haben** and **sein,** namely **ich hätte** and **ich wäre**. 1st pers. sing. pluperf. subjunctive of **sprechen** is **ich** — **gesprochen.**

317

hätte	38. 7 3rd pers. sing. pluperf. subjunctive of **sprechen** is **er** — —.
hätte gesprochen	38. 8 1st pers. pl. pluperf. subjunctive of **machen** is **wir** — —.
hätten gemacht	38. 9 1st pers. sing. pluperf. subjunctive of **kommen** (remember it is a verb of change of position) is **ich** — —.
wäre gekommen	38. 10 3rd pers. sing. pluperf. subjunctive of **kommen** is **er** — —.
wäre gekommen	38. 11 3rd pers. pl. pluperf. subjunctive of **gehen** is **sie** — —.
wären gegangen	38. 12 Here to sum up is the pluperfect subjunctive of a verb conjugated with **haben**:

38. 12

1 Sing. **ich hätte gefragt**   Plur. **wir hätten gefragt**
2   **du hättest gefragt**   **ihr hättet gefragt**
3   **er hätte gefragt**   **sie hätten gefragt**

Go to next item when you are satisfied that you know this.

38. 13
And here is the pluperfect subjunctive of a verb
conjugated with **sein**:

1 Sing. **ich wäre geblieben**   Plur. **wir wären geblieben**
2   **du wärest geblieben**   **ihr wäret geblieben**
3   **er wäre geblieben**   **sie wären geblieben**

Go to next section when you are satisfied that you know
this.

318

39. Indirect Speech (3) — Where Subjunctive is Indistinguishable from Indicative

39. 1
Up to now we have dealt with the following cases of indirect speech — (i) where the original words were in the present indicative; in indirect speech (e.g. **er sagte, die Frau komme**) such words are given in the — subjunctive.

present

39. 2
... (ii) where the original words were in a past tense; in indirect speech (e.g. **sie sagten, er sei geblieben**) such words are given in the — —.

perfect subjunctive

39. 3
... and (iii) where the original words were in the future indicative; in indirect speech (e.g. **er sagte, er werde hinausgehen**) such words are given in the — —.

future subjunctive

39. 4
However in all the examples we have had so far the subjunctive is clearly different from the corresponding tense of the indicative. Thus 3rd pers. sing. pres. indicative of **haben** is **er hat** and the subjunctive is — —.

er habe

39. 5
1st pers. sing. pres. indicative of **sein** is **ich bin** and the subjunctive is — —.

ich sei

39. 6
However, as you noticed, there are many cases in which the subjunctive and the indicative are the same. 1st pers. sing. pres. indicative of **haben** is **ich habe** and the subjunctive is — —.

ich habe

39. 7
3rd pers. pl. pres. indicative of **haben** is **sie haben** and the subjunctive is — —.

sie haben

39. 8

Where the present subjunctive does not differ from the present indicative it must not be used in indirect speech. Thus for *He said they were coming* you could not say **Er sagte, sie kommen** because the 3rd pers. pl. pres. subjunctive of **kommen** is the same as the — —.

present indicative

39. 9

You will understand why this should be so if you imagine yourself listening to someone saying **Er sagte, sie kommen,** namely that it does not sound like indirect speech at all, but like — speech. (It sounds like: **Er sagte 'Sie kommen'.**)

direct

39. 10

In such cases therefore the imperfect subjunctive is used instead of the present subjunctive. So the German for *He said they were coming* is **Er sagte, sie —.**

kämen

39. 11

Similarly for *He said I had a ball* you cannot say **Er sagte, ich habe einen Ball** because in the 1st pers. sing. the pres. indicative of **haben** is no different from the pres. subjunctive. You must therefore say instead **Er sagte, ich — einen Ball.**

hätte

39. 12

For *He said they went for a walk* you could not say **Er sagte, sie machen einen Spaziergang;** the imperfect subjunctive must be used – **Er sagte, sie — einen Spaziergang.**

machten

39. 13

Similar cases may arise with other tenses. Thus with *They said they had spoken* the perfect subjunctive **sie haben gesprochen** cannot be used because it is the same as the — —.

320

perfect indicative	**39. 14** . . . and the pluperfect subjunctive must be used instead. *They said they had spoken* is therefore **sie sagten, sie — —.**
hätten **gesprochen**	**39. 15** *You said I had seen you* is not **du sagtest, ich habe dich gesehen,** but **du sagtest, ich — dich gesehen.**
hätte	**39. 16** *They said we had not helped* is not **sie sagten, wir haben nicht geholfen** but **sie sagten, wir — nicht geholfen.**
hätten	**39. 17** Similarly in some persons the future subjunctive is the same as the future —.
indicative	**39. 18** In such cases the conditional must be used. *They said they would come* is therefore not **sie sagten, sie werden kommen,** but **sie sagten, sie — kommen.**
würden	**39. 19** . . . and *You said I would go* is **du sagtest, — — —.**
ich würde gehen	**39. 20** You will probably find these changes easy to remember – the general principle is that in reported speech when subjunctive and indicative are the same the subjunctive is moved one stage back into the past. Thus present subjunctive becomes — subjunctive . . .
imperfect	**39. 21** . . . perfect subjunctive becomes — subjunctive . . .
pluperfect	**39. 22** . . . and future subjunctive becomes —.
conditional	

40. Viel and Wenig

40. 1

The adjectives **viel** and **wenig** are declined like other adjectives when used in the plural. Thus *many houses* is — —.

viele Häuser

40. 2

Few men is — —.

wenige Männer

40. 3

The many books is — — —.

die vielen Bücher

40. 4

However, when used in the singular (to mean *much* and *little* respectively) **viel** and **wenig** are not usually declined. Thus *much wine* is **viel Wein**. *Little wine* is — —.

wenig Wein

40. 5

I have much wine is — — — —.

ich habe viel
Wein

40. 6

With little money (**Geld** is n.) — — —.

mit wenig Geld

40. 7

The same applies to **ein wenig** which means *a little* (as distinct from *little*). Both words remain undeclined. *With a little cheese* is — — — **Käse**.

mit ein wenig

40. 8

There is however one expression, *many thanks,* in which **viel** is declined in the singular. The word for *thanks* is **Dank** m., and it is used in the singular. *Many thanks* is **vielen Dank,** so that the expression is in the — case.

40. 9

Many thanks is — —.

accusative

vielen Dank

322

41. Use of Subjunctive with Wenn and Als Ob

41.1

The imperfect or pluperfect subjunctive is used after **wenn** relating to unfulfilled conditions (such as *If I were you* etc.) The position is the same in English, but as the imperfect subjunctive of all English verbs except *to be* is identical with the imperfect indicative we do not often realize that we are using it. Go to next item.

41.2

If I had money I should be rich is **Wenn ich Geld hätte, würde ich reich sein.** *If I were king, you would be queen* is **Wenn ich der König —, würdest du die Königin sein.**

wäre

41.3

Remember how the imperfect subjunctive is formed (for weak verbs it is identical with the imperfect indicative; strong and irregular verbs add an Umlaut and an E to the imperfect indicative.) *If I knew that, I should be wise* is **Wenn ich das —, würde ich weise sein.**

wüßte

41.4

I would come if I could is **ich würde kommen, wenn ich es —.**

könnte

41.5

So far the examples have all been of the imperfect subjunctive. The pluperfect subjunctive is used in the same cases as in English (*If you had told me* etc.). Go to next item.

41.6

If I had had money I should have been rich is **Wenn ich Geld gehabt hätte, würde ich reich gewesen sein.**
If I had been king, you would have been queen is **Wenn ich der König — —, würdest du die Königin gewesen sein.**

gewesen wäre	**41. 7** *If I had had money I should have been rich* is **Wenn ich Geld — —, würde ich reich gewesen sein.**
gehabt hätte	**41. 8** *If I had known that I should have been wise* is **Wenn ich das — —, würde ich weise gewesen sein.**
gewußt hätte	**41. 9** *I would have come if I had been able* is **Ich würde gekommen sein, wenn ich es — —.**
gekonnt hätte	**41. 10** When a sentence of this kind has begun with **wenn** it is common to insert the word **so** (equivalent to English *then*) before the second half of the sentence – e.g. **Wenn ich Geld hätte, so würde ich reich sein. Wenn ich könnte, würde ich kommen** could be written **Wenn ich könnte, — — — —.**
so würde ich kommen	**41. 11** It is fairly common to omit the **wenn** at the beginning of such a sentence and to invert the verb instead. Thus instead of **Wenn ich könnte** ... we find **Könnte ich** ... Instead of **Wenn ich das wüßte** ... we might have — — —.
Wüßte ich das	**41. 12** This construction is still found in English. We may still hear people say *Had I known* or *were I to go* instead of the more common — *I had known* or — *I were to go.*
If	**41. 13** In German instead of **Wenn ich der König wäre** we may find — — — —.
wäre ich der König	**41. 14** ... and instead of **Wenn ich das gewußt hätte** ... we may find — — — —.

324

Hätte ich **das gewußt**	**41. 15** Where **wenn** is omitted and the verb inverted in this way **so** must be inserted before the second half of the sentence. Thus we must say **Hätte ich Geld, — würde ich reich sein.**
so	**41. 16** . . . and for *If I could, I would come* (omitting **wenn**) we must say **Könnte ich, — — — —.**
so würde ich **kommen**	**41. 17** The subjunctive is also used after **als ob** (*as if*). **Er sprach, als ob er krank wäre** – *He spoke as if he were ill. It seemed as if he were coming* is **Es schien, — — — —.**
als ob er käme	**41. 18** *He looked as if he were dead* (**tot**) is **Er sah aus, — — — — —.**
als ob er tot **wäre**	**41. 19** The **ob** can be omitted and the verb inverted. Thus for . . . **als ob er käme** you could say . . . **— — —.**
als käme er	**41. 20** . . . and instead of . . . **als ob er tot wäre** you could say . . . **— — — — —.**
als wäre er tot	

42. Relative Pronouns in 1st and 2nd Persons

42. 1

There is a tendency in both English and German to regard relative pronouns as being of the 3rd person, so that it comes as something of a surprise when it is necessary to say for example *I, who — only   a poor student . . .*

325

am	 **41. 2** . . . or *Our Father, which — in Heaven* . . .
art	**42. 3** To avoid this sort of surprise in German, when a relative pronoun has a first or second person as its antecedent the pronoun is repeated after the relative pronoun. *I, who am so old* . . . is <u>ich,</u> <u>der</u> <u>ich</u> <u>so alt</u> —.
bin	**42. 4** *Thou who art from Heaven* is **du, — — von dem Himmel —.**
der (or **die**) **du . . . bist**	**42. 5** *We who come to England* is **—, — — nach England —.**
wir, die wir . . kommen	**42. 6** Sometimes this repetition of the pronoun is felt to be a little heavy, but in that case it is the first mention of the pronoun, not the second, which is omitted. Thus instead of **du, der du von dem Himmel bist,** Goethe writes **— — von dem Himmel —.**
der du . . . bist	

43. More about the Passive Voice

43. 1
The passive can usually be formed by taking the direct object of an active verb and making it the subject of the passive. Instead of *He throws a ball* (*ball* being the direct object) you can say *A ball — — by him.*

43. 2
Instead of *The cat eats the mouse* you can say *The mouse — — by — —.*

is thrown

326

is eaten by	**43. 3**
the cat	The same applies in German, where, you will remember, the verb **werden** is used to form the passive. Instead of **er wirft den Ball** you can say **der Ball — von ihm geworfen.**
	43. 4
wird	Instead of **die Katze frißt die Maus** you can say **die Maus — von der Katze —.**
	43. 5
wird gefressen	Notice how to say *by* with passive constructions: **der Ball wird von ihm geworfen.** *By* is expressed by the preposition — + the — case.
	43. 6
von dative	*The ball is thrown by her* is **der Ball wird — — geworfen.**
	43. 7
von ihr	*The mouse is eaten by the cat* is **die Maus wird — — — gefressen.**
	43. 8
von der Katze	You must be very careful to turn only the <u>direct</u> object of an active verb into the subject of a passive in German. Take the sentence *He tells (to) me.* Since we have been able to insert the word *to* without altering the meaning *me* is *direct/indirect* object.
	43. 9
indirect	*He tells (to) me.* In English we can say *I am — by him.*
	43. 10
told	In German such a sentence is quite impossible. Take another example. *He gives me a book.* In English we can say *I — — a book by him.*
	43. 11
am given	If you try to say it like that in German (**ich werde gegeben**) it means *I — — (away to someone).*

327

am given	**43. 12** Since the abolition of slavery such an action is normally impossible. **Erzählen** (*to tell, to recount*) is another verb with which you must be on your guard against this temptation. *He tells (to) me a story* is **er — mir eine Geschichte.**
erzählt	**43. 13** Notice the cases. *He tells (to) me a story* is **er erzählt —** (Dative) **eine Geschichte.**
mir	**43. 14** *He tells (to) me a story* is **er erzählt mir — —** (Accusative).
eine Geschichte	**43. 15** **Er erzählt mir eine Geschichte.** You can take the direct object (Accusative) and make it the subject of a passive: thus *A story is told (to) me* is **— — — mir erzählt.** (You will remember that the prefix **GE** is not used with inseparable verbs).
eine Geschichte wird	**43. 16** . . . but you cannot make the <u>indirect</u> object (Dative) into the subject of a passive in German, even though in English you can say *I — — a story*.
am told	**43. 17** You must therefore be on your guard when trying to turn into the passive any verb which takes a dative. **Helfen** you will remember, is such a verb. Thus *I am helped can/cannot* be translated literally into German.
cannot	**43. 18** However, verbs requiring the dative can be put into the passive if used <u>impersonally</u> (i.e. with *it* as the subject). Thus for *I am helped* you can say **— is helped to me.** (If you have done Latin you will remember that verbs requiring the dative are similarly used.)

It	**43. 19**
	I am helped (=*It is helped to me*) is — — **mir geholfen.**
es wird	**43. 20**
	I am helped is — — — —.
es wird mir	**43. 21**
geholfen	Similarly for *I am told* you can say *It is told to me* — — **mir erzählt.**
es wird	**43. 22**
	I am told is — — — —.
es wird mir	**43. 23**
erzählt	The reason why verbs such as **helfen** and **erzählen** must be used impersonally in the passive is that they are verbs which require the — case.
dative	**43. 24**
	This impersonal passive is also used with verbs not requiring the dative where it is not clear by whom an action is done. Thus where in English we might say *There is dancing* (**tanzen** = *to dance*) it is possible to say in German *It is danced:* **es — getanzt.**
wird	**43. 25**
	There is dancing is — — —.
es wird getanzt	**43. 26**
	The **es** of this impersonal passive is often omitted. Instead of **es wird mir geholfen** you may say **mir wird geholfen.** Instead of **es wird mir erzählt** you may say — — —.
mir wird erzählt	**43. 27**
	Instead of **es wird heute getanzt** you may say **Heute** — —.
wird getanzt	**43. 28**
	In general the passive is slightly less used in German than in English. Often it is avoided by the use of **man**; thus instead of **mir wird geholfen** you may say *One helps me* – — **hilft mir.**

man

43. 29
I am helped (= *One helps me*) is — — —.

man hilft mir

43. 30
Instead of **es wird mir erzählt** (or **mir wird erzählt**)
you may say — — —.

man erzählt mir

44. Was Für

——————

44. 1
Was für means *what kind of.* It is invariable and does
not affect case in any way. *What kind of house?* is — —
ein Haus?

was für

44. 2
What kind of a house? is — — — —.

was für ein Haus?

44. 3
You should realize that the **für** is not being used as a
preposition in this idiomatic expression and therefore does
not require to be followed by an accusative. *What sort of a
man is he?* is **Was für** — — **ist er?**

ein Mann

44. 4
What sort of a boy came? (use **der Junge**) is — —
— — **kam?**

was für ein Junge

44. 5
Of course the rest of the sentence may still require the
noun to go into the accusative. In the sentence *What
sort of a car have you?* the words *What sort of a car* are
the object of the verb and must therefore be in the
accusative. *What sort of a car* (use **der Wagen**) *have
you?* is — — — — **haben Sie?**

330

was für einen Wagen	**44. 6** After a preposition requiring the dative **was für** remains unchanged but the following noun and article will be dative: *With what sort of a man did he come ?* is **mit** — — — — **kam er?**
was für einem Mann	**44. 7** Sometimes the **für** may be separated from the **was** as in the example *What kind of things are those ?* – — **sind das** — **Sachen?**
was sind das für Sachen?	

45. Use of Subjunctive instead of Conditional

45. 1
Apart from indirect speech one of the most important uses of the subjunctive in German is as an alternative to the conditional or conditional perfect. Go to next item.

45. 2
Instead of the conditional it is possible to use the imperfect subjunctive. This also used to be very commonly done in English; the Bible, hymns and Shakespeare are full of examples. *It were better for him that a millstone were hanged about his neck* means *It — — better for him . . .*

would be	**45. 3** When Macbeth says *If it were done when 'tis done, then 'twere well it were done quickly,* by *'twere well* he means *it — — well.*
would be	**45. 4** *Sad were our lot* (from a hymn) means *Our lot — — sad.*
would be	**45. 5** So in German today instead of **ich würde gehen** you can use the imperfect subjunctive, **ich ginge;** instead of **ich würde kommen** you could say — —.

331

ich käme	**45. 6** Instead of **ich würde müssen** you could say — —.
ich müßte	**45. 7** Instead of **er würde krank sein** you could say — — —.
er wäre krank	**45. 8** Of course this alternative to the conditional can only be used where the imperfect subjunctive differs from the imperfect indicative as otherwise the meaning would not be clear. Instead of **ich würde es machen** you *could/could not* say **ich machte es.**
could not	**45. 9** In particular this use of the subjunctive is common in place of the conditional perfect, which is felt to be clumsy. The tense to be used here is of course the pluperfect. For **ich würde gemacht haben** therefore you may well find **ich — gemacht.**
hätte	**45. 10** Instead of **wir würden gesprochen haben** you may find **wir — gesprochen.**
hätten	**45. 11** Instead of **er würde gemacht haben** you could have — — —.
er hätte gemacht	**45. 12** Instead of **er würde gekommen sein** (remember this time the auxiliary is **sein** not **haben**) you can say — — —.
er wäre gekommen	**45. 13** For **ich würde es getan haben** you may have — — — —.
ich hätte es getan	

46. Other uses of Subjunctive

46.1

There are several other ways of using the subjunctive but we need consider only two of them here. One is the use of the present subjunctive as a 3rd person imperative. We use it in the same way in English: *God be with you.* – **Gott — mit euch.**

46.2

sei

Es lebe die Königin (**leben** = *to live*) is *Long — the Queen.*

46.3

live

Thanks be to God! is **Gott — Dank!** (Note that in German (i) **Gott** is in the dative; (2) **Dank** is singular.)

46.4

sei

Let him do whatever he likes! is **er —, was er wolle.**

46.5

tue

The other use of the subjunctive which you should know is after a verb of wishing – again somewhat as in English: **Ich wünsche, sie wäre hier,** is *I wish she — here.*

46.6

were

I wish I had spoken earlier is **ich wünsche, ich — früher gesprochen.**

46.7

hätte

I want him to be happy (note that in German you must say *I wish that he be happy*) is **ich will, — — glücklich—.**

daß er . . . sei

47. Formation and Use of Present Participle

47.1

The present participle is that part of the verb which in English ends in *—ing.* You will already have noticed that present participles are used much less frequently in German than in English. Go to next item.

333

47. 2

The present participle is formed by adding the letter **D** to the infinitive. The present participle of **machen** is —.

machend

47. 3

The present participle of **gehen** is —.

gehend

47. 4

With a few verbs such as **sein** and **tun** whose infinitives end in a vowel other than **E** + **N** it may be necessary to insert an **E** before the **N**. Present participle of **tun** is —.

tuend

47. 5

Present participle of **sein** is —.

seiend

47. 6

The present participle may be used either as part of a verb (e.g. *seeing me, he laughed*) or as an adjective (e.g. *sleeping dogs*). Go to next item.

47. 7

A present participle should not be used as part of a verb unless two actions, one of which is represented by the participle, are going on simultaneously. *Seeing me, he laughed.* Here the two actions are *the —ing* and *the —ing.*

seeing laughing

47. 8

Coming up to me, she said . . . Here the two actions are *the —ing* and *the —ing.*

coming saying

47. 9

Present participles used as part of a verb show no agreement and like other non-finite verbs come at the end of the phrase. *Coming up to me* (**auf mich zu**) *she said* . . . is — — — —, **sagte sie** . . .

334

auf mich zu kommend

47. 10

Of course you well know by now that present participles cannot be used with the verb *to be* as in English. *I am going* can/cannot be translated into German by using a present participle.

cannot

47. 11

Present participles are more commonly used in German as adjectives and are declined in the same way as adjectives. *A sleeping dog* is **ein — Hund.**

schlafender

47. 12

Sleeping dogs is — —.

schlafende Hunde

48. Participial Phrases

48. 1

A very characteristic feature of German is its use of participial phrases. In English we are used to such expressions as *a sleeping dog* or *the broken glass,* but in German additional words may be added to the participle to give such results as *the last night by my sister broken glass.* Go to next item.

48. 2

Let us build such a phrase up to understand exactly how it works. The past participle of **brechen** (*to break*) is **gebrochen.** Since it is being used as an adjective it must decline like one. *A broken glass* is **ein — Glas** (neut.)

gebrochenes

48. 3

You already know that a participle must come last in its phrase (in this case, as it is being used as an adjective, last before the noun). Any additional words inserted into the phrase must therefore go *before/after* the participle.

before

48. 4

At present we have **ein gebrochenes Glas.** Let us now add the word **gestern** (*yesterday*) so that the meaning will be *a glass broken yesterday* – **ein — — —.**

**gestern
gebrochenes Glas**

48. 5

The order of adverbial expressions, you will remember, is Time, Manner, Place (TMP). **Gestern** represents *Time/Manner/Place.*

Time

48. 6

If therefore we add an adverbial expression of Manner it will come *before/after* **gestern.**

after

48. 7

. . . and, as the participle must come last before the noun, such an adverb of manner will come *before/after* the participle.

before

48. 8

We already have **ein gestern gebrochenes Glas.** Let us now add, in the only possible place, the words **von meiner Schwester** (*by my sister*) so that the meaning will be *a glass broken yesterday by my sister:* **ein — — — — — Glas.**

**gestern von
meiner
Schwester
gebrochenes**

48. 9

If we now add an adverbial expression of Place it can only come *before/after/between* the expressions of Time and Manner.

after

48. 10

We now have **ein gestern von meiner Schwester gebrochenes Glas** (*a glass broken yesterday by my sister*). Adding the words **zu Hause in Berlin** in the correct place for an adverbial expression of Place, we get **ein — — — — — — — — Glas.**

gestern von meiner Schwester zu Hause in Berlin gebrochenes

vorbeigehender

before

48. 11

Such participial phrases can be built up also on present as well as past participles, so that we could choose as a basis for a similar construction *a passing schoolboy* – **ein** — **Schüler** (*to pass* = **vorbeigehen**).

48. 12

Few people would claim that the lengthier of such phrases are elegant, but they are used, and you should know how to deal with them. Most of the difficulties disappear once you realize that the participle comes just *before/after* the noun in German but cannot be left there in translation.

48. 13

The easiest thing is to translate such participial phrases into English by relative sentences – e.g. *the glass which was broken by my sister yesterday at home* etc. Go to next section.

49. Factitive Verbs

49. 1

You may have noticed how in English there are often pairs of verbs with allied meaning but differing by a vowel (and sometimes by a consonant as well) – *fall, fell; sit, seat; lie, lay.* Go to next item.

49. 2

In each such pair of verbs one is transitive (which means simply that it can take a direct object) and one is intransitive. You cannot fall something, or sit something or lie something. The verbs *fall, sit* and *lie* are therefore *transitive/intransitive.*

intransitive

A weak verb in English has a past participle ending in
D or *T* and not showing a change of vowel. Are the
intransitive members of these pairs of verbs weak or
strong? You cannot say *I have falled*, or *sitted* or *lied*, so
that the intransitive verbs are *weak/strong*.

49. 4

strong

Let us consider the other verb of each pair. You can say
I have felled a tree, and *seated someone* and *laid a table*
so that these verbs are both *transitive/intransitive* and
weak/strong.

49. 5

transitive   weak

In each case the transitive-weak verb has the meaning of
making someone or something do the action described by
the intransitive-strong verb. Thus with *fall, fell*, if you fell
a tree you — *it fall*.

49. 6

make

With *sit, seat* if you seat a man by the window you —
him sit there.

49. 7

make

. . . and with *lie, lay* if you lay your coat down you —
it lie.

49. 8

make

The verb in each pair which has the meaning of making
someone do the action referred to by the other verb is
called a factitive verb (from the Latin *facere, to make*).
To fell is the factitive version of — —.

49. 9

to fall

To lay is the — version of *to lie*.

factitive	**49. 10** The situation is the same in German – there are numbers of intransitive-strong verbs, usually conjugated with **sein** which are paired by transitive-weak verbs conjugated (like all transitive verbs in German) with —.
haben	**49. 11** Thus we have **fahren** (strong, intransitive, conjugated with **sein**) meaning *to travel* and **führen** (weak, transitive, conjugated with **haben**) meaning *to make to travel* and thus *to lead*. *I have travelled* is **ich** — —.
bin gefahren	**49. 12** *I have led him* (**führen**, weak, transitive, conjugated with **haben**) is **ich** — — —.
habe ihn geführt	**49. 13** **Fallen, fällt, fiel, gefallen** (intransitive, requiring **sein**) means *to fall*. *I have fallen* is **ich** — —.
bin gefallen	**49. 14** **Fällen** (weak, transitive) means *to fell*. *I have felled a tree* is **ich** — **einen Baum** —.
habe . . . gefällt	**49. 15** **Hangen, hängt, hing, gehangen** (intransitive, requiring **sein**) means *to be hanging*. *I have been hanging* is **ich** — —.
bin gehangen	**49. 16** **Hängen** (weak, transitive) means *to make to hang* or *to hang up*. *I have hung up the washing* is **ich** — **die Wäsche auf**—.
habe die Wäsche aufgehängt	**49. 17** In English too we used to have a pair of verbs like **hangen, hängen** with the same differences, but the only trace of this now remaining is in the weak past tense of *hang* meaning *to execute* – *They* — *my poor Billy.*

hanged	**49. 18** **Liegen, liegt, lag, gelegen** (transitive, but this time conjugated with **haben**) means *to be lying. I have been lying* is **ich** — —.
habe gelegen	**49. 19** **Legen** (weak, transitive) means *to lay down. I have laid the foundation stone* is **ich** — **den Grundstein** —.
habe . . . gelegt	**49. 20** **Sinken, sinkt, sank, gesunken** (intransitive, requiring **sein**) means *to sink. She has sunk* is **sie** — —.
ist gesunken	**49. 21** **Senken** (weak, transitive) means *to sink* (*something*). *They have sunk the ship* is **sie** — **das Schiff** —.
haben . . . gesenkt	**49. 22** **Sitzen, sitzt, saß, gesessen** (intransitive but this time again requiring **haben**) means *to sit. I have sat* is — — —.
ich habe gesessen	**49. 23** **Setzen** (weak, transitive) means *to set* or *to put. I have put my hat on my head* is **ich** — **meinen Hut auf den Kopf** —.
habe . . . gesetzt	**49. 24** There are other pairs of verbs like these. If you appreciate their relationship to one another you will not be confused by the vowel changes involved. Go to next section.

50. Use of ES as Genitive

50. 1
Some uses of the pronoun **es** may cause puzzlement unless it is realized that this is an old genitive form. Thus **sie sind es müde** means *they are tired* — —.

340

of it	**50. 2** This form of words is very frequently used with the adjective **satt** meaning also *tired* (compare Latin *satis*). *I am tired of it* is **ich bin — satt.**
es	**50. 3** *I am tired of it* is — — — —.
ich bin es satt (or müde)	**50. 4** When **satt** or **müde** are used with a noun the latter is in the normal genitive form. *To be tired of a thing* (**Sache** fem.) is — — **satt sein.**
einer Sache	

51. Sein + Past Participle Distinguished from Passive Voice

	51. 1 You remember that the passive voice is made by using **werden** + past participle. Thus *The window is* (= *gets*) *closed* is **das Fenster — geschlossen.**
wird	**51. 2** *The door is* (=*gets*) *opened* is **die Tür — geöffnet.**
wird	**51. 3** In all cases where **werden** is used with the past participle in this way we are thinking of the action which is carried out—e.g. the act of someone opening the door. In **die Maus wird gefressen** therefore we are thinking of the — of the mouse being eaten.
action	**51. 4** However, we may want to speak of the state of the door after it has been opened, or of the mouse after it has been eaten – e.g. to say *The door is* (*already*) *opened*. In such a case **sein** is used with the past participle. *The mouse is* (*already*) *eaten* is **die Maus — (schon) gefressen.**

341

ist	**51. 5** *The door is (already) opened* is **Die Tür — (schon) geöffnet.**
ist	**51. 6** *The window is (already) opened* is **das Fenster — (schon) —.**
ist geöffnet	**51. 7** *She is (= gets) caught (i.e. the action)* is **sie — gefangen.**
wird	**51. 8** *She is (already) caught (i.e. the state)* is **— — (schon) —.**
sie ist gefangen	**51. 9** As you can see from the above examples, if it is correct to use **sein** the word *already* can be inserted without radically distorting the meaning. Go to next item.
	51. 10 *She asks for air, so the window is opened* is **sie bittet um Luft, darum ist/wird das Fenster geöffnet.**
wird	**51. 11** *It is very hot, as the door is closed* is **es ist sehr heiß, da die Tür geschlossen ist/wird.**
ist	

52. Quasi-Modal Verbs

52. 1
There is a group of verbs which, although they are noι modal verbs, share some of their characteristics, and which may conveniently be called quasi-modal verbs. (*Quasi* comes from Latin and means *as if* or *a sort of*). Go to next item.

342

52. 2
Hören, lassen and **sehen,** all of which you have already met, are the most important of these verbs. Like the modal verbs they do not need **zu** with an infinitive. *I hear you speak* is **ich höre dich** —.

sprechen

52. 3
He lets me come is **er läßt mich** —.

kommen

52. 4
We saw her do it is **wir sahen sie es** —.

tun

52. 5
This absence of **zu** need not surprise us greatly as the equivalent verbs in English, along with our own modal verbs, work the same way: *Will you let me (go/to go)?*

go

52. 6
Sometimes in English the second verb is in the present participle but of course this does not affect the German: *I hear you speaking* (= *speak*) is **ich höre Sie sprechen.** *I see you coming* is **ich sehe Sie** —.

kommen

52. 7
I hear you running is — — **Sie** —. ·

ich höre Sie
laufen

52. 8
She lets us go is — — — —.

sie läßt uns gehen

52. 9
These verbs are like modal verbs in another way too – the past participle is replaced by the infinitive when the verb governs another infinitive. *I have heard you go* is **ich habe Sie gehen gehört/hören** . . .

hören

52. 10
We had seen her come is **wir hatten sie kommen** —.

343

sehen	**52. 11** *I have let him wait* (or as we would usually say, *kept him waiting*) is **ich habe ihn warten** —.
lassen	**52. 12** *I have heard her speak* is — — — — —.
ich habe sie sprechen hören	**52. 13** **Helfen** is another verb which usually shares these peculiarities (and note that in English we seem uncertain whether it is right to say *Help me to do it* or *Help me do it*). *He helps me to do it* is **er hilft mir es** —.
tun	**52. 14** *He has helped me to do it* is **er hat mir es tun** —.
helfen	**52. 15** *He has helped me to do it* is — — — — — —.
er hat mir es tun helfen	**52. 16** **Lehren** (*to teach*), **lernen** (*to learn*) and **machen** (*to make*) also sometimes behave in this way. *I have taught him to speak German* is **ich habe ihn Deutsch sprechen** —.
lehren	**52. 17** *It makes me laugh* (**lachen**) is — — — —.
es macht mich lachen	**52. 18** *One must learn to read* (**lesen**) is **Man muß** — —.
lesen lernen	**52. 19** However **lehren** and **lernen** may be used with **zu** if they precede the infinitive. *One must learn to speak German* is **man muß lernen,** — — —.
Deutsch zu sprechen	**52. 20** As you already know, verbs which are neither modal nor quasi-modal verbs require **zu** with an infinitive as a general rule. **Wünschen** means the same as **wollen,** namely *to* —.

344

wish (or want)	**52. 21** However, **wünschen,** you will remember, is not a modal verb, and **wollen** is. Using **wollen,** *I want to sleep* is — — —.
ich will schlafen	**52. 22** But using **wünschen,** *I want to sleep* is — — — —.
ich wünsche zu schlafen	### 53. Actions Previously Begun and Still Continuing
	53. 1 With actions begun some time ago but still going on, English thinks principally of the past time at which the action began and so uses the progressive perfect tense: *I have been learning German for a year.* Go to next item.
	53. 2 Obviously however it is just as important that the action is still going on now. Clearly we could say *I have been learning German for a year and I — still learning it now.*
am	**53. 3** It would therefore be quite logical to put the verb in the present tense, and this is what German and many other languages do. *I have been learning German for a year* is **ich — Deutsch seit einem Jahr.** (You can compare this with the use of *depuis* in French.)
lerne	**53. 4** Notice that in this connexion the word used to translate *for* is **seit** which you already know as a preposition requiring the dative. Its literal meaning of course is *since. I have been learning German for (= since) a year* is **ich lerne Deutsch — — —.**
seit einem Jahr	**53. 5** *I have been learning German for a year* is — — — — — —.

ich lerne Deutsch seit einem Jahr	53. 6 *I have been in England for 10 years (and still am)* is **ich — seit zehn Jahren in England.**
bin	53. 7 *I have been in England for 10 years* is — — — — — **in England.**
ich bin seit 10 Jahren	53. 8 *We have been waiting (***warten***) for an hour (and still are waiting)* is — — — — **Stunde** (fem.)
wir warten seit einer Stunde	53. 9 *We have been waiting for an hour* is — — — — —.
wir warten seit einer Stunde	53. 10 The same principle applies where in English we use the progressive pluperfect: *In 1962 I had been learning German for two years.* Here we could add . . . *and still — learning it at that time.*
was	53. 11 The addition . . . *was still learning* will show us what tense is required in German, namely the —.
imperfect	53. 12 *In 1962 I had been learning German for 2 years* is **im Jahre 1962 (neunzehnhundertzweiundsechzig) — — Deutsch seit zwei Jahren.**
lernte ich	53. 13 *In 1962 I had been learning German for 2 years* is **im Jahre 1962 lernte ich Deutsch — — —.**
seit zwei Jahren	53. 14 *In 1962 I had been learning German for 2 years* is **im Jahre 1962 — — — — — —.**

lernte ich Deutsch seit zwei Jahren	53. 15 *I had been in England for 10 years (and still was)* is — — **seit 10 Jahren in England.**
ich war	53. 16 *I had been in England for 10 years* is — — — — — **in England.**
ich war seit 10 Jahren	53. 17 *We had been waiting for 2 hours (and still were waiting)* is **wir — seit zwei Stunden.**
warteten	53. 18 *We had been waiting for 2 hours* is — — — — —.
wir warteten seit zwei Stunden	53. 19 In practice the word **schon** (meaning *already* but simply not translated into English) would always be added before the **seit.** *I have been waiting for a week* is **ich warte — seit einer Woche.**
schon	53. 20 *I have been in England for 10 years* is — — — **seit 10 Jahren in England.**
ich bin schon	53. 21 Have you noticed how often Germans, even if they speak perfect English, reveal that they are German by using the the word *already* (a translation of **schon**) in places where we would not use it at all? Go to next section.

54. Word Order — Dependent Sentences with Two Infinitives

54. 1
You already know that with the modal and quasi-modal verbs in the perfect tenses we may get two infinitives at the end. Thus *I have been able to come* is **ich habe kommen —.**

können	**54. 2** *I have had to go* (using **müssen**) is **ich habe** — —.
gehen müssen	**54. 3** The quasi-modal verbs you remember were **hören, lassen, sehen** and one or two others. They show this same characteristic. *I have heard her sing* is **ich habe sie** — —.
singen hören	**54. 4** *You have let me go* is **Sie haben** — — —.
mich gehen lassen	**54. 5** Two infinitives may also arise with these verbs in the future and conditional: *I shall have to speak* (using **müssen**) is **ich werde** — —.
sprechen müssen	**54. 6** *You would be required to work* (using **sollen**) is **du würdest** — —.
arbeiten sollen	**54. 7** Whenever two infinitives occur together in this way they must come at the end even in a dependent sentence, and the auxiliary verb (finite verb) must come immediately before them. **Ich werde heute gehen müssen,** but **ich glaube, daß ich heute** — — —.
werde gehen müssen	**54. 8** **Ich habe gestern kommen können** but **ich bleibe, weil ich gestern** — — —.
habe kommen können	**54. 9** **Ich habe sie singen hören** but **ich bin froh** (*glad*), **daß ich** — — — —.
sie habe singen hören	**54. 10** **Er würde morgen kommen wollen** but **er wußte nicht, ob er** — — — —.
morgen würde kommen wollen	

348

55. The More . . . The More

55. 1

The more, the better is **je mehr, desto besser**, so that the first comparative is preceded by —.

55. 2

je

Je mehr, desto besser. The second comparative is preceded by —.

55. 3

desto

There may however be verbs to deal with. *The more it freezes, the colder it gets* is **je mehr es friert, desto kälter wird es.** The first sentence of such an expression is therefore the dependent sentence with the verb at the —.

55. 4

end

Je mehr es friert, desto kälter wird es. The second sentence of such an expression, beginning with **desto** is therefore the main sentence and as we have not begun the expression with the subject, but with a dependent sentence, the verb and subject are —.

55. 5

inverted

The earlier I come, the earlier I go, is — — — —, **desto eher gehe ich.**

55. 6

je eher ich komme

The earlier I come, the earlier I go is **je eher ich komme,** — — — —.

55. 7

desto eher gehe ich

The earlier I come, the earlier I go is — — — —, — — — —.

55. 8

je eher ich komme, desto eher gehe ich

The hotter it becomes, the more it rains is **je heißer es wird, desto mehr** — —.

regnet es	**55. 9** *The hotter it becomes, the more it rains* is **Je heißer es wird,** — — — —.
desto mehr regnet es	**55. 10** *The hotter it becomes, the more it rains* is — — — —, **desto mehr regnet es.**
je heißer es wird	**55. 11** *The hotter it becomes, the more it rains* is — — — —, — — — —.
je heißer es wird, desto mehr regnet es	**55. 12** You may be puzzled by the rather odd appearance of the word **desto.** It is really two words: **des,** (which you know as **dessen,** the genitive of the demonstrative and relative pronouns) plus the definite article, so that in **desto weniger** we are really saying **des die weniger,** meaning *by that the less.* Go to next section.

56. Conditional Perfect of Modal Verbs

56. 1

You remember that in an earlier section you were told that the pluperfect subjunctive was often used instead of the conditional perfect. This is especially important with modal and quasi-modal verbs since there is often an extra infinitive to work in, and the full form of the conditional perfect would be very cumbersome. Go to next item.

56. 2

I have been able to come (remember what you know about past participles of modal verbs where there is a governed infinitive) is **ich habe kommen** —.

350

können	**56. 3** *I would have been able to come* (remember that in such cases the infinitives of modal verb + governed infinitive must come last) is **ich würde haben — —.**
kommen können	**56. 4** **Ich würde haben kommen können.** You can see how inconvenient this is. Fortunately you know that instead of **ich würde haben** you can use the imperfect subjunctive of **haben,** namely — —.
ich hätte	**56. 5** Instead of **ich würde haben kommen können** therefore, you can say **ich — — —.**
hätte kommen können	**56. 6** Instead of **er würde es haben tun müssen** you can say **er — — — —.**
hätte es tun müssen	**56. 7** Instead of **wir würden haben gehen sollen** you can say **wir — — —.**
hätten gehen sollen	**56. 8** Instead of **Sie würden mich haben sprechen lassen** you can say **Sie — — — —.**
hätten mich sprechen lassen	

57. Modal Verb in Simple Tense with Perfect Infinitive

57. 1

There is a small number of cases in which modal verbs can be used as in English – i.e. in a simple tense such as the present, followed by a perfect infinitive; for example *He must have died* – **er muß** (present) **gestorben sein** (perfect infinitive). In all such cases however there is a logic about the situation linking it up with the present. Go to next item.

57. 2

Thus in the sentence *He must have done it* the meaning is that we presume (now, and therefore present tense) that he has done it. The German therefore is (using **müssen**) – **er — es getan haben.** (The principal parts of **tun** are **tun, tut, tat, getan.**)

57. 3

muß

She must have said it is **sie** — — — —.

57. 4

muß es gesagt haben

He may have come (meaning that it is possible that he has come) is (using **können**) **er** — — —.

57. 5

kann gekommen sein

You remember that one of the meanings of **sollen** was *to be said to. He is said* (i.e. now) *to have done it* is **er** — — — —.

soll es getan haben

58. Active Infinitive with Passive Meaning

58. 1

An infinitive in German, whilst keeping its active form, often has a passive meaning, especially after **sein.** *What was to be done?* – **Was war zu tun.** *What was to be seen?* is — — — —.

58. 2

was war zu sehen?

There was nothing to be heard is **es war nichts zu hören.** *There was nothing to be told* (using **erzählen**) is **es war** — — —.

58. 3

nichts zu erzählen

The active infinitive with passive meaning is also frequently to be found with the verb **lassen** (*to let* or *to have something done*). *He has a glass fetched* (i.e. *lets it be fetched*) is **er läßt ein Glas holen.** *I have a house built* (**bauen** = *to build*) is — — — — —.

352

ich lasse ein Haus bauen	**58. 4** *He had Rome burnt* (**brennen** = *to burn*) is **er ließ Rom —.**
brennen	**58. 5** *He has himself washed* is — — — —.
er läßt sich waschen	**58. 6** The position may be compared with French *faire faire quelquechose.* Go to next section.

---

59. The English Preposition —plus—Gerund Construction

59. 1

The gerund is the English verbal noun ending in *-ing*, e.g. *the doing* of something. German has no gerund and the infinitive does not always serve the same purpose, even when used as a neuter noun. How then do we translate such sentences as *Thank you for coming?* Go to next item.

59. 2

Here is an example. *She thanks me for coming* – **Sie dankt mir dafür, daß ich gekommen bin.** The first thing that strikes us is that the English simple sentence has been split up into a main sentence and a — sentence.

dependent

59. 3

She thanks me for coming. **Sie dankt mir dafür, daß ich gekommen bin.** The second thing to notice is that the *for* has been left in the main sentence, where it has been turned into an adverb beginning with —.

da-

59. 4

She thanks me for coming. **Sie dankt mir dafür, daß ich gekommen bin.** The literal translation of the German is *She thanks me therefor,* — — — —.

353

that I have come	**59. 5** For *I insist on your coming* we should say (in English) *I insist there-* —, — — —.
thereon that you <u>come</u>	**59. 6** For *we rely on your working* we should say (in English) *We rely* —, — — —.
thereon that you work	**59. 7** Let us now translate these into German. *I insist on your coming*. You discovered above that this was: *I insist thereon that you come*. **Bestehen auf** means *to insist on*. **Ich bestehe** —, — — —.
darauf, daß Sie kommen	**59. 8** *We rely on your working*. You rephrased this as *We rely thereon that you work*. **Sich verlassen auf** means *to rely on*. **Wir verlassen uns** —, — — —.
darauf, daß Sie arbeiten	**59. 9** *By* + gerund is rather a special case as it is normally translated by **indem** which literally means *whilst*. *He became rich by working* (= *whilst he worked*) is **er wurde reich,** — — —.
indem er arbeitete	**59. 10** *We live by eating* (= *whilst we eat*) is **wir leben,** — — —.
indem wir essen	**59. 11** *One grows wise by learning* is **man wird weise,** — — —.
indem man lernt	

354

EXERCISES

In all the following exercises the sentences given should be entirely rewritten, making the changes indicated at the head of each exercise. Answers are given on pages 367-376.

I. PLUPERFECT (Section 1)

Put the verbs into the pluperfect.

1. Sie machen einen Spaziergang.
2. Ich gehe in die Schule.
3. Wir wohnen nicht in der Stadt.
4. Hört ihr euren Vater?
5. Du sprichst schon mit der Lehrerin.
6. Herr Schmidt holt seinen Wagen jeden Morgen.
7. Sie ist eine gute Schülerin.
8. Sie fährt heute langsam nach Hause.
9. Ich gebe meiner Mutter ein interessantes Buch.
10. Ich komme in das Haus, weil es regnet.

II. 'WISSEN' AND 'KENNEN' (Section 2)

Insert the correct part of wissen *or* kennen, *whichever you think is required.*

1. Ich — nicht Herrn Lange. (*Present tense.*)
2. Er —, daß das Wasser kalt ist.
3. — du, was dieses Wort bedeutet?
4. Dieses Wort — ich nicht.
5. Wir — nichts (*imperfect*) von dieser Nachricht.

III. INFINITIVE WITH AND WITHOUT 'ZU' (Section 4)

Fill in the missing words in German so as to make the meaning correspond with the English shown in brackets.

1. (We must work), wenn wir lernen wollen. (*Use* müssen.)
2. (I want to know), warum er kein Geld hat. (*Use* wollen.)
3. (She is allowed to swim), wenn das Wasser nicht zu kalt ist. (*Use* dürfen.)
4. (They want to learn), wie man diese Fragen beantwortet. (*Use* wünschen.)
5. Jeden Tag fahre ich in die Stadt (in order to see my friends).
6. (You are to ask), wenn du die Antwort nicht weißt. (*Use* sollen.)
7. Herr Schmidt kam ins Haus (without seeing me).

355

8. (If you want to learn), müßt ihr besser arbeiten. (*Use* wünschen.)
9. Gehen Sie zu Bett, wenn (you like to sleep well). (*Use* mögen.)
10. Ich lese immer Bücher, (instead of eating).

IV. MODAL VERBS, PRINCIPAL PARTS (Section 5)
Put the verbs into the tense shown.
1. Ich muß jeden Tag in die Schule gehen. (*Imperfect.*)
2. Warum tust du das? – Ich soll. (*Perfect.*)
3. Wir dürfen all diese Bücher lesen. (*Imperfect.*)
4. Ich mache einen Spaziergang, aber er will nicht. (*Perfect.*)
5. Sie können zu Hause bleiben, wenn Sie wollen. (*Imperfect.*)
6. Ich mag diesen Mann nie. (*Perfect.*)
7. Du kannst heute nicht mitkommen. (*Imperfect.*)
8. Morgen sollen sie nicht in die Schule gehen. (*Imperfect.*)
9. Gehst du wirklich nach Hause? – Ja, ich muß. (*Perfect.*)
10. Können Sie jemals Deutsch? (*Perfect.*)

V. COMPARISON OF ADJECTIVES (Sections 6 & 8)
Insert the comparative or superlative of the adjective shown in brackets, whichever the sense may require.
1. Ich bin — als du. (jung.)
2. Franz ist — — von allen. (stark.)
3. Herr Schmidt ist — als seine Frau. (alt.)
4. Mein Anzug (= *suit*) ist — als der deinige. (grau.)
5. Das Wetter ist morgens — —. (kalt.)
6. Dieses Buch ist — —, das ich je gelesen habe. (gut.)
7. Meine Schule ist — als Ihr Haus. (groß.)
8. Dieser Baum ist — als die anderen. (hoch.)
9. Diese Lampe (= *lamp*) gibt — Licht, als jene. (viel.)
10. Hannover ist die — Stadt. (nah.)

VI. COMPARISON OF ADVERBS (Section 9)
Insert the comparative or superlative of the adverb shown in brackets, whichever the sense may require.
1. Er singt — als Sie, aber ich singe — —. (schön.)

2. Meine Lehrerin spricht französisch — als englisch, aber sie spricht deutsch — —. (gut.)
3. Ich laufe — als meine Frau, aber meine Tochter läuft — —. (schnell.)
4. Der Bus kommt — als der Zug an, aber das Flugzeug wird — — hier sein. (bald.)
5. Ich esse — als ich lese, aber — — schlafe ich. (gern.)

VII. 'THERE IS' AND 'THERE ARE' (Section 11)

Insert the correct expression for there is *or* there are. (*In this exercise a dash may stand for one or more missing words.*)

1. — ein Mann in unserem Haus. (*Present.*)
2. — einen Gott im Himmel (=*heaven*).
3. — zwei Frauen vor dem Hause.
4. In unserem Hause — drei Jungen.
5. Im Himmel — einen Gott.
6. — jemand hier —. (*Perfect.*)
7. — gestern viele Leute in der Stadt. (*Imperfect.*)
8. — nur einen Adam —. (*Perfect.*)
9. In jenem Zimmer — kein Licht. (*Imperfect.*)
10. Wenn es kalt ist, — viel Schnee —. (*Future.*)

VIII. FUTURE PERFECT, CONDITIONAL AND CONDITIONAL PERFECT (Sections 10 & 12)

Put the verb into the tense shown in each case.

1. Wir machen einen langen Spaziergang. (*Future Perfect.*)
2. Ich komme jeden Tag in die Schule. (*Conditional.*)
3. Die Katze frißt die flinke Maus. (*Conditional Perfect.*)
4. Du fährst morgen nach Berlin. (*Conditional Perfect.*)
5. Die Mädchen arbeiten besser am Abend. (*Future Perfect.*)
6. Das Wetter wird im Sommer viel schöner. (*Conditional.*)
7. Mein Vater ist jetzt nicht so krank. (*Conditional Perfect.*)
8. Ich habe genug Geld, um einen Wagen zu kaufen. (*Conditional Perfect.*)
9. Ihr bleibt den ganzen Tag im Bett. (*Conditional.*)
10. Seine Frau wird nach dem Abendessen sehr müde. (*Future Perfect.*)

EXERCISES

IX. THE DEFINITE ARTICLE (Section 13)

In the following sentences the definite article is sometimes required and sometimes not. A dash is inserted in each case, whether or not there has been an omission. Insert the correct form of the definite article where necessary.

1. Bist du früher in — Deutschland gewesen?
2. Was hat sie nach — Mittagessen getan?
3. In — Türkei spricht man türkisch.
4. Meine Katze frißt sehr gern — Mäuse.
5. — Zeit arbeitet für uns.
6. — schöne Luise ging gestern abend ins Theater.
7. In — Winter ist das Wetter oft sehr kalt.
8. Trinkst du gern — Milch?
9. — Menschen glauben gern, was sie wünschen.
10. In — Schweiz spricht man französisch, deutsch und italienisch.

X. MODAL VERBS IN PERFECT TENSES (Section 14)

Put the verbs into the Perfect Tense.

1. Ich mag nie starken Tee.
2. Will er mit mir nach Süddeutschland fahren?
3. Wir mögen gern ins Theater gehen.
4. Kannst du andere Sprachen?
5. Darf Frau Braun mit Ihnen kommen?
6. Ich kann mein Buch zu Hause lesen.
7. Er bleibt zu Hause, wenn er will.
8. Was sollst du heute machen?
9. Sie wollen gar nicht mitkommen.
10. Ihr müßt euren Hund zu Hause lassen.

XI. GENITIVE OF PERSONAL PRONOUNS (Section 15)

Insert the missing words as indicated by the English shown in brackets.

1. Weil wir nicht gehen konnten, sind sie (instead of us) gegangen.
2. Du sagtest, wir sollten nicht kommen, aber wir kamen (in spite of you).
3. Wenn du das nicht für mich tun willst, tue es (for his sake).
4. Ich öffnete die Tür und fand Herrn Braun (instead of her).
5. Ich glaube, daß du nur (on account of me) Deutsch lernst.

358

XII. POSSESSIVE ADJECTIVES AND PRONOUNS AND 'EINER' ETC. (Section 16)
Put the word or words shown in brackets into the correct form (if not already correct).
1. Dies Buch ist (mein).
2. Er ist (ein) von meinen Freunden.
3. (Sein) Vater wohnt in Hannover.
4. Ich kenne deinen Lehrer, aber nicht (der seinige).
5. Meine Tante hat zwei Häuser, und ich habe (kein).
6. Unsere Katze haben wir gern, (ihr) aber nicht.
7. (Kein) von diesen Wagen ist groß genug.
8. Sie spricht nicht mit ihrem Mann, sondern mit (der deine).
9. (Euer) Hund geht nicht sehr oft spazieren.
10. Sollen wir in deinem Wagen oder in (unser) fahren?

XIII. PASSIVE VOICE (Section 17)
Put the verb into the passive voice – e.g. Man macht das Mittagessen: das Mittagessen wird gemacht.
1. Man sieht den kleinen Hund.
2. Gestern spielte man hier Fußball.
3. Man hat das neue Buch gelesen.
4. Hier spricht man deutsch.
5. In der Schule sah man nur Mädchen.
6. Man hatte den Ball zu weit geworfen.
7. Mit Käse fängt man Mäuse.
8. Man hat einen langen Brief auf Deutsch geschrieben.
9. Endlich begann man die schwere Arbeit.
10. Man hatte den Hund jeden Tag gewaschen.

XIV. HOW TO EXPRESS TIME (Section 18)
Put the expressions shown in brackets into the correct case and add a preposition if you think one is necessary.
1. (Jeder Tag) lernt sie zehn deutsche Wörter.
2. (Ein Morgen) fand ich einen Apfel auf der Straße.
3. (Der siebzehnte November) ist ihr Geburtstag.
4. Hannover (der erste Mai). (*Heading to a letter.*)

5. Er hatte Frau Permaneder (der vorige Tag) gesehen.
6. Wir wollen (ein ganzer Monat) in Deutschland bleiben.
7. Das Jahr beginnt (der erste Januar).
8. Man arbeitet micht während der Nacht, sondern (der Tag).
9. Mein Bruder wird (der ganze Tag) bleiben.
10. (Ein Tag) werden Sie Deutsch besser sprechen können.

XV. PASSIVE VOICE – FUTURE AND CONDITIONAL (Section 20)

Put the verb into the passive voice – e.g. Man wird das Mittagessen machen: das Mittagessen wird gemacht werden.

1. Man wird den kleinen Hund sehen.
2. Man würde die Kinder jeden Tag waschen.
3. Morgen wird man hier Fußball spielen.
4. Man wird einen langen Brief auf Deutsch geschrieben haben.
5. Endlich würde man diese Arbeit begonnen haben.

In the following questions join sentence (b) to sentence (a), making any necessary changes in word order.

6 (a). Mein Bruder glaubte, daß . . .
  (b). Das neue Buch würde gelesen werden.
7 (a). Es ist zu hoffen (= *it is to be hoped*), daß . . .
  (b). Die Mäuse werden mit Käse gefangen werden.
8 (a). Man wird den Ball wieder finden, obgleich (= *although*) . . .
  (b). Er wird zu weit geworfen worden sein.
9 (a). Der Fremde fragte, ob . . .
  (b). Man würde in London deutsch sprechen.
10 (a). Während der Ferien (= *holidays*) war niemand in der Schule, so daß . .
  (b). Keine Jungen würden dort gesehen worden sein.

XVI. NOUNS (STRONG, WEAK AND MIXED)

Put the words in brackets into the correct form.

1. Wie ist der Name dieses (Junge)?
2. Ich habe einen langen Brief an meine (Tante) geschrieben.
3. Man muß (der Mensch) nehmen, wie er ist.
4. Er ist ein Mann nach (mein Herz).

5. Was ist die Bedeutung dieses (Name)?
6. Diesem (Mann) möchte ich gerne helfen.
7. Wo ist das Büro des (Präsident)?
8. Seine Frau hat zu viel Stärke des (Wille).
9. Ein junges Kind ist vom (Fels) gefallen.
10. Geht in (Friede)!

XVII. ADJECTIVES – USED AS NOUNS AND AFTER INDEFINITE PRONOUNS (Sections 19 & 24)
Add the correct endings in place of the dashes.
1. Er ist ein Verwandt— von mir.
2. Wenig Gut— ist geschehen.
3. Sprich nicht mit jenem Deutsch—.
4. Ich wünsche dir alles Gut—.
5. Einige Fremd— können kein Deutsch.
6. Nichts Recht— wird aus ihm werden.
7. Eine kleine Katze kam mit dem Reisend—.
8. Sie denkt immer Gut— von mir.
9. Er spricht immer von etwas Neu—.
10. Sie bleibt bei einer Alt—.

XVIII. PRESENT SUBJUNCTIVE AND INDIRECT SPEECH (1) (Sections 26 & 27)
Rewrite the following sentences as indirect speech, beginning each one with 'Er sagte, daß . . .' or 'Er fragte, ob . . .', according to whether it is a statement or a question – e.g. Bist du müde?: er fragte, ob du müde seiest.
1. Meine Mutter ist krank.
2. Geht ihr heute aus?
3. Herr Schmidt hat einen neuen Wagen.
4. Mein Bruder fährt morgen nach Hause.
5. Regnet es heute morgen?
6. Kommst du mit deinen Freunden?
7. Gibt es etwas Neues?
8. Er liest immer sehr alte Bücher.
9. Ich mag diesen Hund gar nicht.
10. Sie spricht den ganzen Tag.

EXERCISES

XIX. INDEFINITE PRONOUNS (Section 28)

Put the pronouns in brackets into the correct form if they are not already correct.

1. Mein Vater hat (jedermann) gesehen.
2. Man muß (man – *possessive adjective*) Arbeit aufs Beste tun.
3. Ich habe heute (jemand) auf der Straße gesehen.
4. Seine Söhne lieben (einander) gar nicht.
5. Wenn Herr Schmidt (man) sieht, geht er immer über die Straße.
6. Ist das (jemand – *Genitive*) Buch?
7. (Jedermann – *Genitive*) Zeit ist zu teuer.
8. Wenn die Lehrerin (man) sieht, spricht sie immer mit (man).
9. Das habe ich (niemand) erzählt.
10. Diese drei Freunde kommen immer mit (einander) an.

XX. DEMONSTRATIVE PRONOUNS (Section 31)

Put the demonstrative pronouns in brackets into the correct form if they are not already correct.

1. (Derjenige), die mir das sagte, hat selbst keine Bücher.
2. Mein Vater sprach mit allen (derjenige), die nicht kommen konnten.
3. Wer war das? (Der) kenne ich gar nicht.
4. Viele (derjenige–*Genitive Plural*), die nicht intelligent sind, wollen nicht lernen.
5. Das ist nicht mein Buch, sondern (derjenige) meiner Frau.
6. Die Freunde kamen mit ihrem Hund und mit (derjenige) des Doktors.
7. Hast du meinen Hut oder (der) meines Onkels gesehen?
8. Wessen Katze ist das? – (Derjenige) meines Bruders.
9. Ist dieses Buch von deiner Lehrerin oder von (derjenige) der anderen Schule geschrieben worden?
10. (Der – *Dative Singular*) wollte ich kein Geld geben.

XXI. INDIRECT SPEECH (2) (Section 33)

Rewrite the following sentences as indirect speech, beginning each one with 'Er sagte, daß . . .' or 'Er fragte, ob . . .' according to whether it is a statement or a question – e.g. Warst du müde?: er fragte, ob du müde gewesen seiest.

1. Seid ihr heute ausgegangen?

2. Seine Mutter wurde krank.
3. Euer Bruder fuhr gestern nach Hause.
4. Herr Heide hat einen neuen Wagen.
5. Regnete es letzte Woche?
6. Es gab nichts Neues.
7. Warst du mit deinen Freunden angekommen?
8. Er hat immer die neuesten Bücher gelesen.
9. Sie sprach den ganzen Tag.
10. Du mochtest jenen Hund gar nicht.

XXII. EXPRESSIONS OF QUANTITY (Section 37)
Put the words in brackets into the correct form if they are not already correct.

1. Eine Flasche (gute Milch).
2. Zwei Glas (Wein).
3. Viele Flaschen (guter Wein).
4. Die Tasse (= *cup*) ist nicht voll (kalte Milch).
5. Ein Glas voll (Wasser).

XXIII. INDIRECT SPEECH (3) (Sections 35, 36, 38 & 39)
Rewrite the following sentences as indirect speech, beginning each one with 'Er sagte, daß . . .' *or* 'Er fragte, ob . . .' *according to whether it is a statement or a question –
e.g.* Ich habe keine Katze: er sagte, daß ich keine Katze hätte.

1. Wird man das alles glauben?
2. Ich habe keine Antwort darauf.
3. Werden Sie das nächste Mal (= *time*) mitkommen?
4. Wir haben nicht zu oft mit Herrn Bergmann gesprochen.
5. Ich habe einen neuen Wagen gekauft.
6. Wird ihr Bruder morgen nach Hause fahren?
7. Gab es nichts Neues?
8. Wir haben alle sehr gut geschlafen.
9. Werde ich Sie morgen sehen?
10. Ich habe nicht immer die besten Bücher zu Hause.

EXERCISES

XXIV. VIEL AND WENIG (Section 40)

Put the words in brackets into the correct form if they are not already correct.

1. Mein Vater hat (wenig) Geld.
2. (Viel) Bücher sind nicht sehr interessant.
3. Nur (wenig) Männer können schnell lernen.
4. (Viel) Dank!
5. Ich bin mit (ein wenig) Geld nach Deutschland gefahren.

XXV. WENN AND ALS OB (Section 41)

Put the verbs in brackets into the correct tense and mood – e.g. (a) Ich würde kommen, wenn ich (können): ich würde kommen, wenn ich könnte. (b) Ich würde gekommen sein, wenn ich (können): ich würde gekommen sein, wenn ich gekonnt hätte.

1. Ich würde ihn gesehen haben, wenn ich (kommen).
2. Er sah aus, als ob er reich (sein).
3. Mein Freund sprach, als ob er aus Deutschland (kommen).
4. Wäre ich reich, so (haben) ich mehr Geld.
5. Wenn du mich gefragt hättest, (sagen) ich es dir.
6. Wenn du das (wissen), würdest du so weise als ich sein.
7. Mein Freund lief so schnell, als ob er mich nicht sehen (wollen).
8. Wenn ihr das gewußt hättet, (bleiben) ihr zu Hause.
9. Frau Duden sagte 'Guten Tag', als ob sie meinen Namen nicht (vergessen).
10. Wenn die Katze die Mäuse gefangen hätte, (sein) wir alle sehr glücklich.

XXVI. PASSIVE VOICE (VERBS REQUIRING DATIVE AS DISTINCT FROM ACCUSATIVE IN ACTIVE VOICE) (Section 43)

Put the sentences into the Passive Voice – e.g. (a) Mein Mutter hilft mir: es wird mir von meiner Mutter geholfen. (b) Die Mädchen sahen mich: ich wurde von den Mädchen gesehen.

1. Meine Frau erzählt mir eine lange Geschichte.
2. Oft wirft der Junge den Ball zu hoch.
3. Man half den Lehrern in der Schule.

4. Hat der Vater den kleinen Jungen gesehen?
5. Gestern tanzte man den ganzen Tag.
6. In diesen Häusern fand der Alte viele schöne Bücher.
7. Der Lehrer hat mir die neuesten Bücher gezeigt.
8. Der Schüler wird die Milch getrunken haben.
9. Gestern sagte man mir, daß ich zu Hause bleiben solle.
10. Ihr Onkel wird Ihnen einen neuen Wagen geben.

XXVII. USE OF SUBJUNCTIVE INSTEAD OF CONDITIONAL (Section 45)

Substitute the imperfect or pluperfect subjunctive for the conditional or conditional perfect respectively – e.g. (a) Was würden wir tun können?: was könnten wir tun? (b) Wir würden angekommen sein: wir wären angekommen.

1. Wie würde es sein, wenn wir nach Hause gingen?
2. Wenn wir nicht angekommen wären, würden wir Sie nicht gesehen haben.
3. Wenn sie zu spät kämen, würde es keine Zeit geben.
4. Was würden Sie tun, wenn wir zu Hause blieben?
5. Wenn wir Geld gehabt hätten, würden wir reich gewesen sein.
6. Er würde mir geholfen haben, wenn seine Frau es gewollt hätte.
7. Du würdest arbeiten müssen, wenn du mehr Geld haben wolltest.
8. Wenn wir das gewußt hätten, würden wir früher gekommen sein.
9. Sie würden schnell weglaufen, wenn Sie ihn sähen.
10. Wenn sie mir das erzählen wollte, würde sie mir einen Brief schreiben.

XXVIII. SEIN + PAST PARTICIPLE DISTINGUISHED FROM PASSIVE VOICE (Section 51)

Omit the brackets and insert the correct part of either sein *or* werden *to make the best sense.*

1. Da die Tür geschlossen (war/wurde), konnte ich nicht hineingehen.
2. Als ich da stand, (war/wurde) die Tür vor mir geschlossen.
3. Das Zimmer ist sehr kalt, weil das Fenster geöffnet (ist/wird).
4. Ich konnte die Milch nicht sehen, weil sie schon getrunken (war/wurde).
5. Jeden Morgen um acht Uhr (ist/wird) die Tür der Schule geöffnet.

XXIX. QUASI-MODAL VERBS (Section 52)

Omit the brackets and select whichever of the alternative versions given is correct.

1. Frau Schmidt läßt den Doktor (kommen/zu kommen).
2. Sie haben gelernt, Deutsch (sprechen/zu sprechen).
3. Ich hörte das Kind (schreien/zu schreien).
4. Ich habe den Lehrer kommen (lassen/gelassen).
5. Wir hatten die Mädchen sprechen (sehen/gesehen).

XXX. ACTIONS PREVIOUSLY BEGUN AND STILL CONTINUING (Section 53)

Omit the brackets and put the verb into the correct form to translate the English.

1. Ich (arbeiten) hier seit drei Jahren. (have been working.)
2. Wir (warten) schon seit einer Woche. (had been waiting.)
3. Er (essen) sein Mittagessen seit zwei Stunden. (has been eating.)
4. Sie (sein) schon seit vier Jahren in England. (have been.)
5. Im Jahre 1965 (lernen) ich Deutsch seit einem Jahr. (had been learning.)

XXXI. WORD ORDER – DEPENDENT SENTENCES WITH TWO INFINITIVES (Section 54)

Join the following pairs of sentences together, making the necessary changes in word order.

1 (a). Ich esse viel, weil . . .
 (b). ich habe gestern nichts essen können.
2 (a). Er fragt, ob . . .
 (b). werden Sie morgen abreisen müssen ?
3 (a). Wir glauben, daß . . .
 (b). wir werden früher aufstehen sollen.
4 (a). Mein Vater sagte, daß . . .
 (b). er würde in der Nacht nicht singen dürfen.
5 (a). Sie fragte mich, ob . . .
 (b) ich hätte je laufen mögen.

ANSWERS TO THE EXERCISES ON PAGES 355 TO 366
OF PART 2

Where the exercise calls for a change in one or two words, only those words are given. Otherwise the whole sentence is reproduced.

I.   PLUPERFECT
1. Sie hatten einen Spaziergang gemacht
2. Ich war in die Schule gegangen
3. Wir hatten nicht in der Stadt gewohnt
4. Hattet ihr euren Vater gehört?
5. Du hattest schon mit der Lehrerin gesprochen
6. Herr Schmidt hatte seinen Wagen jeden Morgen geholt
7. Sie war eine gute Schülerin gewesen
8. Sie war heute langsam nach Hause gefahren
9. Ich hatte meiner Mutter ein interessantes Buch gegeben
10. Ich war in das Haus gekommen, weil es geregnet hatte

II.   WISSEN AND KENNEN
1. kenne
2. weiß
3. Weißt
4. kenne
5. wußten

III.   INFINITIVE WITH AND WITHOUT ZU
1. Wir müssen arbeiten
2. Ich will
3. Sie darf
4. Sie wünschen zu lernen

ANSWERS

5. , um meine Freunde zu sehen
6. Du sollst fragen
7. , ohne mich zu sehen
8. Wenn ihr zu lernen wünscht
9. Sie gut schlafen mögen
10. statt zu essen

IV.   MODAL VERBS, PRINCIPAL PARTS
1. Ich mußte jeden Tag in die Schule gehen
2. Warum hast du das getan?—Ich habe gesollt
3. Wir durften all diese Bücher lesen
4. Ich habe einen Spaziergang gemacht, aber er hat nicht gewollt
5. Sie konnten zu Hause bleiben, wenn Sie wollten
6. Ich habe diesen Mann nie gemocht
7. Du konntest heute nicht mitkommen
8. Morgen sollten Sie nicht in die Schule gehen
9. Bist du wirklich nach Hause gegangen?—Ja, ich habe gemußt
10. Haben Sie jemals Deutsch gekonnt?

V.   COMPARISON OF ADJECTIVES
1. jünger
2. der stärkste
3. älter
4. grauer
5. am kältesten
6. das beste
7. größer
8. höher
9. mehr
10. nächste

VI.   COMPARISON OF ADVERBS
1. schöner . . . am schönsten
2. besser . . . am besten
3. schneller . . . am schnellsten

4. früher . . . am frühesten
5. lieber . . . am liebsten

VII.   THERE IS AND THERE ARE
  1. Es ist
  2. Es gibt
  3. Es sind
  4. sind
  5. gibt es
  6. Es ist . . . gewesen
  7. Es waren
  8. Es hat . . . gegeben
  9. gab es
 10. wird es . . . geben

VIII.   FUTURE PERFECT, CONDITIONAL AND CONDITIONAL PERFECT
  1. Wir werden einen langen Spaziergang gemacht haben
  2. Ich würde jeden Tag in die Schule kommen
  3. Die Katze würde die flinke Maus gefressen haben
  4. Du würdest morgen nach Berlin gefahren sein
  5. Die Mädchen würden besser am Abend arbeiten
  6. Das Wetter würde im Sommer viel schöner werden
  7. Mein Vater würde jetzt nicht so krank gewesen sein
  8. Ich würde genug Geld gehabt haben, um einen Wagen zu kaufen
  9. Ihr würdet den ganzen Tag im Bett bleiben
 10. Seine Frau wird nach dem Abendessen sehr müde geworden sein

IX.   THE DEFINITE ARTICLE
  1. [no addition]
  2. dem
  3. der
  4. [no addition]
  5. Die
  6. Die
  7. dem [or Im]

ANSWERS

8. [no addition]
9. Die
10. der

X.   MODAL VERBS IN PERFECT TENSES

1. Ich habe nie starken Tee gemocht
2. Hat er mit mir nach Süddeutschland fahren wollen?
3. Wir haben gern ins Theater gehen mögen
4. Hast du andere Sprachen gekonnt?
5. Hat Frau Braun mit Ihnen kommen dürfen?
6. Ich habe mein Buch zu Hause lesen können
7. Er ist zu Hause geblieben, wenn er gewollt hat
8. Was hast du heute machen sollen?
9. Sie haben gar nicht mitkommen wollen
10. Ihr habt euren Hund zu Hause lassen müssen

XI.   GENITIVE OF PERSONAL PRONOUNS

1. statt unser
2. trotz deiner
3. seinethalb
4. statt ihrer
5. meinetwegen

XII.   POSSESSIVE ADJECTIVES AND PRONOUNS AND EINER, ETC.

1. meines [or meins]
2. einer
3. Sein
4. den seinigen
5. keines [or keins]
6. ihren
7. Keiner
8. dem deinen
9. Euer
10. unserem

XIII.   PASSIVE VOICE
1. Der kleine Hund wird gesehen
2. Fußball wurde gestern hier gespielt
3. Das neue Buch ist gelesen worden
4. Deutsch wird hier gesprochen
5. Nur Mädchen wurden in der Schule gesehen
6. Der Ball war zu weit geworfen worden
7. Mäuse werden mit Käse gefangen
8. Ein langer Brief ist auf Deutsch geschrieben worden
9. Endlich wurde die schwere Arbeit begonnen
10. Der Hund war jeden Tag gewaschen worden

XIV.   HOW TO EXPRESS TIME
1. Jeden Tag
2. Eines Morgens
3. Der siebzehnte November
4. den ersten Mai
5. am vorigen Tag
6. einen ganzen Monat
7. am ersten Januar
8. des Tages
9. den ganzen Tag
10. Eines Tages

XV.   PASSIVE VOICE—FUTURE AND CONDITIONAL
1. Der kleine Hund wird gesehen werden
2. Die Kinder würden jeden Tag gewaschen werden
3. Morgen wird Fußball hier gespielt werden
4. Ein langer Brief wird auf Deutsch geschrieben worden sein
5. Endlich würde diese Arbeit begonnen worden sein
6. Mein Bruder glaubte, daß das neue Buch gelesen werden würde
7. Es ist zu hoffen, daß die Mäuse mit Käse gefangen werden werden
8. Man wird ben Ball wieder finden, obgleich er zu weit geworfen worden sein würde

9. Der Fremde fragte, ob man in London deutsch sprechen würde
10. Während der Ferien war niemand in der Schule, so daß keine Jungen dort gesehen worden sein würden

XVI.   NOUNS (STRONG, WEAK AND MIXED)
1. Jungen
2. Tante
3. den Menschen
4. meinem Herzen
5. Namens
6. Mann [or Manne]
7. Präsidenten
8. Willens
9. Felsen
10. Frieden

XVII.   ADJECTIVES—USED AS NOUNS AND AFTER INDEFINITE PRONOUNS
1. Verwandter
2. Gutes
3. Deutschen
4. Gute
5. Fremden
6. Rechtes
7. Reisenden
8. Gutes
9. Neuem
10. Alten

XVIII.   PRESENT SUBJUNCTIVE AND INDIRECT SPEECH (1)
1. Er sagte, daß meine Mutter krank sei
2. Er fragte, ob ihr heute ausgehet
3. Er sagte, daß Herr Schmidt einen neuen Wagen habe
4. Er sagte, daß mein Bruder morgen nach Hause fahre
5. Er fragte, ob es heute morgen regne
6. Er fragte, ob du mit deinen Freunden kommest

7. Er fragte, ob es etwas Neues gebe
8. Er sagte, daß er immer sehr alte Bücher lese
9. Er sagte, daß ich diesen Hund gar nicht möge
10. Er sagte, daß sie den ganzen Tag spreche

XIX.   INDEFINITE PRONOUNS

1. jedermann
2. seine
3. jemanden
4. einander
5. einen
6. jemandes [or jemands]
7. Jedermanns
8. einen, einem
9. niemandem
10. einander

XX.   DEMONSTRATIVE PRONOUNS

1. Derjenige
2. denjenigen
3. Den
4. derjenigen
5. dasjenige
6. demjenigen
7. den
8. Diejenige
9. derjenigen
10. Dem

XXI.   INDIRECT SPEECH (2)

1. Er fragte, ob ihr heute ausgegangen seiet
2. Er sagte, daß seine Mutter krank geworden sei
3. Er sagte, daß euer Bruder gestern nach Hause gefahren sei
4. Er sagte, daß Herr Heide einen neuen Wagen habe
5. Er fragte, ob es letzte Woche geregnet habe

ANSWERS

6. Er sagte, daß es nichts Neues gegeben habe
7. Er fragte, ob du mit deinen Freunden angekommen seiest
8. Er sagte, daß er immer die neuesten Bücher gelesen habe
9. Er sagte, daß sie den ganzen Tag gesprochen habe
10. Er sagte, daß du jenen Hund gar nicht gemocht habest

XXII.   EXPRESSIONS OF QUANTITY
1. guter Milch
2. Wein
3. guten Weins
4. kalter Milch
5. Wasser

XXIII.   INDIRECT SPEECH (3)
1. Er fragte, ob man das alles glauben werde
2. Er sagte, daß ich keine Antwort darauf hätte
3. Er fragte, ob Sie das nächste Mal mitkommen würden
4. Er sagte, daß wir nicht zu oft mit Herrn Bergmann gesprochen hätten
5. Er sagte, daß ich einen neuen Wagen gekauft hätte
6. Er fragte, ob ihr Bruder morgen nach Hause fahren werde
7. Er fragte, ob es nichts Neues gebe
8. Er sagte, daß wir alle sehr gut geschlafen hätten
9. Er fragte, ob ich Sie morgen sehen würde
10. Er sagte, daß ich nicht immer die besten Bücher zu Hause hätte

XXIV.   VIEL AND WENIG
1. wenig
2. Viele
3. wenige
4. Vielen
5. ein wenig

XXV.   WENN AND ALS OB
1. gekommen wäre

2. wäre
3. gekommen wäre
4. hätte
5. hätte ich es dir gesagt
6. wüßtest
7. wollte
8. wäret ihr zu Hause geblieben
9. vergessen hätte
10. wären

XXVI.   PASSIVE VOICE (VERBS REQUIRING DATIVE AS DISTINCT FROM
ACCUSATIVE IN ACTIVE VOICE)
1. Es ist mir eine lange Geschichte von meiner Frau erzählt worden
2. Der Ball wird von dem Jungen zu hoch geworfen
3. Es wurde den Lehrern in der Schule geholfen
4. Sind die kleinen Jungen von dem Vater gesehen worden?
5. Gestern wurde den ganzen Tag getanzt
6. Viele schöne Bücher sind in diesen Häusern von dem Alten
gefunden worden
7. Die neuesten Bücher sind mir von dem Lehrer gezeigt worden
8. Die Milch wird von dem Schüler getrunken worden sein
9. Es ist mir gestern gesagt worden, daß ich zu Hause bleiben solle
10. Ein neuer Wagen wird Ihnen von Ihrem Onkel gegeben werden

XXVII.   USE OF SUBJUNCTIVE INSTEAD OF CONDITIONAL
1. Wie wäre es, wenn wir nach Hause gingen?
2. Wenn wir nicht angekommen wären, hätten wir Sie nicht gesehen
3. Wenn sie zu spät kämen, gäbe es keine Zeit
4. Was täten Sie, wenn wir zu Hause blieben?
5. Wenn wir Geld gehabt hätten, wären wir reich gewesen
6. Er hätte mir geholfen, wenn seine Frau es gewollt hätte
7. Du müßtest arbeiten, wenn du mehr Geld haben wolltest
8. Wenn wir das gewußt hätten, wären wir früher gekommen
9. Sie liefen schnell weg, wenn sie ihn sähen
10. Wenn sie mir das erzählen wollte, schriebe sie mir einen Brief

ANSWERS
XXVIII. SEIN AND PAST PARTICIPLE DISTINGUISHED FROM PASSIVE VOICE
1. war
2. wurde
3. ist
4. war
5. wird

XXIX. QUASI-MODAL VERBS
1. kommen
2. zu sprechen
3. schreien
4. lassen
5. sehen

XXX. ACTIONS PREVIOUSLY BEGUN AND STILL CONTINUING
1. arbeite
2. warteten
3. ißt
4. sind
5. lernte

XXXI. WORD ORDER—DEPENDENT SENTENCES WITH TWO INFINITIVES
1. . . . ich gestern nichts habe essen können
2. . . . Sie morgen werden abreisen müssen
3. . . . früher werden aufstehen sollen
4. . . . er in der Nacht nicht würde singen dürfen
5. . . . ich je hätte laufen mögen

VOCABULARY

GERMAN – ENGLISH

NOTES: (1) Plurals of nouns are shown in brackets but -(e)n endings of regular feminine nouns in the plural are not shown.

(2) In the case of weak and mixed nouns the genitive singular ending is also shown in brackets, before the plural.

(3) Verbs not marked as strong or irregular are weak. Principal parts of strong and irregular verbs, if not shown under the item given, will be found in Part I.

(4) The numerical reference is to the item in which the meaning is first given.

der **Abend** (-e), evening 18. 13
das **Abendessen** (-), supper 13. 9
    abmarschieren, to march off 34. 3
    alles, all, everything 32. 1
    als, than 6. 33
    als ob, as if 41. 17
    alt, old 6. 17
der **(die) Alte,** old man (woman) 19. 21–22
    anstatt (+ Gen.), instead of 4. 17
der **Apfel** (⁻), apple 13. 1
der **April,** April 18. 5
    arbeiten, to work 18. 2
    arm, poor 13. 6
die **Armee** (-n), army 13. 11
    aufhängen (sep.), to hang up 49. 16
    auf mich zu, up to me 47. 9
der **August,** August 18. 6
    aussehen (sep., strong), to look, appear, seem 41. 18

    backen (strong), to bake 21. 7
    bald, soon 9. 9
der **Ball** (⁻e), ball 17. 23
    bauen, to build 21. 8
der **Baum** (⁻e), tree 49. 14
    bedeuten, to mean 2. 17
die **Bedeutung,** meaning 23. 4
    beginnen (strong), to begin 33. 7
der **Bein** (-e), leg, bone 21. 2
der **Berg** (-e), mountain 21. 5
    besser, better 8. 2
der **(die, das) beste,** best 8. 2
    bestehen (strong) **auf** (+ Acc.), to insist on 59. 7
das **Bett** (-en), bed 4. 12
das **Bild** (-er), picture 6. 37
    bitten (strong) **um,** to ask for 51. 10
    bleiben (**sein,** strong), to stay 18. 4
    blind, blind 13. 2
das **Blut,** blood 23. 22

das Böse, evil 19. 26
    braun, brown 6. 20
    brechen (strong), to break 48. 2
    brennen (irreg.), to burn 58. 4
das Brot (-e), bread 9. 20
das Buch (ᵁer), book 8. 4
der Buchstabe (-ns, -n), letter of
    alphabet 23. 19

    da, there 28.9; as, since, because
    51. 11
    dafür, therefor, for it 59. 2
die Dame, lady 31. 11
der Dank, thanks 40. 8
    danken (+ Dat.), to thank 59. 2
    darauf, thereon, on it 59. 7
    darum, so, therefore 51. 10
    das (pro.) that 32. 1
der (die, das) dein(ig)e, yours 16. 10
    der, die, das (rel. pro.), that,
    which, who 32. 1
    derjenige, diejenige, dasjenige,
    the one 31. 1
    desto – see **je.**
    Deutsch, German 52. 16
der (die) Deutsche, the German 19 26
    Deutschland (neut.), Germany
    13. 5
der Dienstag, Tuesday 18. 5
    dieser, diese, dieses, this 11. 5
    dort, there 11. 19
der Drache (-ns, -n), dragon, paper
    dart 23. 19
    drängen, to press 13. 2

der (die, das) dreißigste, thirtieth
    18. 8
dürfen (irreg.), to be allowed, may
    5. 9

edel, noble 6. 23
einander, one another 28. 14
einer, eine, eines (eins), one
    (pro.) 16. 17
der Engländer (-), Englishman 19. 26
    erzählen, to tell, recount 43. 12
    essen (strong), to eat 4. 14
    etwas, something 32. 1
    ewig, eternally 32. 7

    fahren (sein, strong), to travel 9. 2
    fallen (sein, strong), to fall 49. 13
    fällen, to fell 49. 14
    falsch, wrong 32. 2
    fangen (strong), to catch 20. 1
der Fels (-ns, -n), Felsen (-), rock 23. 9
das Fenster (-), window 51. 1
der Fisch (-e), fish 9. 16
die Flasche, bottle 37. 3
das Fleisch, meat 9. 11
    fragen, to ask 27. 21
    fragen, sich, to wonder 20. 11
der Franzose (-n, -n), Frenchman
    19. 26
die Frau, woman 6. 35; wife 16. 14
    fremd, foreign 19. 3
der (die) Fremde, foreigner 19. 3
    fressen (strong), to eat (of animals)
    17. 19
die Freude, pleasure 8. 5

378

freuen, to please 32. 6
der **Freund** (-e), friend 4. 13
die **Freundschaft,** friendship 15. 13
der **Friede** (-ns, -n), **Frieden** (-),
  peace 23. 15
  frieren (strong), to freeze 55. 4
  froh, glad 54. 9
  führen, to lead 49. 11
der **Funke** (-ns, -n), spark 23. 19

  ganz, whole 18. 1
das **Gebäck,** cakes 21. 7
das **Gebäude** (-), building 21. 8
das **Gebein,** skeleton 21. 2
  geben (strong), to give (there is,
  are) 11. 17
das **Gebirge** (-), mountain range 21. 5
der **Geburtstag** (-e), birthday 18. 8
der **Gedanke** (-ns, -n), thought 23. 11
  gedenke mein, remember me 15. 20
  gehen (sein, strong), to go, walk 1. 27
das **Gehen,** going, walking 7. 2
das **Gelände** (-), landscape, tract of
  land 21. 4
das **Geld,** money 33. 3
das **Gemüse,** vegetable(s) 21. 9
das **Gepäck,** luggage 21. 7
  gern, gladly 9. 11
die **Geschichte,** story 43. 12
das **Geschrei,** crying 21. 1
das **Gestein,** stonework 21. 3
  gestern, yesterday 6. 46
das **Glas** (-̈er), glass 37. 1
der **Glaube** (-ns, -n), faith, belief 23. 19

glauben, to believe 54. 7
das **Glück,** fortune 13. 2
  glücklich, happy 46. 7
der **Gott** (-̈er), God 13. 4
  grau, gray 6. 21
  groß, big 8. 4
die **Größe,** size 23. 10
  grün, green 6. 12
der **Grundstein** (-e), foundation stone
  49. 19
  gut, good, well 9. 7
das **Gute,** good 19. 29

  haben (irreg.), to have 1. 25
  halb, halber ($+$ Gen.), for the
  sake of 15. 13
  hangen (sein, strong), to be
  hanging 49. 15
  hängen, to hang up 49. 16
der **Haufe** (-ns, -n), **Haufen** (-),
  heap 23. 18
das **Haus** (-̈er), house 11. 5
  Hause, nach, home(wards) 27. 7
  heiß, hot 51. 11
das **Herz** (-ns, -n), heart 23. 20
  helfen (strong) ($+$ Dat.), to help
  28. 3
  heute, today 27. 11
  hier, here 11. 16
der **Himmel** (-), Heaven 42. 4
  hinausgehen (sep., sein, strong),
  to go out 39. 3
  hoch, high 8. 6
  holen, to fetch 17. 21

hören, to hear 34. 8
der Hund (-e), dog 47. 11
hungrig, hungry 8. 14
der Hut (-̈e), hat 16. 9

ihr, ihre, ihr, their 16. 6; her 16. 8
ihrer, ihre, ihres, hers 16. 4
der (die, das) ihr(ig)e, hers 16. 13
ihretwegen, on account of them 15. 14
Ihretwillen, um, for your sake 15. 19
indem, whilst (by + Gerund) 59. 9
intelligent, intelligent 6. 32

je . . . desto, the more . . . the more 55. 1
jeder, jede, jedes, every 10. 6
jedermann, everyone 28. 5
jemand, someone, anyone 11. 12 28. 8
jener, jene, jenes, that (dem. adj.) 2. 17
jung, young 6. 39
der Junge (-n, -n), boy 11. 5
der Juni, June 18. 8

kalt, cold 6. 18
der Käse, cheese 40. 7
die Katze, cat 43. 4
kein, keine, kein, no, not any 16. 20
kennen (irreg.), to know, recognize 2. 14
klein, small, little 6. 14

der Knabe (-n, -n), boy 16. 18
kommen (sein, strong), to come 1. 28
der König (-e), king 41. 2
die Königin (-nen), queen 3. 3
können (irreg.), can, to be able 5. 12
der Kopf (-̈e), head 49. 23
krank, ill 27. 4

lachen, to laugh 52. 17
das Land (-̈er), land 21. 4
langsam, slow 6. 22
lassen (strong), to let 52. 2
laufen (sein, strong), to run 34. 5
leben, to live 11. 13
legen, to lay down 49. 19
lehren, to teach 52. 16
der Lehrer (-), master 31. 15
lernen, to learn 52. 16
lesen (strong), to read 52. 18
letzt, last 18. 3
das Licht (-er), light 8. 11
lieben, to love 13. 3
liegen (strong), to be lying 49. 18
der Löwe (-n, -n), lion 6. 46
die Luft (-̈e), air 51. 10
die Lust (-̈e), joy 7. 5

machen, to make, do 1. 17
das Mädchen (-), girl 6. 32
man, one (pro.) 28. 1
der Mann (-̈er), man 6. 50
der März, March 13. 7

380

die **Maus** (-̈e), mouse 17. 20
mehr, more 8. 11
meiner, meine, meines (meins),
  mine 16. 3
meinethalb, for my sake 15. 15
meinetwegen, on account of me
  15. 14
meinetwillen, um, for my sake
  15. 18
der (die, das) **mein(ig)e,** mine 16. 9
meist, most 8. 12
der **Mensch** (-en, -en), Man 13. 4
die **Milch,** milk 6. 25
mögen (irreg.), to like, may 4. 9
der **Monat** (-e), month 18. 4
der **Montag,** Monday 13. 8
der **Morgen** (-), morning 18. 10
morgen früh, tomorrow morning
  22. 3
müde, tired 6. 24
der **Müller** (-), miller 7. 5
die **Musik,** music 13. 3
müssen (irreg.), must, to have to
  4. 7

nach (+ Dat.), according to
  23. 13
der **Nachmittag** (-e), afternoon 18. 11
nächst, next, nearest 8. 10
die **Nacht** (-̈e), 18. 15
nachts, at night, 6. 46
nah, near 8. 9
der **Name** (-ns, -n), name 2. 19
nehmen (strong), to take 26. 26

nichts, nothing 32. 1
niemand, no one 28. 8

ob, whether 20. 11
ob, als, as if 41. 17
oben, upstairs 11. 4
öffnen, to open 51. 2
ohne (+ Acc.) without 4. 14

packen, to pack 21. 7

regieren, to reign 3. 3
regnen, to rain 27. 1
reich, rich 41. 2
reisend, travelling 19. 17
der (die) **Reisende,** traveller 19. 17
reiten (sein, strong), to ride (on
  horseback) 34. 7
richtig, right 32. 4
der **Rundfunk,** radio 23. 19

die **Sache,** thing 44. 7
sagen, to say 26. 1
der **Same** (-ns, -n), **Samen** (-), seed
  23. 17
satt, tired 50. 2
sauer, sour 37. 8
schade, a pity 32. 7
schaffen (strong), to create 13. 4
scheinen (strong), to seem 41. 17
das **Schiff** (-e), ship 49. 21
schlafen (strong), to sleep 4. 17
schließen (strong), to close 51. 1
schon, already 51. 4

schön, beautiful 6. 27

der Schrei (-e), cry 21. 1

schreiben (strong), to write 9. 4

die Schule, school 6. 39

der Schüler (-), schoolboy 48. 11

die Schweiz, Switzerland 13. 10

die Schwester, sister 27. 5

schwimmen (strong), to swim 9. 3

sehen (strong), to see 4. 16

sein (irreg.), to be 1. 30

sein, seine, sein, his (adj.) 16. 3

seiner, seine, seines (seins), his (pro.) 16. 5

der (die, das) sein(ig)e, his (pro.) 16. 9

seinethalb, for his sake 15. 15

seit (+ Dat.), since 53. 3

senken, to sink (trans.) 49. 21

der September, September 18. 12

setzen, to set, put 49. 23

singen (strong), to sing 7. 3

das Singen, singing 7. 3

sinken (sein, strong), to sink (intrans.) 49. 20

sitzen (strong), to sit 49. 22

so . . . wie, as . . . as 6. 41

der Sohn (-̈e), son 8. 2

sollen (irreg.), to be required to, should 5. 21, 10. 14

der Spaziergang (-̈e), walk 39. 12

spielen, to play 14. 11

sprechen (strong), to speak 4. 7

das Sprechen, speaking 7. 4

springen (sein, strong), to jump 34. 6

die Stadt (-̈e), town 2. 18

stark, strong 6. 16

die Stärke, strength 23. 14

statt (+ Gen.), instead of 4. 17

der Stein (-e), stone 21. 3

sterben (sein, strong), to die 57. 1

stillstehen (sep., strong), to stand still, at attention 34. 2

studieren, to study 3. 2

die Stunde, hour 53. 8

der Tag (-e), day 10. 6

tanzen, to dance 43. 24

tapfer, bold 6. 50

der Tee, tea 13. 1

teuer, dear 6. 23

der Tisch (-e), table 8. 6

die Tochter (-̈), daughter 16. 4

tot, dead 41. 18

tragen (strong), to carry 30. 16

trinken (strong), to drink 13. 1

trotz (+ Gen.), in spite of 15. 2

tun (strong), to do 9. 12

die Tür, door 51. 2

die Türkei, Turkey 13. 11

um . . . willen, for the sake of 15. 17

unser, unsere, unser, our 16. 4

unserer, unsere, unseres, ours 16. 6

unsertwegen, on account of us 15. 16

unsertwillen, um, for our sake 15. 19

der **Vater** (-̈), father 28. 12
   vergelten (strong), to repay 19. 29
   vergessen (strong), to forget 28. 4
   vergißmeinnicht, forget-me-not
     15. 20
   verlassen (strong) **auf, sich,** to
     rely on 59. 8
   verwandt, related 19. 14
der (die) **Verwandte,** relative 19. 14
   viel, much 8. 11, 32. 1
   vier, four 2. 16
der (die, das) **vierte,** fourth 18. 7
   voll, voller, full 37. 5, 37. 7
   von (+ Dat.), of, from 6. 38
   vorbeigehen (**sein,** sep., strong),
     to pass 48. 11
   vorig, previous 18. 9

der **Wagen** (-), car 11. 19
   wandern, to walk 7. 5
das **Wandern,** walking 7. 5
   warten, to wait 52. 11
   was (rel. pro.), which 32. 1
   was für, what kind of 44. 1
die **Wäsche,** washing 49. 16
   waschen, sich (strong), to wash
     (oneself) 58. 5
das **Wasser** (-), water 37. 4
   wegen (+ Gen.), on account of
     15. 13
der **Wein** (-e), wine 37. 1
   weise, wise 41. 3
   welcher, welche, welches, that,
     which, who 32. 1

   wenig, little 40. 1
   wenig, ein, a little 40. 7
   wenn, if, whenever, when 41. 1
   wer? who? 27. 21
   werden (**sein,** strong), to become
     1. 29
   werfen (strong), to throw 17. 23
das **Wesen,** existence, being 7. 6
das **Wetter,** weather 6. 46
   wie, as 6. 41; how 23. 2
der **Wille** (-ns, -n), will 23. 13
   willen, um Gottes, for God's
     sake 15. 15
der **Winter** (-), winter 13. 7
   wissen (irreg.), to know (facts) 2. 1
   wo, where 29. 1
die **Woche,** week 53. 19
   woher, where from, whence 29. 5
   wohin, where to, whither 29. 3
   wohnen, to dwell, live 31. 12
   wollen (irreg.), to want, be willing
     4. 8, 10. 12
das **Wort** (-̈er or -e), word 2. 17
   wünschen, to want, wish 4. 6

   zehn, ten 53. 6
die **Zeit,** time 13. 2
   zornig, angry 28. 2
   zu, to, in order to 4. 11
der (die, das) **zwanzigste,** twentieth
     18. 6
   zwei, two 2. 16
   zweimal, twice 2. 16
der (die, das) **zweite,** second 18. 5

able – see 'be able'.

according to, **nach** (+ Dat.) 23. 13

account of, on, **wegen** (+ Gen.) 15. 13

account of me, on, **meinetwegen** 15. 14

account of them, on, **ihretwegen** 15. 15

account of us, on, **unsertwegen** 15. 16

afternoon, **der Nachmittag** (-e) 18. 11

air, **die Luft** (-̈e) 51. 10

all, **alles** 32. 1

allowed – see 'be allowed'.

already, **schon** 51. 4

angry, **zornig** 28. 2

anyone, **jemand** 28. 8

apple, **der Apfel** (-̈) 13. 1

April, **der April** 18. 5

army, **die Armee** 13. 11

as (= since, because), **da** 51. 11

as . . . as, **so . . . wie** 6. 41

as if, **als ob** 41. 17

to ask, **fragen** 27. 21

to ask for, **bitten** (strong) **um** 51. 10

August, **der August** 18. 6

to bake, **backen** (strong) 21. 6

ball, **der Ball** (-̈e) 17. 23

to be, **sein** (irreg.) (**sein**) 1. 30

to be able, **können** (irreg.) 5. 12

to be allowed, **dürfen** (irreg.) 5. 9

to become, **werden** (irreg., **sein**) 1. 29

bed, **das Bett** (-en) 4. 12

to begin, **beginnen** (strong) 33. 7

being, **das Wesen** 7. 6

belief, **der Glaube** (-ns, -n) 23. 19

to believe, **glauben** 54. 7

best, **der** (**die, das**) **beste** 8. 2

better, **besser** 8. 2

big, **groß** 8. 4

birthday, **der Geburtstag** (-e) 18. 8

blind, **blind** 13. 2

blood, **das Blut** 23. 22

bold, **tapfer** 6. 50

bone, **der Bein** (-e) 21. 2

book, **das Buch** (-̈er) 8. 4

bottle, **die Flasche** 37. 3

boy, **der Junge** (-n, -n) 11. 5; **der Knabe** (-n, -n) 16. 18

bread, **das Brot** (-e) 9. 20

to break, **brechen** (irreg.) 48. 2

brown, **braun** 6. 20

to build, **bauen** 21. 8

building, **das Gebäude** (-) 21. 8

to burn, **brennen** (irreg.) 58. 4

cakes, **das Gebäck** 21. 6

can (verb), **können** (irreg.) 5. 12

car, **der Wagen** (-) 11. 19

to carry, **tragen** (strong) 30. 16

cat, **die Katze** 43. 4

to catch, **fangen** (strong) 20. 1

cheese, **der Käse** 40. 7
to close, **schließen** (strong) 51. 1
cold, **kalt** 6. 18
to come, **kommen** (**sein**, strong) 1. 28
to create, **schaffen** (strong) 13. 4
cry, **der Schrei** (**-e**) 21. 1
crying, **das Geschrei** 21. 1

to dance, **ranzen** 43. 24
daughter, **die Tochter** (ⁱ) 16. 4
day, **der Tag** (**-e**) 10. 6
dead, **tot** 41. 18
dear, **teuer** 6. 23
to die, **sterben** (**sein**, strong) 57. 1
to do, **tun** (strong) 9. 12
dog, **der Hund** (**-e**) 47. 11
door, **die Tür** 51. 2
dragon, **der Drache** (**-ns, -n**) 23. 19
to drink, **trinken** (strong) 13. 1

to eat, **essen** (strong) 4. 14; **fressen**
(strong) (of animals) 17. 19
Englishman, **der Engländer** (**-**)
19. 26
eternally, **ewig** 32. 7
evening, **der Abend** (**-e**) 18. 13
every, **jeder, jede, jedes** 10. 6
every one, **jedermann** 28. 5
everything, **alles** 32. 1
evil, **das Böse** 19. 29
existence, **das Wesen** 7. 6

faith, **der Glaube** (**-ns, -n**) 23. 19
to fall, **fallen** (**sein**, strong) 49. 13

father, **der Vater** (ⁱ) 28. 12
to fell, **fällen** 49. 14
to fetch, **holen** 17. 21
fish, **der Fisch** (**-e**) 9. 16
foreign, **fremd** 19. 3
foreigner, **der** (**die**) **Fremde** 19. 3
to forget, **vergessen** (strong) 28. 4
forget-me-not, **vergißmeinnicht**
15. 20
fortune, **das Glück** 13. 2
foundation stone, **der Grundstein**
(**-e**) 49. 19
four, **vier**
fourth, **der** (**die, das**) **vierte** 18. 7
to freeze, **frieren** (strong) 55. 3
Frenchman, **der Franzose** (**-n, -n**)
19. 26
friend, **der Freund** (**-e**) 4. 13
friendship, **die Freundschaft** 15. 13

German, **deutsch** 52. 16
German, the, **der** (**die**) **Deutsche**
19. 26
Germany, **Deutschland** (neut.) 13. 5
to get (= become), **werden** (**sein**,
strong) 17. 10
girl, **das Mädchen** (**-**) 6. 32
to give, **geben** (strong) 11. 17
glad, **froh** 54. 9
gladly, **gern** 9. 11
glass, **das Glas** (ⁱ**er**) 37. 1
to go, **gehen** (**sein**, strong) 1. 27
to go out, **hinausgehen** (**sein**, sep.,
strong) 39. 3

385

God, **der Gott** (-̈er) 13. 4
good (adj.), **gut** 7. 2
good (noun), **das Gute** 19. 29
gray, **grau** 6. 21
green, **grün** 6. 12

to hang up, (**auf**)**hängen** (sep.) 49. 16
hanging, to be, **hangen** (**sein,**
strong) 49. 15
happy, **glücklich** 46. 7
hat, **der Hut** (-̈e) 16. 9
to have, **haben** (irreg.) 1. 25
to have to, **müssen** (irreg.) 4. 9
head, **der Kopf** (-̈e) 49. 23
heap, **der Haufe** (**-ns, -n**), **Haufen**
(**-**) 23. 18
to hear, **hören** 34. 8
heart, **das Herz** (**-ns, -n**) 23. 20
Heaven, **der Himmel** (**-**) 42. 4
to help, **helfen** (strong) (+ Dat.) 28. 3
her (adj.), **ihr, ihre, ihr** 16. 7
here, **hier** 11. 16
hers, **ihrer, ihre, ihres** 16. 4; **der**
(**die, das**) **ihr**(**ig**)**e** 16. 13
high, **hoch** 8. 6
his (adj.), **sein, seine, sein** 16. 3
his (pro.), **seiner, seine, seines**
(**seins**) 16. 5; **der** (**die, das**)
sein(**ig**)**e** 16. 9
home(wards), **nach Hause** 27. 7
hot, **heiß** 51. 11
hour, **die Stunde** 53. 8
house, **das Haus** (-̈er) 11. 5
how, **wie** 23. 2

hungry, **hungrig** 8. 14

if, **wenn** 41. 1
if, as, **als ob** 41. 17
ill, **krank** 27. 4
to insist on, **bestehen** (strong) **auf** 59. 7
instead of, (**an**)**statt** (+ Gen.) 4. 17
intelligent, **intelligent** 6. 32

joy, **die Lust** (-̈e) 7. 5
to jump, **springen** (**sein,** strong) 34. 6
June, **der Juni** 18. 8

king, **der König** (**-e**) 41. 2
to know (facts), **wissen** (irreg.) 2. 1
to know (= recognize), **kennen** (irreg.)
2. 14

lady, **die Dame** 31. 11
land, **das Land** (-̈er) 21. 4
landscape, **das Gelände** 21. 4
last, **letzt** 18. 3
to laugh, **lachen** 52. 17
to lay down, **legen** 49. 19
to lead, **führen** 49. 12
to learn, **lernen** 52. 16
leg, **der Bein** (**-e**) 21. 2
to let, **lassen** (strong) 52. 2
letter of alphabet, **der Buchstabe**
(**-ns, -n**) 23. 19
to lie – see 'lying, to be'.
light, **das Licht** (**-er**) 8. 11
to like, **mögen** (irreg.) 4. 9
lion, **der Löwe** (**-n, -n**) 6. 46

little (= small), **klein** 6. 14; (= not much), **wenig** 40. 1

little, a, **ein wenig** 40. 7

to live, **leben** 11. 13; (= dwell), **wohnen** 31. 12

to look, **aussehen** (sep., strong) 41. 18

to love, **lieben** 13. 3

luggage, **das Gepäck** 21. 7

lying, to be, **liegen** (strong) 49. 18

to make, **machen** 1. 17

Man, **der Mensch** (-n, -n) 13. 4

March, **der März** 13. 7

to march off, **abmarschieren** (sep.) 34. 3

master, **der Lehrer** (-) 31. 15

may, **mögen** (irreg.) 4. 9

to mean, **bedeuten** 2. 17

meaning, **die Bedeutung** 23. 4

meat, **das Fleisch** 9. 11

milk, **die Milch** 6. 25

miller, **der Müller** (-) 7. 5

mine, **meiner, meine, meines** (**meins**) 16. 3; **der** (**die, das**) **mein(ig)e** 16. 9

Monday, **der Montag** 13. 8

money, **das Geld** 33. 3

month, **der Monat** (-e) 18. 4

most, **meist** 8. 12

more, **mehr** 8. 11

more, the . . . the more, **je . . . desto** 55. 1

morning, **der Morgen** (-) 18. 10

mountain, **der Berg** (-e) 21. 5

mouse, **die Maus** (-̈e) 17. 20

much, **viel** 8. 11; **vieles** 32. 1

music, **die Musik** 13. 3

must, **müssen** (irreg.) 4. 7

name, **der Name** (-ns, -n) 2. 19

near, **nah** 8. 9

nearest, **nächst** 8. 10

night, **die Nacht** (-̈e) 18. 15

night, at, **nachts** 6. 46

no (adj.), **kein, keine, kein** 16. 20

no one, **niemand** 28. 8

noble, **edel** 6. 23

none, **keiner, keine, keines** (**keins**) 16. 20

nothing, **nichts** 32. 1

of, **von** (+ Dat.) 6. 38

old, **alt** 6. 17

old man, **der Alte** 19. 21

old woman, **die Alte** 19. 22

one (indef. pers. pro.), **man** 28. 1

one (pro.), **einer, eine, eines** (**eins**) 16. 17

one, the, **derjenige, diejenige, dasjenige** 31. 1

one another, **einander** 28. 14

to open, **öffnen** 51. 2

order to, in, **um . . . zu** 4. 11

our, **unser, unsere, unser** 16. 4

ours, **unserer, unsere, unseres** 16. 6

ENGLISH–GERMAN VOCABULARY

to pack, **packen** 21. 7

paper dart, **der Drache** (-ns, -n) 23. 19

to pass, **vorbeigehen** (sein, sep., strong) 48. 11

peace, **der Friede** (-ns, -n), **Frieden** (-) 23. 15

picture, **das Bild** (-er) 6. 37

pity, a, **schade** 32. 7

to play, **spielen** 14. 11

to please, **freuen** 32. 6

pleasure, **die Freude** 8. 5

poor, **arm** 13. 6

to prefer – see 'gladly' (**gern**) 9. 16

to press, **drängen** 13. 2

previous, **vorig** 18. 9

to put, **setzen** 49. 23

queen, **die Königin** (-nen) 3. 3

radio, **der Rundfunk** 23. 19

to rain, **regnen** 27. 1

range of mountains, **das Gebirge** (-) 21. 5

to read, **lesen** (strong) 52. 18

to reign, **regieren** 3. 3

related, **verwandt** 19. 14

relative, **der (die) Verwandte** 19. 14

to rely on, **sich verlassen** (strong) **auf** (+ Acc.) 59. 8

remember me, **gedenke mein** 15. 20

to repay, **vergelten** (strong) 19. 29

required to, to be, **sollen** (irreg.) 5. 21

rich, **reich** 41. 2

to ride (on horseback), **reiten** (sein, strong) 34. 7

right, **richtig** 32. 4

rock, **der Fels** (-ns, -n), **Felsen** (-) 23. 9

to run, **laufen** (sein, strong) 34. 5

sake, for God's, **um Gottes willen** 15. 17

sake, for his, **seinethalb** 15. 16

sake, for my, **meinethalb** 15. 15 **um meinetwillen** 15. 18

sake, for our, **um unsertwillen** 15. 19

sake, for your, **um Ihretwillen** 15. 18

sake of, for the, **halb, halber** 15. 13; **um . . . willen** 15. 17

to say, **sagen** 26. 1

school, **die Schule** 6. 39

schoolboy, **der Schüler** (-) 48. 11

second, **der (die, das) zweite** 18. 5

to see, **sehen** (strong) 4. 16

seed, **der Same** (-ns, -n), **Samen** (-) 23. 17

to seem, **scheinen** (strong) 41. 17

September, **der September** 18. 12

to set, **setzen** 49. 23

ship, **das Schiff** (-e) 49. 21

should, **sollen** (irreg.) 10. 14

since (prep.), **seit** (+ Dat.) 53. 3; (conj.), **da** 51. 11

to sing, **singen** (strong) 7. 3

to sink (intrans.), **sinken** (**sein,** strong) 49. 20

to sink (trans.), **senken** 49. 21

sister, **die Schwester** 27. 5

to sit, **sitzen** (strong) 49. 22

size, **die Größe** 23. 10

skeleton, **das Gebein** 21. 2

to sleep, **schlafen** (strong) 4. 17

slow, **langsam** 6. 22

small, **klein** 6. 14

so (= therefore), **darum** 51. 10

someone, **jemand** 11. 12

something, **etwas** 32. 1

son, **der Sohn** (**-e**) 8. 2

soon, **bald** 9. 9

sour, **sauer** 37. 8

spark, **der Funke** (**-ns, -n**) 23. 19

to speak, **sprechen** (strong) 4. 7

speaking, **das Sprechen** 7. 4

spite of, in, **trotz** (+ Gen.) 15. 2

to stand still, at attention, **stillstehen** (sep., strong) 34. 2

to stay, **bleiben** (**sein,** strong) 18. 4

stone, **der Stein** (**-e**) 21. 3

stonework, **das Gestein** 21. 3

story, **die Geschichte** 43. 12

strength, **die Stärke** 43. 12

strong, **stark** 6. 16

to study, **studieren** 3. 2

supper, **das Abendessen** (**-**) 13. 9

to swim, **schwimmen** (strong) 9. 3

Switzerland, **die Schweiz** 13. 10

table, **der Tisch** (**-e**) 8. 6

to take, **nehmen** (strong) 26. 26

tea, **der Tee** 13. 1

to teach, **lehren** 52. 16

to tell, **erzählen** 43. 12

ten, **zehn** 53. 6

than, **als** 6. 33

to thank, **danken** (+ Dat.) 59. 2

thanks, **der Dank** 40. 8

that (dem. adj.), **jener, jene, jenes** 2. 17; (dem. pro.), **das** 32. 1

their, **ihr, ihre, ihr** 16. 6

there, **dort** 11. 19; **da** 28. 9

there is, are – see Section 11

therefor (= for it), **dafür** 59. 3

therefore, **darum** 51. 10

thereon (= on it) **darauf** 59. 7

thing, **die Sache** 44. 7

thirtieth, **der** (**die, das**) **dreißigste** 18. 8

this, **dieser, diese, dieses** 11. 5

thought, **der Gedanke** (**-ns, -n**) 23. 11

to throw, **werfen** (strong) 17. 23

tired, **müde** 6. 24; **satt** 50. 2

time, **die Zeit** 13. 2

today, **heute** 27. 11

tomorrow morning, **morgen früh** 22. 3

town, **die Stadt** (**-e**) 2. 18

tract of land, **das Gelände** (**-**) 21. 4

to travel, **fahren** (**sein,** strong) 9. 2

traveller, **der** (**die**) **Reisende** 19. 17

travelling, **reisend** 19. 17

tree, **der Baum** (**-e**) 49. 14

Tuesday, **der Dienstag** 18. 5
Turkey, **die Türkei** 13. 11
twentieth, **der (die, das) zwanzigste**
18. 6
twice, **zweimal** 2. 16
two, **zwei** 2. 16

up to me, **auf mich zu** 47. 9
upstairs, **oben** 11. 4

vegetable(s), **das Gemüse** 21. 9

to wait, **warten** 52. 11
to walk, **wandern** 7. 5; **gehen (sein,**
strong) 7. 2
walk (noun), **der Spaziergang (-̈e)**
39. 12
walking, **das Gehen,** 7. 2; **das**
Wandern 7. 5
to want to, **wollen** (irreg.) 4. 8;
wünschen 4. 6
to wash (oneself), **sich waschen**
(strong) 58. 5
washing, **die Wäsche** 49. 16
water, **das Wasser** (-) 37. 4
weather, **das Wetter** 6. 46
week, **die Woche** 53. 19
well, **gut** 9. 7
what kind of, **was für** 44. 1
when, **wenn** 41. 1
whence, **woher** 29. 5
where, **wo** 29. 1

where from, **woher** 29. 5
where to, **wohin** 29. 3
whether, **ob** 20. 11
which, **der, die, das** 32. 1; **was**
32. 1; **welcher, welche, welches**
32. 1
whilst, **indem** 59. 9
whither, **wohin** 29. 3
whole, **ganz** 18. 1
wife, **die Frau** 16. 14
will, **der Wille (-ns, -n)** 23. 13
willing, to be, **wollen** (irreg.) 10. 12
window, **das Fenster** (-) 51. 1
wine, **der Wein** (-e) 37. 1
winter, **der Winter** (-) 13. 7
wise, **weise** 41. 3
to wish, **wollen** (irreg.) 4. 8; **wünschen**
4. 6
without, **ohne** (+ Acc.) 4. 14
woman, **die Frau** 6. 35
to wonder, **sich fragen** 20. 11
word, **das Wort (-̈er** or **-e)** 2. 17
to work, **arbeiten** 18. 2
to write, **schreiben** (strong) 9. 4
wrong, **falsch** 32. 2

year, **das Jahr** (-e) 3. 3
yesterday, **gestern** 6. 46
young, **jung** 6. 39
yours, **der (die, das) dein(ig)e**
16. 10

390